GRASSROOTS II
901-E N. SALISBURY BLVD
SALISBURY, MD 21801

BLACK LABOR, WHITE WEALTH

The Search for Power and Economic Justice

Claud Anderson, Ed.D

Duncan & Duncan, Inc.,
Publishers

a publication of

Duncan & Duncan, Inc.
Publishers

We gratefully acknowledge permission to reprint the following: Quotes from *Two Nations: Black and White, Separate, Hostile, Unequal* by Andrew Hacker © 1992, Charles Scribner's Sons; Quotes from *Plural But Equal* by Harold Cruse © 1987, Quill-William Morrow; Quotes from *The Politics of Black Empowerment* by James Jennings © 1992, Wayne State University Press; Quote from *Effects of Black on Blacks' Perceptions of Relative Power and Social Distance* by Arthur S. Evans and Michael W. Giles © 1986, Journal of Black Studies; Quote from *The Crisis of the Negro Intellectual: A Historical Analysis of the Failure of Black Leadership* by Harold Cruse © 1984, Quill Books; Quote from *A People's History of the United States* by Howard Zinn © 1990, Harper Perennial; Quote regarding Clarence Thomas from *The Washington Post* by Jack Anderson © 1994, The Washington Post; Quote from *Toward a Theory of Black Politics: The Black and Ethnic Models Revisited* by Leslie McLemore © 1972, Journal of Black Studies; Quote from *Black Men: Obsolete, Single, Dangerous?* by Haki R. Madhubuti © 1990, Third World Press;

(continued on last page of book)

Second Printing-Revised

Duncan & Duncan, Inc.
Publishers
2809 Pulaski Highway, P.O. Box 1137
Edgewood, MD 21040
410-538-5579

Edited by: *Edward D. Sargent and Reginald B. Scott, Jr.*

Library of Congress Catalog Card Number: 93-72794

Anderson, Claud, 1935—
  Black Labor, White Wealth
1. African-American history 2. American history 3. Slavery 4. Blacks, economic empowerment of 5. Race relations, economic aspects of 6. Race relations, political aspects of 7. Wealth, formation of in America

ISBN: 1-878647-11-3

9 8 7 6 5 4 3 2

Dedication

For My Youngest Brother, John Wesley,
Who I Love With All My Being.
I Will Always Keep In My Heart His Laughter,
Creative Spirit, Warmth and Caring Ways.

Acknowledgments

I must give special acknowledgment to my wife, Joann and my children Paige and Brant, for their inspiration, advice and unwavering support. I am also grateful to the many friends who encouraged me to write a book of this nature and supported my effort. They willingly and unwillingly engaged in endless discussions to help me analyze the complex racial issues that I explore in this book.

I must also recognize and acknowledge the family in which I grew up for its support and encouragement: my mother, Essie and my brothers and sisters, James, Charles, Wesley, Bessie and Cleopatra.

For their reviews, critiques and practical suggestions, I am indebted to Hugh Wells, Dr. Alfred Cooke, Dr. James B. Christensen, Dr. Noelle Clark, Miguel Lawson, Dr. Hattie Washington, Celeste James and Karen James Cody.

Contents

Foreword

I t is not often that people of Dr. Claud Anderson's stature will take the risk of stepping out from the pack. However, his book *Black Labor, White Wealth,* breaks away from the pack. Dr. Anderson has written in a straight forward manner about the sensitive issues of race and ethnicity in America.

Many blacks and far too many whites still believe that blacks contributed little or nothing to the creation of wealth and power in this country. Dr. Anderson forcefully proves the contrary. Of course, there are many people who have heard of the cotton gin or blood plasma (as though these were the only important creations of blacks), but few people of the world know of the historic economic and monetary contributions of black folk. *Black Labor, White Wealth* shows how the labor of black men and women from days of slavery to the present helped to lay the wealth building foundation for this country.

One would think that such a feat would be enough for one book, but Dr. Anderson didn't stop there. He was bold enough to ask and then answer the $64,000 question: Since blacks originated from one of the oldest civilizations, why are blacks still so far behind economically as compared to whites and other immigrants? Again, Dr. Anderson reveals startling information! His examination of the methods whites used (and still use) to gain wealth and power provides examples of ways that blacks can adopt to build bases of wealth and power throughout the country. This book is provocative and powerful!

Tony Brown
Tony Brown's Journal

Introduction

*R*acism against black people has been a virulent undercurrent in our society for hundreds of years. In various forms, it insinuates itself into all aspects of our lives. Yet, it is not an acceptable topic for discussion anywhere, neither the conference room nor the living room, especially across racial lines. It is as if we believe that if we ignore the facts of racism, they will not exist. That is not the reality. It is time for a serious dialogue and a change in black strategies.

Neither the dialogue nor the strategies can be emotional or superficial. Instead, they must be based on facts and knowledge and considered for the purpose of understanding, not just the symptoms that we see all around us, but also how things came to be as they are and how as blacks we can reverse our misfortunes and strengthen ourselves as a racial group.

It is critical that we strengthen our group, because while as individuals some of us may hold high-ranking positions in corporate America, government agencies and our own businesses, and some of us may reside far from the scenes of black despair, all blacks are identifiable members of one racial group. Furthermore, as a racial group, we are powerless, impoverished and increasingly unable to compete in America. And whether they intend to or not, those outside of our group see us as one group.

The predominantly marginal living conditions of black America did not happen by accident. They resulted from much forethought and planning by whites. European whites who came to this country in 1607 were the first power group in America. They wielded power in a manner that is natural to the human race. They had a chance to start a new government in a country filled with resources and potential for wealth. They seized a unique opportunity to structure a government and a system to their sole advantage. To secure their advantage and increase their power, they subordinated and exploited another race of people — blacks.

The purpose of this book is to illuminate and examine the strategies and techniques that were used by whites to accomplish their goal of solidifying power and privilege. Once black Americans understand the strategies and techniques that whites used to build their power, they can use those same tools to build black empowerment.

The history of slavery and the struggles for equality serve as a guide for the future. While the dire conditions of black Americans can be traced back to measures that colonial governments used against blacks, it does not end there. We have further handicapped ourselves by some of our own beliefs and behaviors. Our dogged pursuit of integration is one example. In so doing, we have destroyed our communities, diluted our numerical strength and become dependent upon others. We have been further handicapped by our inability to practice group economics in a capitalistic democracy.

We have always been a key capitalistic element in the national empowerment plans of others — as a source of free or cheap labor. Yet, we have never had a national empowerment plan of our own. We have never used our collective intellectual resources to create a national plan with explicit policies and strategies for our own economic and political gain. *Black Labor, White Wealth* provides useful information and a conceptual framework to stimulate thought, discussion and planning toward that end.

Chapter One describes and analyzes the present day conditions of black America and establishes links with the antebellum condition of slaves. Chapter Two discusses concepts of power and focuses on the ways groups acquire and institutionalize power. Chapter Three describes the social and economic impediments to black empowerment, including certain behavior patterns and ideological beliefs that diffuse and weaken our sense of direction and unity. Chapters Four and Five explain why blacks were selected for enslavement and why we cannot change our conditions by emulating Asians, Hispanics or other ethnic and racial groups that immigrated into this country.

Chapter Six tracks the nature and development of black-white relationships in connection with the wealth-building process. Using comparative tables, charts, illustrations, drawings and visual timelines, this chapter covers five centuries of social practices and devices that created wealth and power imbalances between blacks and whites. Chapter Seven explains the national public policy that has guided institutions in their manipulative use of blacks. The conditioning and supportive systems for controlling and keeping blacks a powerless minority are also discussed.

Chapter Eight explains why certain major problems will converge within the next generation to make blacks a permanent underclass, unless black Americans take immediate preventive actions to avoid this catastrophe. To that end, Chapter Eight offers practical courses of action that blacks can take to achieve community cohesiveness, change detrimental social-psychological behavior patterns and to develop a new type of leadership that will help black America develop itself into a competitive group in a rapidly developing pluralistic society.

Finally, Chapter Nine describes the concept of building vertical businesses or structuring a system of businesses around an area of black dominance, such as the music industry. This chapter also includes discussion of sports, another area where blacks have a strong dominance, which, if properly leveraged, could create vertical business opportunities.

Some readers may think this book is too pessimistic, because it doesn't pay homage to the positive aspects of black-white relationships. Others may question a book on black history that does not highlight the individual successes of black people. But such black achievements have been recognized and discussed by many other writers. This book breaks new ground by offering a hard and honest look at how to best resolve a 400-year-old problem that black and white, conservatives and liberals would like to wish away or bury beneath debates on less complex issues, such as abortion, sexual harassment, or a balanced budget amendment. *Black Labor, White Wealth* is written to re-engage the reader emotionally and intellectually in the profoundly unresolved black/white race issue.

The purpose of this book is not to criticize any group of people, but to analyze history and propose a reasonable solution. All too frequently, blacks are admonished to forget slavery. But to do so would be foolhardy especially at this time, because the major problems facing black America are rooted in slavery. Thus, we must squarely face that tragedy and learn from it, lest we be doomed to be shackled by it *forever*.

Dr. Claud Anderson

1

The Nature of the Problem

*"It isn't that they can't see the solution.
It is that they can't see the problem."[1]*

T he Los Angeles, California riot had subsided, but the acrid smell of burned wood and tar still hung heavy in the early morning air. A local television reporter scanned the crowd and spotted a familiar black community activist standing by a burned-out grocery store. Sensing a good sound bite, the reporter asked for an interview. The bright lights came on and the reporter began:

Three decades after the Civil Rights Movement transformed the nation, why is the black community dissatisfied? Why have they rioted and destroyed their own neighborhood? What is the problem?"

The activist cocked his head and in a voice mixed with anger and indignation, responded, "Surely, the gains of the Civil Rights Movement in the '60s were important, but they turned out to be superficial and largely symbolic. We can sit at lunch counters and vote, but economically, civil rights gains took more from us than they gave. Some blacks got important big-paying jobs in white businesses or government. Sure, we have our Colin Powells and Oprahs, but the black masses were left behind. So, you see, integration came at the expense of the black community. Now things are worse than ever.

We have more killings and crime, more school dropouts and drug users. Integration killed our communities. We have no black economic structure to solve the problems of our community. Our black churches and families are weak and struggling. We have yet to gain control of our communities and our destinies. The Vietnamese, Koreans, Indians, Iranians and Mexicans are putting up profitable businesses in our neighborhoods. And we are still hopelessly vulnerable to every danger — from police brutality to violence and poverty. The next time we go to the Supreme Court, instead of integration, maybe we should seek 'separate but equal.'"

The white newscaster forced a smile and said, "But, with all the civil rights laws and blacks who have been elected to public office, surely things are better for blacks. What happened to the dream that Dr. King spoke of so eloquently more than 20 years ago?"

Exasperated, the activist shook his head and walked away. At home he waited for his interview to appear on the evening news. He had tried to explain the causes of black peoples' pain, confusion, disappointment and anger. He cursed himself for not talking about black peoples' tiredness. How tired they were of being the world's underdog. Even so, he hoped the world would be watching and listening. As the riot coverage aired on television, he saw close-up shots of the faces of distressed blacks. Looters scrambled in the background. He heard an elected official saying now was the time for healing and a coming together among blacks and whites. He watched, but his interview never aired. The words of the reporter played again and again in his head, "Surely things are better for blacks."

As the black activist pushed the off button on his television set, a chipper weatherman concluded the news, saying, "Sunny skies tomorrow."

The Problem and Its Root

The newscaster's assumption is shared by millions of Americans. We ask each other what has gone wrong in the black community? What's wrong with blacks? Why can't they act like other ethnic or racial groups in America? Talk shows seek the answers from leading black personalities, who, when asked about the problems of black America, mouth well-worn platitudes. Perhaps they are fearful of raising the ire of mainstream America or perhaps they are simply naive.

Nevertheless, the solutions these blacks urge address only the symptoms afflicting black America, not the causes. The root of the problem within black America is not teenage pregnancy, drugs, the decline in family values, anger, rap music, unemployment or even the epidemic of violent crime. These are only symptoms of the deeper problem.

The root problem in black communities across America is race and the unjust distribution of our nation's wealth, power and resources. One race, the descendents of white Europeans, seemingly has checkmated blacks' efforts to improve themselves. Whites live in privileged conditions, with nearly 100 percent ownership and control of the nation's wealth, power, businesses and all levels of government support and resources. White society has a monopoly of ownership and control.

This monopoly of control resulted directly from centuries of abusive exploitation and expropriation of the labor of a darker race, black Americans of African descent. Though black Americans reside in the richest nation on earth, their standard of living is comparable to that of a Third World nation. Blacks own and control less than two percent of the wealth, power and resources of the nation, so they have little control over their lives and the conditions in which they are forced to live.

Both the disparity between white and black living conditions and inequitable allocation of resources are centuries-old problems. They are a major legacy of the "peculiar institution" called slavery. It was that social system that a white patriarchal society consigned blacks to live in the most inhumane conditions, doing the harshest labor, without just compensation. The dominant white society felt that by stripping the black slave of his humanity, all of his worldly possessions, his personal freedom, and keeping him hopeless that blacks would be forever non-competitive and powerless. Needless to say, the dominant society's experiment in social engineering worked.

The living conditions of a people, enslaved or free, tend to reflect their status and power within the larger society. Conditions in black America are no more or less than what was planned for them centuries ago. Solomon Northrup, a free black who was kidnapped into slavery, but later escaped, described the living standards of slaves in 1841 as befitting beasts of the field. He wrote about extraordinarily dehumanizing conditions that stripped slaves of their individuality, their labor and often their lives.

Slaves lived in dilapidated, damp, dark cabins, and their worldly possessions consisted of a few rags. A small board and a stick of wood, served as their beds and pillows. There were no physical, financial, nor psychological comforts for them, and worst of all, slaves were intentionally kept without hope. A slave's life was committed to producing wealth and comfort for white masters.[2] The slaves suffered in silence, but routinely asked in their prayers and work songs, "When will life get better for us, Lord?" Their descendants collectively still await an answer.

Legal and extra-legal measures were taken to keep both the free blacks, like the slaves, in a dependent state and excluded from enjoying the fruits of a nation that their labor was building. Free blacks were forced to survive or perish off of the marginal resources that extended into their communities. One of the first lessons that free blacks learned was that without money and power, freedom for a black-skinned person was freedom in theory only. They were still bound by their conditions and non-white skin color. The larger society kept them bound by making black skin color a badge of inferiority and degradation. Blacks who escaped the plantations were not permitted to escape the boundaries of their own flesh. In reality, the socioeconomic conditions for blacks outside of slavery were only slightly better than those within the slavery system.

Being free for a black person meant being quasi-free. A black was free as long as he could prove he was free. And even then he had only a marginally greater choice concerning how he lived compared to his enslaved brethren. In 1841, while Solomon Northrup lamented the terrible conditions of more than four million black slaves, approximately 386,290 quasi-free blacks throughout the North were being subjected to "Jim Crow" practices, a multiplicity of local ordinances and social sanctions that prohibited them from sharing fully in an affluent American society. They were forced to survive in poverty and social decay. In the shadows of the American dream, blacks' freedom was little more than a cruel and sadistic joke.

Local ordinances and social sanctions in the North and South restricted free blacks from earning competitive incomes (See the Appendix). Their labor was sold for just barely above the cost of slave labor. Without sufficient income, few were able to secure decent food, health care, or housing. They remained legally free but sought safe havens in large urban areas in the North, such as Philadelphia, Cincinnati, and Boston. The free black populations in and around these or any other large cities rarely exceeded two percent of the total population. These blacks lived off low quality food and had few worldly possessions.

According to Leonard P. Curry, author of *The Free Black in Urban America, 1800-1850,* more than a third of the black population in cities like Boston lived in blind alleys, cellars and lofts. Their poor and unsanitary living conditions created rampant health problems and shortened their life spans. Curry further stated that in 1855 Boston's City Register, Dr. Josiah Curtis found that the death rate among blacks was 99 times higher than whites'.[3] Today, 150 years later, the mortality gap between whites and blacks has narrowed only a little. Social pathology and inferior living conditions, not genetics, continue to control the life expectancy of blacks.

In the mid-1800s the living conditions for free blacks were so desperate that nearly 50 percent had no choice but to seek some form of public welfare. In order to survive, large numbers of blacks publicly acknowledged that they were in a helpless state and were incapable of feeding, protecting, sheltering and educating themselves and their children. Many black families became so desperate that they voluntarily re-entered slavery to survive. Others turned to public charity.

But nearly every black who sought some form of public relief was refused. They were chastised for being uneducated and were called lazy and irresponsible for bearing children that they could not support. Curry indicates that in Cincinnati, a typical northern urban area, out of 3,269 cases in which the city granted relief to the needy only 10 recipients were black. And the assistance offered these fortunate black recipients was only for their own burial expenses.

Public assistance tended to be distributed to whites only, including able-bodied male immigrants, while aid was denied to black widows with small children.[4] With the exception of a small number of abolitionists, dominant society was indifferent to the living conditions of free blacks. Rather than blaming white racism and slavery, white society blamed blacks for their conditions, even though the conditions were not unique to Cincinnati or Boston.

Similar horrendous conditions existed throughout the North and eventually gave rise to what became urban black ghettos that symbolized the conditions of blacks. The Emancipation Proclamation and subsequent Constitutional Amendments legally freed all blacks and granted them citizenship, but without social and economic resources these newly granted rights amounted to little more than paper rights.

The government refused to compensate blacks for their prolonged servitude by providing them with the necessary tools and resources to transition from a dependent labor class to independent, competitive citizens. Instead of aiding blacks, whites expected and urged the newly freed slaves to fend for themselves. They could work, seek public assistance, steal, or disappear.

Since free blacks could not find work, were denied public assistance and often could not leave the country, they had no choice but to accept what the dominant society offered them: sharecropping, which was only but another form of servitude controlled by white plantation owners.

No Light at the End of the Tunnel

One hundred and thirty years after slavery, American society has become more pluralistic and competitive, but blacks' marginal conditions remain relatively unchanged. In some respects, they have worsened. The socioeconomic inequalities that existed between whites and blacks during and shortly after slavery are now structural.

For example, on the eve of the Civil War, records indicated that more than 50 percent of free blacks were paupers; all free blacks collectively held less than one-half of one percent of the nations's wealth, with wealth being defined as a great quantity of money or valuable goods or resources within both the private and public sectors. A century later, in the 1960s, an era considered by many as "great decade of progress for blacks," more than 55 percent of all the blacks in America were still impoverished and below the poverty line. And, blacks barely held one percent of the nation's wealth. According to the 1990 Census, approximately 40 percent of all black families are receiving public assistance and the number is increasing, with more than 56 percent of all black female-headed households beneath the poverty level.

Black unemployment has not significantly improved, in comparative terms, over the last century. According to Curry, an historian, black unemployment exceeded 40 percent in the 1850s. The National Urban League's (NUL) 1992 State of Black America Report differed with the U.S. government figures indicating that the hidden and true unemployment rate is approximately 28 percent for black adults and nearly 55 percent for black youth.

The NUL's discomfort index further indicated that black unemployment worsened between 1960 and 1990, while economic conditions for white society improved. Blacks' lack of progress was reflected in the fact that blacks earned 53 percent of what whites earned in 1948. In the 1990s, after nearly 50 years of civil rights activities and affirmative action programs, blacks earn 59 percent of what whites earn. Further, the 1990 Census indicated that black per capita net worth is $9,359 versus $44,980 for whites.[5]

Like their ancestors, blacks today have the same set of options. And they still lack employment opportunities in public jobs or black businesses, because most white businesses are inaccessibly in the suburbs. They still are denied or expunged from public assistance rolls. And they have yet to learn how to disappear. Many blacks have turned to crime. They are therefore criminalized in order to seek sustenance and wealth. And, just as in the previous centuries, blacks continue to be disproportionately represented in the prison system.

Curry indicated that in 1850, for example, blacks constituted 60 percent of all persons incarcerated in Maryland and half of them were under 16 years of age. During the same time period, in the states of New York, New Jersey and Pennsylvania, blacks made up more than 50 percent of the prison populations. Today's prison rolls show similar percentages of blacks. Approximately 38 percent of all black males in America are either in prison, on parole or probation. Still, they are luckier than many of their counterparts, who annually fall victim to the homicide crisis, which each year claims more lives than the total number of American soldiers killed in either the Korean or Vietnam Wars.

In the final analysis, black America remains trapped in a dire dilemma. Some organizations have tried to call the nation's attention to the plight of blacks. In 1990, a five-year report by the National Research Council (NRC), a Washington-based research organization, indicated that the infinitesimal social and economic gains that blacks made during the 1950s and 1960s largely ended in the 1970s. *The Washington Post,* in June 1990 summarized the study reporting: "There has been no significant black progress for the last 20 years and a great socioeconomic gulf now separates blacks from European and other ethnic groups in America." Unfortunately, the NRC study received little media coverage or public response, even from black civil rights organizations.

Most blacks are concerned about what is happening in their communities and to their race, even if the media and the power structure are not. They actively participate in the political process and complain to their elected representatives about the worsening conditions, but the political system seems unable to stimulate change. Harold Cruse, a black historian, believes that among those who do care about the black problem, "Nothing is being done, because no one knows what to do about it."[6]

Considering the magnitude of black America's impoverished and powerless state, Cruse is probably right. But, why is it that society does not know what to do? Is it that the leaders of this society lack the knowledge or resources to solve the problems of black America? Or is it that they lack the incentive and commitment to create viable means for blacks to empower themselves as a group? Why should this nation's leaders do something to address the fundamental problems affecting blacks? The answer is simple. The United States' superiority among the industrial and agricultural world powers was achieved because of the exploitation of blacks. This exploitation established and now maintains a privileged racial class whose wealth and power explains and legitimizes the system's inequalities. Wealthy, conservative whites control both public and private sector resources and tools that have kept blacks impoverished and powerless in a racially competitive society.

Conservative Forces: The Bane of Black Society

Conservative social forces are the protectors of the status quo and the "good ole days." After using government to amass wealth, power and resources, conservative white power structures have long espoused sociopolitical policies that reflect their "pull up the gangplank" mentality. Powerful white conservatives profess commitment to capitalism and insist that wealth stays in the hands of the private, wealthy class, which has most benefited from the inequalities in the system.[7] They rigidly oppose any societal changes regarding race and resources. This places them in direct opposition to and in conflict with blacks.

Conservatism, of course, comes from the root word to conserve or hold on to what one has. In essence, the conservative attitude towards blacks is, "If you do not have it, we are not going to let you get it." When considering what should be done for black people, conservatives have espoused a role and solution for blacks that has not changed an iota since the country was founded. Conservatives believe in a natural ordering of human beings and have always preferred that blacks play a servile role in society.

In many ways, white liberal policies have been as injurious to blacks as those of conservatives. Neither the liberals nor the conservatives have offered any programs or resources for improving the overall socioeconomic condition of blacks. While conservatives have consistently sought to sink blacks' ship, liberals have simply rearranged the deck chairs on the sinking ship, so that blacks would be more comfortable.

Conservatives and liberals have historically approached black issues differently. Compared to ambiguous liberal approaches, conservatism is typically straightforward concerning the issue of race. It is not difficult to uncover conservative intentions in programs and public policies. Conservatives boldly proclaim that their positions reflect the sentiments of mainstream society as well as the principles of the first European settlers, who established a self-serving system that made it easy for them to horde wealth and power. It is this imbalance that conservatives seek to conserve. They frequently say that blacks are poor because they have unacceptable attitudes and behaviors and have failed to take advantage of opportunities, because they are basically inferior human beings.[8]

Over the past three decades, national opinion surveys have reported a growing conservatism among white society. Undoubtedly, some of it is a response to the growing uncertainty of the times. Societal clashes on such issues as abortions, family values, immigration, taxation, gender issues and crime have contributed to the popularity of conservatism. However, the core issue of white conservatives springs from race. They oppose government policies and programs that hint at the redistribution of public and private resources and power to benefit blacks.[9]

Modern conservatism began its ascendance in the late 1960s as a white backlash to the Civil Rights Movement, black power protests and urban riots. The demands of the black protests for improved living conditions through more wealth, power and community control shocked and frightened white society, which responded as it frequently does in times of civil turmoil and uncertainty. The privileged class appealed to conservatism to reassert the supremacy of white authority and its exclusive claim to power and wealth.

Breeding Black Conservatism

Black conservatism is as old as black enslavement. But three decades of popular white conservatism, coupled with the social and economic devastation of black America, has attracted an increasing number of blacks to the conservative political movement. Black conservatives represent a potential danger to their race because of their alignment with white conservatives, who have always been anti-black. When black-white conservative alignments occur, black conservatives become a liability to blacks and an asset to whites.

By mouthing the social and economic views of white conservatives, black conservatives convert confusion of their personal racial identity to a confusion in the minds of black people about the real issue facing them.

Black conservatives operate under misleading colors. As an old farmer said, "They run with the hounds while pretending friendship and brotherhood with the rabbits." The confusion caused by their schizophrenic behavior provides a public cover for anti-black attitudes and activities and makes them appear as nothing more than white racists in black face minstrel makeup.

Becoming a conservative has historically provided personal rewards to individual blacks, with few down sides, because of the powerlessness of the black community to hold accountable those members who turn against it. Blacks found that it was not difficult to establish beneficial relations with whites once they accepted a subordinate position and committed themselves to placing the welfare of the white class first. Once that was agreed upon, tacitly or otherwise, blacks were then entitled to various forms of paternalistic protection, Christian charity, and meritorious recognition. White conservatives then conferred special status and recognition to conservative blacks as exceptional or acceptable.

Accordingly, black conservatives who place their personal advancement above the welfare of their race often gain significant personal and financial benefits, recognition and access to power. They are anointed by whites as "leaders" and touted as role models. In political and social situations, a black conservative is closely akin to Sambo in Harriet Beecher Stowe's *Uncle Tom's Cabin*. In an historical context, a Sambo was black America's worst nightmare. The stereotypical Sambo was more than a minstrel man, a buffoon, and a plantation "darkie." Sambo represented the extraordinary success of social control, which was the ultimate goal of a slavery conditioning process that transplanted a white mindset into a black personality.[10]

The Symbolic Betrayal of the Black Race

The term Uncle Tom is not an appropriate label for an individual who is "white on the inside and black on the outside" and sells out his race by placing his personal gains with whites ahead of the rights and gains of his people. Contrary to popular usage of the label, the character Uncle Tom was not the culprit in *Uncle Tom's Cabin*. Uncle Tom was a brave man with dignity who cared about his family and race. The real villain was another black slave named Sambo. He was totally committed to the white master and used every opportunity to undermine the other slaves.

Sambo, in many respects, was like today's black conservatives. Sambo always followed the white slave master, Simon Legree, and offered to show him how to "tree the coons." It was Sambo who beat Uncle Tom to death both for refusing to whip a black female slave or sell out his people. Uncle Tom tried to empower his people by understanding and beating the social and political structure wherever he could. Uncle Tom felt it was important to get his people across the river to freedom. He risked his life to do so.[11]

The Sambo character personified a very successful social control created by conservatives. He was such a successful phenomenon that the concept he personified became a greater danger to blacks than Uncle Tom. As blacks move towards structuring policies of racial accountability, it will be very important for them to know who helps and who hurts the race.

Sambo was the black slave character in numerous novels and movies who was willing to pick up a weapon and defend his white master against the approaching Union army or hide the master's silver from Northern carpetbaggers. What is the difference between the fictional Sambo characters and today's real-life blacks who join the conservative movement to argue against affirmative action, black reparations and set-asides? They declare that the world is now color blind and are opposed to any policies requiring whites to share the socioeconomic burden that centuries of slavery and second-class citizenship have imposed on blacks.

Isn't espousing a color blind, race-neutral, melting pot society, a modern way of hiding the master's silver? What are black conservatives conserving when black America is burdened by poverty, crime, unemployment, homelessness and other social pathologies?

Based upon historical treatment alone there should be a general antagonism between blacks and conservatives. Though conservatives claim that they are not racist, for centuries they have opposed programs and policies to help blacks. Andrew Hacker, a white writer, provided insight on this in his book, *Two Nations: Black and White, Separate, Hostile, Unequal.* Hacker asserted that: "There persists the belief that members of the black race represent an inferior strain of the human species . . . Of course, the belief is seldom voiced in public. Most whites who call themselves conservatives hold this view about blacks and proclaim it when they are sure of their company."[12] Since white conservatives share their true feelings only in the privacy of other whites, there is a strong possibility that black conservatives do not know how white conservatives truly feel about them.

The Black-Jewish Alliance

It is often a conclusion of "popular history" that blacks and Jews have always shared a strong alliance. However, in their struggles to escape bondage and second-class citizenship, blacks have had few temporary and no permanent allies. At various times, abolitionists, liberals and individual Jews have provided visible support to black causes and sometimes at great personal risk and expense. They have lobbied state and federal legislative branches of government, contributed financial resources, provided surrogate leadership and given their lives to assist blacks. But, these contributions were made by individuals and not by Jews as a class, religious or racial body of Samaritans.[13] Prior to the 20th century, there were no known recorded public commitments of Jewish organizations to help blacks.

Beyond their good intentions, neither the abolitionists nor individual Jews achieved great success in helping blacks due to major philosophical flaws in their strategies. The flaw in the abolitionists' strategy was that they did not recognize or treat slavery as the economic issue that it was. They made the abolishment of slavery a moral issue, which it was not. As a moral issue, the abolitionists appealed to the conscience of slaveholders' concerning right and wrong. These appeals did not damage the slaveholders' profits from slavery.

By not treating slavery as an economic issue, they, perhaps unwittingly, supported slavery and undermined their own anti-slavery arguments. They continued to use, rather than boycott, slave-produced products, such as cotton goods, tobacco products, table foods, alcoholic beverages, iron products, and jewelry made from gold and silver. They could have withheld their monies from the shoe industry, insurance and shipping companies and other businesses that directly and indirectly made their profits from black slavery.

After Reconstruction, the efforts of individual Jews to assist blacks were flawed, because they encouraged blacks to do something that Jews themselves did not want to do — assimilate into the broader white culture. Jews helped blacks to secure civil and voting rights, but these legal rights, though important in principle, gave the appearance of making blacks self-sufficient, when in fact, these gains could not appreciably change blacks' wealth and power base. Worse still, the socioeconomic alliance between Jews and blacks did not emphasize blacks' learning the self-sufficiency skills and strategies mastered by Jews.[14]

From the beginning of the alliance in the 1900s, Jews kept their problems and blacks' problems in perspective. Jewish problems came first. Jews did not totally identify with blacks. Jews, fleeing persecution in Europe in the first and second decades of the 20th century entered America just as blacks were being forced back into "separate, but equal" worlds of Jim Crowism. The majority of Jews were poor, liberal and alone. Some were sympathetic to black problems and allied with them against racial bigotry.

In the 1920s and 1930s, blacks returned the favor by aligning with Jews against religious bigotry and oppression. The alliance benefited each group and presented a common front against some common conservative enemies. The alliance ultimately gave blacks access to high levels of government and the corporate world. In return for Jewish support, blacks gave Jews carte blanche access to every aspect of black society. Jews established neighborhood businesses that survived strictly off of black customers. They advised black leaders on public policy matters. Jews also built entire industries around resources that blacks controlled or owned, such as sports, entertainment and music.

For nearly half a century, Jews were officially endorsed as the liberal intermediaries between white and black America.[15] The alliance began to break down as blacks became increasingly disenchanted with their lack of progress and stagnant socioeconomic conditions. As the social fortunes of Jews and blacks began to diverge, the relationship became more paternalistic. Black organizations, such as the National Association for the Advancement of Colored People (NAACP), the National Urban League as well as independent black leaders were advised to pursue social integration, upward mobility within mainstream society and civil rights.

Black leadership was convinced that once blacks had obtained integration and civil rights, the quality of life would naturally improve for all blacks. After all, the strategy worked for the Jews. As the society began to soften its virulent anti-Semitism of the 1940s, Jews used their new found mobility to secure wealth and power for themselves. However, a decade after the 1954 desegregation decision and the Civil Rights Movement, not only had black America's socioeconomic dilemma not been resolved, it was getting worse.

Blacks outside of the traditional civil rights organizations became convinced that the only way to improve the conditions of black America was for blacks to take complete economic and political control of their communities, institutions and culture.[16] Many voiced anti-white sentiments that frightened and threatened the white establishment. Through slogans, symbols and urban riots, black America informed the nation that, having lost faith in the system, they had established alternative black leadership and were committed to achieving black power.

By the mid-1960s, religious attitudes and socioeconomic conditions had significantly changed for Jews in America. They had become the wealthiest and most influential political group in the nation. They had been accepted into the dominant society, with practically unlimited mobility opportunities. They controlled a major share of wealth, businesses, professional and management positions, government influence and access to institutions of higher education. Having made remarkable social and economic achievements, Jews now had a philosophical base for becoming more conservative.[17]

The black power protests of the late 1960s moved many Jews closer to right wing, conservative principles. Jews' increased conservatism was reflected in their reversed attitude towards the role of government. Previously, "Jews and blacks were . . . advocates for a strong governmental role in combating discrimination, alleviating the plight of the poor and aiding social mobility," according to Tom W. Smith. In a 1990 article entitled, "Jewish Attitudes Towards Blacks and Race Relations," published in the American Jewish Committee's Jewish Sociology Papers, Smith wrote that both Jews and blacks encouraged government involvement to improve the lives of the socially disadvantaged through progressive measures such as the New Deal policies.

From the 1930s to the 1950s, they used the legislative and court systems to pursue integration and broad intervention policies.[18] But according to Smith's attitude survey, after blacks demanded specific governmental assistance, Jews changed their minds about the role of government. For instance, Smith reported that today: "A majority of Jews do not favor government measures to help blacks, more government spending for blacks or the use of busing to achieve school integration." In response to the specific question, "Does the government have a special obligation to improve . . . [blacks'] living standards," more than 46 percent of Jews were opposed and 26 percent were either neutral or undecided.[19]

So, according to the Smith report, Jewish attitudes on the question of the government's responsibility to assist a structurally handicapped group, such as Jews were years ago, has now turned 180 degrees. At the start of the 20th century, they were pro-government involvement. By mid-century, they were opposed. Harold Cruse, in his book, *Plural But Equal,* offers his explanation for Jews' turning towards conservatism and away from blacks: "The opposition of Jewish liberalism to the threat of quotas shows that when power enclaves are threatened, sociologically and psychologically the dominant white society will instinctively oppose, limit, and restrict . . . [such changes]. In such manner are the avenues to social and economic power effectively maintained."[20]

While some Jews opposed the vehicle of quotas and affirmative action three decades ago, various Jewish organizations have worked to keep a dialogue going with the black community. Others have continued to feel alienated from blacks. Today, some Jews are upset because of the alignment of some members of the black community with the Nation of Islam, which teaches that Jews have been just as oppressive and exploitive of blacks as any other white groups. According to Smith, though there are heated tensions between the two groups and the ties are not as strong as they were in the early part of the 1900s, Jews have a more positive attitude towards blacks than any other white group. Smith's survey further indicated that the most conservative groups against blacks are Protestants and Baptist fundamentalists.[21]

Government's Conservatism Alienates Blacks

Anti-black conservatism from 1980 to 1992 severed the fragile relationship that was beginning to build between blacks and government. The government established new priorities that reversed most of the progress made by blacks during the 1960s. It withdrew its marginal support of blacks for political and racial reasons, just as it did during the Reconstruction Period following the Civil War.

President Lyndon Johnson acknowledged the social and economic inequities of black life. Through his Great Society Programs, he sought to do what government had failed to do during Reconstruction — to relieve the depressed conditions of black America by redistributing opportunities and self-development tools. But again, the larger society would not tolerate it. There was a backlash against all programs and policies that suggested wealth and power re-distribution between whites and blacks. Conservative whites opposed public policies that mandated busing, affirmative action, quotas, equal housing opportunities, set-asides and racial preferences.

Conservatives insisted that their actions were not racist and that they were committed to equal opportunities for blacks. The hypocritical difference between their rhetoric and actions was similar to the old line that, "Everybody wants to go to heaven, but nobody wants to die." They proclaimed a belief in equality and parity for blacks, but they would not accept the measures that were needed to bring about that equality and parity.

Richard Nixon, the presidential successor to Lyndon Johnson, rode into the highest public office in this nation on the conservative white backlash to black power protests in the late 1960s. Shortly after his 1968 election, his domestic advisor, Daniel Moynihan, sent out the first signal that the federal government was ready to use its powers to put blacks back "in their place" by blaming them, not racism, for the breakdown of the black family and community as well as the widespread poverty and powerlessness that afflicted the black community.

The conservatives' national goal was to abandon the civil rights agenda and move towards a "color-blind" society. In 1970, Moynihan issued his infamous "benign neglect" memorandum that announced the new public policy on blacks. The policy behind the memorandum moved attention away from blacks, saying: "The time may have come when the issue of race could benefit from a period of benign neglect . . . We may need a period in which Negro progress continues and racial rhetoric fades."[22]

Moynihan's memorandum signalled that the old government policy of using blacks as cheap labor was ending and the new policy would declare blacks obsolete. Alphonso Pinkney, in his book, *The Myth of Black Progress*, indicated that Moynihan's memorandum encouraged the supplanting of blacks with other ethnic groups. Moynihan wrote that "Greater attention to Indians, Mexican-Americans and Puerto Ricans would be useful." The government justified supplanting blacks by promoting the myth that "black Americans were making extraordinary progress." The nation swallowed the myth of black progress. Meanwhile, real change in black America's condition never even got off the ground.[23]

Most black Americans did not agree with Moynihan's assessment that blacks had created their social ills through self-inflicted pathologies. And blacks didn't accept the government's claim that they were making extraordinary social and economic progress. "Making progress compared to what and whom?" they asked.

History has taught blacks that they, not the powerful social and economic system, are always blamed for their deplorable living conditions. Dominant society's belief that the negative conditions of black America are self-inflicted is based upon the fact that the conditions that blacks endure are almost peculiar to blacks alone. White society has never been enthusiastic about helping blacks nor has it permitted them to acquire the tools to help themselves. Blaming blacks for their underclass status keeps the larger society free from recriminations or obligations to blacks.

Ironically, if the deplorable conditions of black America were experienced by white America for even a short period of time, the government would not hesitate to declare a national disaster and activate emergency assistance measures. But, since depressive socioeconomic conditions have been peculiar to black America for centuries, no such governmental intervention is to be expected.

The Death of the Black Civil Rights Movement

For everyone but the caretakers of old black civil rights organizations, the Civil Rights Movement for blacks is dead. Civil rightism for blacks had a brief life for the second time within a 100-year period, reached a point of diminishing returns, then died a premature death during the late 1960s. All of the rights gained by the Civil Rights Movement have been bequeathed to groups that are more acceptable to the larger society — women, gays, Hispanics, Asians, handicapped and poor whites. The first black civil rights efforts formally started shortly after the Civil War as slaves realized that they had received paper freedom and unexercisable rights. For nearly a century, they pursued their phantom freedom and rights nationally by way of public forums, courtrooms, schoolhouses, union halls and journalism.

In the 1954 Brown vs. the Board of Education desegregation decision, blacks won a battle, but the decision had incalculable destructive effects on the black community. During the subsequent civil rights protest period, blacks stimulated a rush of new social movements by a melange of social groups which piggybacked on black causes in their own quests for rights and freedoms. This offended the larger society in general and gave conservatives grounds to orchestrate a backlash. Since blacks were the largest, most visible and least acceptable group, they became the primary target of conservatives' angst.

The movement was drowned out by the new groups and out-flanked by the conservatives. In the heat of various civil rights battles for control over jobs, schools, housing, community services, businesses and tax dollars, black leadership ran out of insight, social tools and strategies for effectively dealing with the more subtle and less direct forms of racism that cropped up.

As the other groups began to take away from blacks control of the civil rights agenda, conservative political forces started using their government and media power to diminish the black component of the Civil Rights Movement. They successfully destroyed the legitimate base of the black movement by diluting the movement beyond recognition. They identified every group that could possibly perceive itself as aggrieved and made it equal to blacks. Thus, the public perception of blacks was severely damaged and distorted. The unique problems that they faced were made to appear no more important than the problems faced by other, so-called victims of discrimination.

The black Civil Rights Movement, though spectacularly successful in many respects, had at least four major flaws that diminished the accomplishments of the movement and left critical imperatives for black America:

• The movement's black leadership focused its entire weight of resources on achieving integration. They believed, perhaps naively, that by removing all the symbols of Jim Crowism and acquiring access to various segments of white society, black people would gain equality.

• Black leaders failed to focus on neutralizing the forces behind Jim Crowism or developing effective strategies for black America to use in dealing with the problems that spring forth from the maldistribution and racist control of wealth, power and resources in America.

• They failed to develop a long-term national plan with goals and strategies, spelling out where blacks ought to be going and how best to get there.

• In addition, black leaders failed to construct a national network of institutions to train new generations of blacks who could successfully assume leadership positions and implement a national plan for black empowerment.

The combined effect of these four major failures left the black Civil Rights Movement with no place to go, no way to get there and no leadership to take them.

A few visible black organizations managed to survive by becoming "politically correct" and expanding their focus to include so-called minorities, poor people, gays, women and abused children. They could not survive in the powerful conservative climate by continuing to target the problems of blacks alone. Although black conditions continued to need attention, most black organizations could not raise enough money to survive by focusing solely upon their own people. The surviving black organizations remained visible by continuing to pursue the integration dream. It would not have been necessary for black organizations to abandon their own community if the Civil Rights Movement had established a sense of community cohesiveness founded on group economics and group politics.

The National Urban League and the NAACP are still active, but they have lost much of their influence and membership. The Student Nonviolent Coordinating Committee (SNCC) and the Black Panther Party are defunct. The Congress of Racial Equality joined the conservative ranks of a national political party and the Southern Christian Leadership Conference barely survives. This nation's political apparatus disabled many of the civil rights groups by destroying or neutralizing black leadership: Adam Clayton Powell and Stokely Carmichael were discredited; Martin Luther King, Jr., Malcolm X and Medger Evers were assassinated; Rap Brown, Eldridge Cleaver, Angela Davis and prominent members of the Black Panthers were criminalized.

Many of the others were enticed into mainstream society. Consequently, the large block of black leadership was eradicated, changed or disappeared after just one generation following the great movement. Having failed to address the structural conditions of black America, the 1960s left little structure upon which blacks could build. Instead, that colorful era only left faded memories and soul-stirring songs.

The void created by the death of black civil rights presented the opportunity for a cadre of black neoconservatives to join the popular white conservative movement and proclaim themselves and their new organizations the new black leadership. They were publicly blessed by the highest levels of government and corporate America and they offered black America political and economic ideologies that were taken right from the conservative right-wing political bible. Their politically correct ideologies advocated less government and taxes, free market economies, privatization of government services and race-neutral government policies.[24] Black traditional leadership, like the black masses, was ignored by government and the media, except during times of racial disturbances or anniversaries of the movement.

Conclusion

The problem of race and resources has been festering for hundreds of years, but has yet to arise as the core public issue in America. Whites have inherited the power and wealth of their ancestors through a social and economic structure designed and weighted to the advantage of non-blacks.

Blacks have inherited a legacy of permanent poverty and powerlessness. Black labor made the nation a strong, wealthy, international world power, but nothing has been proposed to seriously bring about remuneration, parity or fairness to black people. It is clear that blacks must both solve their own problems and structure a national plan of action that puts their priorities first and foremost. Self-empowerment is the only road to economic justice, but it requires the support of a national policy and plan of action.

2

Power and Black Progress

"Blacks and power are the oil and water of American politics."
— Source Unknown

P ower plays a critical role in black-white race relationships in
America. Though we cannot see, taste or touch it, we can sense its
presence and attest to its strength and potency. It affects all manner of human relations. Power, in and of itself, is neutral. Only the motives and purposes of the power users make power good or bad. It has been abusively
used to create divisions between black and white people around the world. A
racial and ethnic hierarchy disproportionately distributed nearly 100 percent
control and ownership of wealth, material resources, and privileges to whites
at the top of the social order, while blacks, assigned to the lowest level, were
disproportionately burdened with poverty, powerlessness and social exclusion. The problems created by those power disparities spawned racial inequities that only power realignment can correct.

Dominant society used its power to label blacks lazy, ignorant and criminal, then enacted laws that denied them jobs, education and justice. And,
through the most insidious act of all, dominant society used its social powers

to assign an intensely negative human worth to black skin color, that caused millions of blacks to fear each other and hate themselves.

What Is Power?

Power is defined by *Webster's Dictionary* as the ability to bring about fulfillment of one's desires and needs. Behavioral scientists add another nuance to the meaning by including in the definition the notion of one entity imposing its will on another. Along the same line, Thomas Sowell, an economist, defines the term power in a much broader sense, in his book, The Economics and the Politics of Race, he adds the qualifier, that "Power is not simply the ability to get something done, but to get it done despite the resistance and opposition of others." It is this last definition of power that is used in this book.

A true powerholder can enforce its decisions and will on the less powerful by applying or threatening to apply penalties or force. Or, it can elect to secure compliance to its wishes and decisions by providing or offering rewards. The final decision on the use of any particular form of social control belongs to the powerholder. Those holding power have used it effectively in organizing and controlling blacks to the benefit of the larger society. Power has determined the quality of black life.

Social powers external to black communities have controlled and shaped black peoples' lives and behavior for more than four centuries. The power of dominant society determined whether blacks would walk proudly as free bushmen of West Africa or toil in chains as slaves among the bushes of America. Dominant society's power made blacks the economic locomotive engine that drove civilizations around the world, but assigned blacks to the caboose, so that they could not enjoy the fruits of their own labor.

Kinds of Power

To advance the self-interest of an individual or a group, humans use numerous kinds of powers. The most common forms of power in black-white relations are group power, institutional power, wealth power, numerical population power, political power, and voting power. The dominant society uses power mechanisms, such as government, private corporations, religious and social institutions, to perpetuate its self-interests and secure and maintain control of power-building resources. Black labor was a wealth builder and therefore a power generating resource that dominant society greatly valued and manipulated. To maintain the power generated by black labor, white society used whatever means necessary to keep blacks powerless and under control.

Group Power

The United States' constitutional spirit of individualism notwithstanding, group power was the true and base origin of all rights in American society. Group power is typically manifested when a collection of individuals organize and pool their resources to achieve common goals and shared benefits. Such action is the primary instrument for securing objects of interest and power.

In the founding years of this nation, European whites built their dreams of becoming a wealthy aristocracy within a capitalistic democracy on the backs of black slaves. The collective power resources of many people, nations, religions, and organizations were aligned and concertedly used to exploit blacks. Their strategy illustrates that group power requires general agreement among the participating members on a core issue, but power evolves from the group's collective motives and goals.

Institutional Power

Institutions arise and exist only by means of group behavior. Institutions center their activities around fundamental social, cultural, academic, racial, religious, or financial needs. They permanently unite a group of people in a cooperative task. Once decisions have been made by the larger society, institutions use their resources to confirm and explain why the larger society made such decisions and occasionally, institutions are called upon to play leadership roles.

Institutions can acquire a variety of powers due to their non-biological permanency. If financially supported, they survive aging, political shifts and drastic social changes. An institution's powers are in proportion to and may be measured by its ability to create, store and circulate data, develop and influence public policies, aggregate people around issues, network with other institutions and organizations, and stimulate the development of leadership. Institutions that can do all of these things well become very powerful. The greatest limitation of institutional power is the lack of transferability of its powers to a particular individual, at a particular time, on a particular issue. This institutional limitation promotes institutional leadership instead of charismatic personalities. Considering black America's dire dilemma, the formation of a network of intellectual institutions is imperative for building power bases.

The Impact of Institutionalized Power on Blacks

The superior group power of whites influenced all the institutions they built: government, schools, businesses, churches, and social organizations. Institutions were the means of inculcating values that would perpetually maintain the self-interest of European whites and their descendents. Thus, institutional power has become a major factor in maintaining the power imbalance between blacks and whites. Government was one of the most powerful tools of the dominant society. Without the support and power of government, the white society could not have enslaved and segregated blacks for centuries.

Government, for example, enacted laws that forbade schools to accept black children and made it illegal to teach a black person to read or write. Initially, all formal religious denominations accepted the abuse of blacks and even offered Biblical justifications for it. Through government, businesses, churches and other institutionalized powerholders, white society controlled the wealth, power and resources. They also controlled blacks, their primary labor source.

Wealth-Power

Economic power has always been the greatest source of power for individuals and groups in America. Individuals who merge their political or financial resources into a group can become very powerful in a capitalistic democracy. For instance, Jews and White Anglo-Saxon Protestants (WASP) have uncontested control over a disproportionate share of America's wealth. Wealth gives them options. They use their wealth as political tools to open doors to new economic opportunities for their respective groups; to punish other groups and to block the doors of opportunity.

Obviously, all whites do not possess great wealth and power. But, because of their strong sense of racial cohesion and their compulsive belief in keeping economic resources within their communities, the resources of wealthy and powerful whites stay within the white community. They rarely help non-whites, especially blacks. Chancellor Williams, in his book, *The Destruction of Black Civilization*, wrote:

"Caucasians will wage frightful wars against other Caucasians, but will quickly unite, as though by instinct, against non-whites, not only in wars, but in international policies. They have developed a kind of built-in solidarity in their relations with non-Caucasian peoples. This fact, as much as anything else, helps to explain their position as masters of the world."[1]

Together, wealth and politics represent a potent combination of powers, because they are versatile and by working together they can produce other forms of power. They are the root cause of racial stratification, exploitation and the unequal distribution of resources. In the present social structure, maldistribution guarantees that America will never be an "equal opportunity society." Those who hold a disproportionate share of the wealth and power are not inclined to share or relinquish these tools. In combination, political power and wealth become practically synonymous in a capitalistic democracy.[2]

Since wealth remains concentrated and rigidly locked in the hands of whites, black progress will be difficult. As far back as 1790, the richest 10 percent of white households has held half of the nations wealth.[3] By the eve of the Civil War, one percent of the most wealthy whites owned 24 percent of the nation's wealth. One hundred years later, in 1969, they owned 24.9 percent.[4]

During the very same time periods, black wealth remained between one and two percent. It is astounding that the percentages of wealth controlled by whites or blacks have not changed throughout this nation's involvements in the Civil War, emancipation of the slaves and Reconstruction, World War I, the Great Depression, World War II, Korean and Vietnam Wars, and the Civil Rights Movement, which was followed by a second reconstruction period. Through it all, the wealthy white elite collectively held on to everything.[5]

According to Census reports, the great disparity between black and white wealth and income levels continues to increase. The U.S. Department of Commerce, Bureau of the Census in 1986 reported that the average white household had 10 times more wealth than the average black household. The wealth gap is so large that the three richest white Americans, with a collective net worth of $15 billion, had a greater financial net worth than all black businesses combined.[6]

The major driver of the wealth and income gap between blacks and whites is the maldistribution of poverty. The poverty level for blacks is three times that of whites and Hispanics. Nearly one-third of blacks are classified as poor. And 50 percent of all single, black female heads of household are poverty stricken.[7] Poverty is a power impeder.

Numerical Population Power

In a democratic society, the numerical majority wins, rules and decides. The theoretical rights of a minority, may or may not be respected, especially if they are a planned minority. Numerical population power is the power that comes to those groups that acquire power through their sheer size. The black population peaked in the 1750s when slaves and free blacks accounted for approximately 33 percent of the total population.[8] The high numerical strength of blacks caused fear and concern among whites. They feared the loss of their own numerical power. Word of black Haitians' successful slave revolt in the 1790s had spread across America and reportedly ignited several slave revolts in Southern states.

The First U.S. Congress enacted the first naturalization law that declared America to be a nation for "whites only." This naturalization act and other income incentives attracted a massive influx of legal and illegal European ethnics, followed by Asian and Hispanic immigrants a century later. The immigration quota on blacks remained zero until their total percentage of the population declined to nine percent. By making blacks a planned numerical minority, white society assured its dominance in a democratic society where the majority always wins.

Political Power and Its Supportive Concepts

Political power comprises all those activities that relate to the authoritative uses of public and governmental powers under existing traditions, laws and Constitutional authorities of government. But political power can be acquired either through or outside of the normal process of elective or appointed office. Political power is an important power for a depressed group to have because politics is the process that typically decides who shall have what benefits in life. However, groups aspiring to gain political power can only obtain and use it if they have economic power as well. Economic power allows a group to possess and exercise control over its own power rather than seeking access to another's power.

Voting: Illusionary Power

Voting in publicly held elections is a key source of power in any democratic society, if the voting groups have certain collateral forms of power. Emancipation and Amendments to the Constitution gave blacks the legal right to vote. Probably the only instance in which blacks exercise true group power is through block voting. But, without wealth, numerical or social accountability powers, voting becomes a weak form of power for blacks. Voting rights have pacified blacks by allowing them to make choices, but never decisions. They could only vote their choice for candidates about whom the dominant white society had already made decisions. The weakness of blacks' voting power was demonstrated when a white anti-Reconstruction backlash in the South took voting rights from blacks within a generation after they were granted in the mid-1860s. It took nearly another century to restore blacks' access to the ballot box.

Since the 1960s, blacks' consistent level of voter participation indicates that they steadfastly believe that their voting power can significantly change their life conditions. This will not happen, though much effort and expense go into black voter registration and get-out-the-vote projects. Blacks have successfully put black and white candidates into high governmental offices by voting in blocks. But blacks have failed to buttress their block voting with other forms of group power building activity.

Voting itself is a limited, transitory form of power that ends when the polls close. With the block vote, blacks may cast the decisive votes that put a candidate into office, but they cannot make that new office holder deliver. Threats can be made, but voting power cannot be exercised outside of the ballot box. Since elections are held every two or four years, the black electorate can be ignored or further damaged by those they put into public office.

Blacks' limited income and wealth encouraged them to support their political candidates with campaign workers and votes at the ballot boxes. But, "He who pays the piper calls the tune." Black communities in recent years have failed to use their limited financial power and resources to persuade outside forces to create change inside black communities. One of the most noteworthy times that they did was the Alabama bus boycott. Beyond a doubt it was more effective than the ballot box. When money stopped flowing from black to white hands, the white society in Alabama listened and changed a little.

Even when blacks vote blacks into public office, their ballot box victories do not necessarily translate into improved social and economic conditions for black people. Some black elected officials have been reluctant to initiate programs solely targeted to blacks. Many have been convinced that we live in a color-blind society or are simply afraid to push for black causes.

Thus, black political power has yet to become an effective strategy for getting vitally needed resources to black communities. Though the rule of politics is "something for something," black Americans are never specifically rewarded for their overwhelming support for candidates for public office. Black officials are skittish about using the powers of their offices to specifically address the needs of black communities because they are concerned about generating a white backlash. It is easier for them to propose or support programs that are ambiguously designed to assist everybody rather than just blacks. For their political support, blacks have always been denied quid pro quo, or something in return for their votes.

Some black office holders, like their white political counterparts, practice "trickle down" politics. They demonstrate their productivity to blacks by

TABLE 1 Comparison of the Number of Black Elected Officials vs. Black Socioeconomic Conditions*					
Year	Number Elected	Unemployment Percentage (%)	Black Prisoners (%)	Blacks Below Poverty Line (%)	Per Capita Income (%)
1964	103	10.8	33.0	34.0	53.0
1970	1439	08.2	35.8	32.5	60.0
1975	3503	14.7	42.0	31.1	55.0
1988	6793	11.7	45.0	32.0	59.5
1992	8000	14.6	45.3	34.4	59.1

* Figures reported by the National Urban League; they are typically higher and more accurate than government figures, because they include blacks who are not actively seeking unemployment benefits, employment, or are only marginally employed. [9]

pointing to legislation and programs that they supported for civil rights, poor people, minorities, the homeless, immigrants, prison reform, and public works. Few can point to a program or policy that was enacted specifically and solely to relieve the horrendous conditions in black communities. At nearly every level of government and in corporate America, there are some programs or policies that target women, Indians, Asians, Hispanics, handicapped and other aggrieved groups. Once black elected officials buy into the idea of supporting measures to assist everybody, they have, in effect, eliminated the importance of having a black elected official. Mainstream programs and policies have merely maintained the status quo, leaving blacks in the same status that they were in before blacks were elected or appointed to public office.

Since 1960, there has been a sizable increase in the number of black elected officials, an 8,000 percent increase, to be more specific. As indicated in **Table 1**, black conditions have either remained the same or worsened.

Black per capita income, compared to white per capita income, went up over the last two decades, but the gap between poor and middle-class blacks widened. The 8,000 percent rise in the number of black elected officials did little to impede the steady increase of blacks entering the criminal justice system, poverty, homelessness, unwed motherhood, drug abuse activity, or the homicide rolls.

Likely, without the increased number of black elected officials, black conditions would be even worse today. Yet, it is a dramatic statement about the dire condition of black America that it took an 8,000 percent increase in blacks elected to public office to keep blacks where they had always been.

Many black elected officials bewail their inability to change the conditions of blacks. The nation's 36 million blacks are a sleeping giant that, if properly organized and mobilized, could achieve group economic and political power. However, in order to do so, black disposable income must be just as organized and selectively spent as black votes are cast during an election.

James Jennings, a writer and observer of black political activism, summarized the fallacy that voting results in political power for blacks: "Voting in itself is not power . . . nor is having black elected and appointed officials power. These phenomena become power only when they can be used to influence and affect the behavior of . . . white society and others."[10]

The Importance of Power for Black People

Without increased wealth and political power, blacks cannot correct the multitude of social ills that have become imbedded in the fabric of their communities. Nor can they acquire the power they need through a shared power arrangement with the dominant white society. The dominant society will not permit blacks to use the power within white institutions to improve social and economic conditions within black communities, especially since whites as a group generally have neither the interest nor incentive for correcting the conditions. Consequently, blacks must develop their own group and institutional powers then remedy the inequalities that have been historically imposed upon them.

Progress has eluded black people because they have been powerless to get what they wanted and needed, and they have not been able to stop others from depriving them of the necessities of life. Since slavery and the 1954 desegregation decision, blacks have experienced political and civil rights improvements. Blacks have relatively free access to voting booths and can vote for any candidate that the power structure offers. They have access to public rest rooms, lunchroom counters, and the front seat on any bus. However, civil rights did not bring about much change in their ability to pay for the best facilities or seats.

Civil rights have been ineffective for most blacks in terms of improving substandard housing, lowering their unemployment rate, transforming dysfunctional schools, removing massive poverty, reducing high crime or eliminating social rejection by whites, Asians, Hispanics and other ethnics. Black social and economic progress will come about only when blacks muster the power and the commitment to bring forth positive change.

Black Self-Empowerment: The Only Road Open

Self-empowerment is the most effective, if not the only road open for blacks to reach racial competitiveness. But, the first issue to resolve is a common understanding of what the term self-empowerment means. Since the 1960s, the term has been used in unclear and even contradictory ways.

The *American Heritage Dictionary* defines empowerment "to invest with legal power or to authorize." This definition speaks to institutionalized authorities and powers. Quite clearly, this is not what black activists intended when they spoke of empowering black people and black communities in the 1960s. Most community activists were concerned about empowering black people to act in or be in a position to speak for their own people through established systems.

Today, it is politically correct to espouse "empowerment zones" in minority communities throughout the nation. According to one federal official, empowerment zone monies would be invested in infrastructure improvements and preferential tax incentives would be offered to white businesses in order to attract them into the very same black communities that they began abandoning 30 years ago.

How do infrastructure improvements and tax incentives for white wealth holders help blacks? Is the term empowerment zones used to mean self-empowerment? If so, how? Who is really being empowered and how will what the government proposes to do eradicate black communities' dire conditions? Self-empowerment for blacks can only occur when blacks use all of their available resources to accrue wealth and social power through a comprehensive plan involving all segments of their communities.

A properly developed self-empowerment plan that is supported in principle by all of black America could change centuries of deferred dreams into realized visions. Until black America collectively aspires to acquire its own power to alter its marginal conditions, it is highly unlikely that they will ever obtain power. A plan for self-empowerment must begin with a realistic analysis of blacks' assets and lead to the development of strategies to maximize their fullest potential.

True empowerment would give blacks new tools and strengths to deal with the power imbalances that today promote racism in the court systems, educational institutions as well as the government and private corporate sectors. These entities have no accountability to blacks, even though they exert tremendous power over blacks. They are repositories of the cultural power of whites. They have not changed through the centuries, thus, they still safeguard the culture, heritage and social values of the original European settlers.

Organize and Power Will Come

A great writer once said that, "Those who the gods would make powerful must first organize." Few words could be truer for blacks. Whether individual blacks are firm believers in the concepts of integration, segregation or moderation, they must all come together around the goal of improving the living conditions of their race. Although political and other philosophies may differ, blacks are united by their physical commonality. Divided they cannot achieve empowerment. They will be unable to make effective decisions about their future.

Blacks are no longer in servitude. They have a protected right to exercise their freedom of association. They may freely organize in their own best interest. No other ethnic or racial group will organize for nor represent blacks' interest. Society is competitive and becoming increasingly more pluralistic and there are no incentives for others to assist black people.

A plan for organizing will not spontaneously materialize. Blacks must organize in order to direct their own future and long-term best interest. In the past, blacks organized to address specific issues that aggrieved them. The resultant organizations, therefore, lacked permanence. When the issue or the leader died, so did the organization, regardless of its effectiveness. Consequently, blacks have historically been caught in the constant cycle of reorganizing. Moreover, most black single-issue organizations have lacked the human or financial capital to provide a forceful, continuous, adaptive and sustained fight strictly on behalf of blacks.

Though Jews are a minority religious group, they can serve as an empowerment model. Jews wield strong blocks of powers — financial and political — that result from their strong sense of community, control of wealth and organizational networking. Under their religious identification and sense of togetherness, they aggressively protect their domestic and international interests, regardless of criticisms. Unlike blacks, they openly and aggressively use their powers to tilt the government and private resources to support issues and programs that benefit Jews. As a religious minority, Jews understand that in a government that is based on the belief of being of, by and for the people that "the people" are those who can concentrate their power and get what they want.

Harold Cruse, the historian, criticized blacks' failure to develop new organizational leadership for collective decision making. Using Jews as a model of organizing, Harold Cruse lamented that: "History had taught Jews that without a strong, purposeful organization, there was little chance for survival in a hostile world. To this very day, blacks have not learned that lesson."[11]

Blacks are a sleeping giant, with some limited potential for developing economic and social powers. But, regardless of the limited nature of their potential, group power operates upon the very simple principle that whosoever is organized has already established a minimum level of power that they did not have as a scattered people. Blacks seeking to empower themselves will undoubtedly create concerns among whites who have grown accustomed to the historical belief that blacks should always be a powerless, poverty stricken people.

Although it appears that the dominant society would be more comfortable with American Indians, Asians, or Hispanics seeking increased group power, the black race is not so weak that it cannot develop the limited potentials for group power that up until now have been acquired by them only through chance and historical circumstances.

As a powerless group, blacks have at least two choices: They can seek self-empowerment through incremental structural changes or they can seek to share with those groups that already have it. Blacks, to a large degree, have taken the latter route and have looked for access to white powerholders for a share of power. This decision was a natural outgrowth of the slavery conditioning process (as explained later in Chapter Seven) which taught blacks to align their interests with the interests of the masters. This social phenomenon is aptly demonstrated both in the behavior of Sambo in *Uncle Tom's Cabin* and the real life acts of black conservatives.[12]

At best, access to power allows the power seeker the opportunity of being near the powerholder and to secure personal benefits or limited benefits for the needful masses. In seeking to share power with whites, blacks must understand the drawback — that requests for power to improve their conditions must always be passed through and approved by the social and political forces of the major white powerholders, who are rarely generous to blacks in their decision making.

As James Jennings, in his book, the *Politics of Black Empowerment*, stated:

"For all groups in a given society, the prospect for improved incomes, greater holdings of property, and more favorable life chances generally is profoundly influenced by the group's relationship to the instruments of power . . . This means the ability [of blacks] to use all those sanctions, rewards, and inducements, and methods that people in the advanced society use to control their environment and influence the behavior of others."[13]

Unity or group power is the most important ingredient in the advancement of a racial group. Group power is essential to make the most of blacks' access to power, as they endeavor to acquire power itself.

Progress Follows Empowerment

For black progress to occur, there must be a fundamental redistribution of wealth and poverty in America. They are burdened by too much planned impoverishment. Blacks cannot amass power from their individual holdings of wealth until they organize and develop a plan that will attract and retain wealth within black communities. Nearly every black community suffers from historical deprivation, low income levels and the flight of black capital and disposable income to white suburbs. The income that does remain in black communities, usually between two and five percent, is insufficient to maintain public services, support businesses, stimulate employment opportunities. It cannot support a political structure dedicated to advancing black interests nor garner respect from other competitive racial or ethnic groups.

Organizing and Thinking Strategically

It must be clarified that the possession of power does not guarantee wealth. Nor does wealth always guarantee power. But, contrarily, the lack of power can guarantee poverty and poverty can always guarantee powerlessness. Controlling resources, maintaining a strong sense of community, and good organizational planning can produce both power and wealth.

It is the American way to organize groups for the purpose of acquiring and wielding power. While most groups realize that there is strength in numbers, apparently, according to one study, some blacks do not necessarily see strength in grouping themselves with other blacks.

In a study of group power, Evans and Giles reported that: "Increased concentration [of blacks] served to generate higher levels of ethnocentrism among blacks and raised fears among whites."[14] The lower the percentage of blacks in the workplace, for instance, the lower whites fear that blacks will acquire power. This is an important finding and raises questions about the wisdom of integration. If race relations are based on power, the more blacks integrate into white society, the less chance they have to acquire power. Blacks' willingness to dilute their own strength destroys any perception of their having power. The perception of power is the first step towards the reality of power.

The Evans and Giles study revealed significant findings that have an impact on group power for blacks. The authors found that blacks did not conceptualize their potential for group power. And, more detrimental, blacks may actually perceive their group power to diminish when higher concentrations of blacks are present. These perceptions of racial concentrations and power are exactly the opposite of whites. Whites establish barriers, legal and otherwise, to insure their superior numbers and power.

Blacks' belief that something may be wrong when large numbers of them come together without the presence of whites can probably be traced to the conditioning process of slavery, which taught blacks to see themselves through the eyes of a white person. Thus, reversing years of self-deprecating thinking, low self-esteem and slave conditioning and organizing to achieve group empowerment goals will require careful strategic planning. Blacks must organize around new principles and purposes in order to confront the political and economic realities facing them.

To their credit, black intellectuals, in the ante- and post-bellum periods, did try to organize and plan. They shared resources and demonstrated some community-oriented accountability by establishing planning forums and advocacy organizations through churches and benevolent societies. Their effectiveness was limited by their meager financial and material resources, and lack of access to power sources. However, they had an impact on the attitudes of the black masses, especially during the most oppressive times.

Some noteworthy planning organizations that were singularly committed to black people were established during several historical periods: the Negro Convention Movement in 1830; the Niagara Movement in 1905; the African Community League in 1914; The Universal Negro Improvement Association in the early 1900s, and the National Negro Congress in 1936.[15]

Clearly, blacks felt a recurring need for national planning and research, but there was no commonly accepted goal or established public policy for blacks. Differing philosophies and political personalities confused the issues and bogged down the organizations. In the recent past, blacks organized over specific issues, such as discrimination, crime, unemployment or voting rights. As stated earlier, the organizations either faded when the issue faded or lost potency and became nonthreatening advocacy groups. They found it easier to organize advocacy groups whose narrow focuses did not appear as threatening to established powers.

One of the first known and longest lasting attempts by blacks to establish a national planning group was the Negro Convention Movement, which began in 1830 and continued through the Civil War. Black leaders throughout the North got together to identify problems, develop policies and speak as a united voice. This movement was followed by the Niagara Movement. In 1905, W. E. B. Dubois, John Hope, Maurice Trotter and other vocal young black intellectuals met in Niagara Falls, in Ontario, Canada, and founded the Niagara Movement.

This organization was primarily political in its objectives. Its leaders strove to seize the leadership of black America from the more conciliatory emphasis of Booker T. Washington.[16] Further, they wanted to establish a platform from which to condemn the white prejudice that they found all about them. They hoped to resurrect the spirit of the angry abolitionist leadership that preceded the Civil War.

In the early 1920s, chapters of the Universal Negro Improvement Association sprung up all over the nation. It was the largest mass organization in black history. Marcus Garvey led the organization advocating race redemption, black pride, black identity and black solidarity in an African homeland.

Garvey followers were groups of young blacks who were disenchanted with the NAACP and the National Urban League's unwillingness to develop meaningful policies and programs to uplift the economically depressed masses. They organized the National Negro Congress, whose membership included aggressive men, such as Ralph Bunche and A. Philip Randolph.[17]

Members of the National Negro Congress knew that if they did not plan their future, the white power elite most certainly would. And any plans by whites to improve conditions for blacks would be at black peoples' expense.

Nearly a half a century after the Civil Rights Movement and the Black Power Movement, there is still no national black policy or plan for black self-sufficiency or empowerment. Since such a plan would singularly benefit blacks, it is black America's responsibility to build an organization that will develop a national plan. The organization should be an intellectual infrastructure that would not only develop the plan but would analyze and craft road maps to get black America out of its marginal existence and into a socioeconomic competitive position with other racial and ethnic groups.

Strategic Leveling of the Playing Field

Decision making through strategic planning is the wave of the future. The decision to organize and plan is the first step towards acquiring power and increased control over resources. By organizing for self-sufficiency, self-empowerment, and racial accountability, blacks make a conscious decision to both effect and be responsible for their own future. Blacks have paid dearly for entrusting their future to non-blacks. If the lesson has been, learned then it is not too late for blacks to begin leveling the competitive playing field to avoid being locked into a permanent underclass status among racial and ethnic groups in the hyper-competitive decade ahead.

Decision making is based in choosing between the probable and the possible. More specifically, blacks must identify and choose preferred paths based upon their historical experiences, present conditions and future needs. If blacks ignore these factors and continue to be non-involved as a group, it is highly probable that they will get stuck in non-preferred paths in the future.

More to the point, there is a rule of human behavior that states that if we continue to do the same thing that we have always done, then we will continue to get the same results that we have always gotten. If blacks want different results and an improved quality of life, then they must make different decisions as a group. Once blacks design a national plan, even if the plan fails initially, blacks will have at least improved their image as an organized group of people interested in an improved future.

The protracted powerlessness and poverty of black America are the results of planning not chance. The planning was not done by blacks. In the 130 years that blacks have had their legal freedom, they have not had collective long-term planning of public policies for black people. Blacks are concerned about the future of black youth, but sixteen generations of blacks have had to grow up without the benefit of organized lives within a national plan. Professor Harold Cruse prophesied that, "Without a functional philosophy for coping with American realities of white racism, each successive generation of black youth would be born, evolve, hesitate, ponder, persevere, and flounder into the blind anonymity of deferred dreams and frustrated hopes."[18] Cruse's prophecy is being manifested across this nation in the daily statistics on black youth violence and death.

Conclusion

Blacks have made little relative progress from slavery to today because we still have not acquired the necessary sources of power to create positive change in our marginal conditions. People who use their individual means to build collective wealth and power understand that there is strength in numbers. Blacks have yet to recognize or act upon this truth. The black vote alone will not ensure blacks a respectable status or new role in America. The vote must be backed by a national plan of public policies specifically designed to help blacks achieve economic self-sufficiency and self-empowerment.

3

Impediments to Empowerment and Economic Justice

"Blacks ought not swallow beliefs that they cannot digest."
C. Anderson

he U.S. Constitution has historically been and continues to be an impediment to black political and economic empowerment and self-sufficiency. During the formative years of this nation, the Constitution outright excluded blacks from the privileges of citizenship, the acquisition of wealth and power, and the enjoyment of the fruits of their own labor. Moreover, the Constitution shackled blacks so that members of the majority white society and any other ethnic or racial group could use blacks for socioeconomic gains. The social acceptance and grants of wealth that the government has given to European, Asian, and Hispanic immigrants, but withheld from blacks, left blacks decidedly ill-equipped to compete with the more advantaged groups.

Worse, the Constitution is again being used to block even the slightest effort by blacks to redistribute resources to remedy the wealth and power imbalance between blacks and whites. Conservative forces within the court system and government now seek to maintain the status quo of inequality between blacks and whites by mandating that blacks and whites be treated equally in all future endeavors. Any efforts whatsoever to correct past injustices are found to be unconstitutional forms of reverse discrimination against whites. Thus, equal protection has come to mean the equal treatment of fundamentally unequal groups, which in effect perpetuates the unequal distribution of wealth, power and resources.

White society enjoys a virtual monopoly over wealth, power and governmental and business resources, because to a large degree the Constitution decreed that whites would solely possess those advantages. Equality for blacks, therefore, amounts to anything other than the equal ownership and control of resources and power, because the Constitution set the legal, civic and racial tones of the nation and placed numerous impediments and obstacles to black empowerment and self-sufficiency. The following is an analysis of the obstacles that the Constitution has used to impede black peoples' progress:

Obstacle #1

Constitutional Racism: Termites in the Foundation —The Constitution has formed the foundation for the subordination and exploitation of black Americans by perpetrating racist attitudes and hurtful behavior toward blacks.

The Constitution espoused values of individual rights, freedom and opportunities, but gave slave holders the legal right to deny blacks their personal freedom to benefit from their own labor. Further, since the framers of the Constitution did not consider blacks full human beings they did not assign them individual rights. Thus, blacks were never really meant to be included in the Constitution at all. Professor Harold Cruse spoke of this tragedy by stating:

> "The legal Constitution of American society recognizes the rights, privileges and aspirations of the individual, while America has become a nation dominated by the social powers of various ethnic and religious groups. The reality of the power struggles between competing ethnic or religious groups is that an individual has few rights and opportunities in America that are not backed up by the political and social power of one group or another." [1]

America is, in principle, a majority-rule society. However, in areas of the country where blacks constituted the majority of the population, all manner of legal and illegal means have been used to ensure that they nevertheless cannot wrest control from whites. Whether blacks were the majority populations in Mississippi, Louisiana, South Carolina, or the inner cities of many urban areas, a white minority controlled the halls of government. The framers declared the nation to be a democracy while operating a Southern plutocracy, a government run by a wealthy class of plantation owners.

In 1786, the framers of the Constitution laid the legal foundation for a black-white wealth and power imbalance by: 1) counting blacks as three-fifths of a person; 2) postponing for 20 years the effective date for outlawing the slave trade; and 3) obligating the government to defend fugitive slave laws and to use its forces to suppress black insurrections and violence. The federal government was a co-conspirator in black slavery.

The Constitution placed white wealth interests over black personal rights because the framers were wealthy, conservative white men. More than 31 percent of the delegates to the Philadelphia Convention were slave holders who together owned approximately 1,400 slaves.[2] The framers were idealists, but they were also racist. James Madison and George Washington were two of the larger and more prosperous of all the Constitutional delegates.[3] Their capital investment in slaves would be worth approximately $105 million today. They and their fellow delegates protected their own slave investments and the nation's free labor system. The delegates believed that black slave labor was necessary for the development of the nation and the prosperity of white Europeans in this country. All of the nation's power and wealth were in the hands of white males. Any antislavery sentiments that might have been voiced did not prevail. The well-being of blacks was not a concern.

The framers spoke out against concentrated power in the hands of the British, but ignored the concentration of power within their own developing aristocratic ranks. "The accumulation of all powers in the same hands, whether of one, a few, and whether hereditary, self-appointed, or elective," cautioned James Madison, "may justly be pronounced the very definition of tyranny."[4] If the concentration of power in British hands constituted tyranny, why was that not so when it was concentrated in the hands of white colonialists? Blacks became permanent victims of a tyrannical majority, when their lowly role was inscribed into the founding documents. The framers obviously did not foresee a time when blacks would be anything other than slaves.

The Constitution fused the broad concept of property ownership and related rights with English slave laws. Once blacks were classified as property, the English insisted that slaves, as property, had no rights beyond the right to perform as requested. The framers codified in the Constitution their belief that property ownership rights were superior to slaves' human rights. As slave owners, many of the framers believed in the old English Law that whomever discovers or owns a person or thing has inherent rights over them.

Obstacle # 2

Racism in the Supreme Court and the Legal System —The Supreme Court has been a major player in the denigration of blacks. It has exercised powers that the Constitution never gave it in order to overrule the U.S. Congress. In the famous 1857 Dred Scott Decision that concluded that blacks had no rights, the Supreme Court made itself coequal to the U.S. Congress and began issuing rulings that declared congressional acts to aid blacks were unconstitutional.

According to the Constitution, courts were supposed to be sanctuaries of judicial objectivity, fairness and justice. It is ironic, then, that for nearly 200 years, only wealthy, white male lawyers served in the high court. And even today, they are the overwhelming dominant class of judges and justices. The judicial system cannot be fair and impartial to all citizens because judges' decisions naturally reflect their experiences and beliefs. How fair and impartial to all is a judicial system that is composed of 99 percent conservative white males? How unbiased are the courts' decisions when the judges are appointed or elected because of their social and political ideologies?

The Supreme Court's interpretive freedom is both its strength and its weakness, because as political appointees, the justices, to some extent, reflect the views and philosophies of the appointing President and seek to maintain the status quo. In his book, *A People's History of the United States*, historian Howard Zinn lamented the court's biased class interest stating that "despite its look of somber, black robed fairness, the Supreme Court was doing everything it could for the ruling elite."[5]

Only the politically naive would believe that presidents would appoint individuals to the Supreme Court who did not hold social-political views on race matters that were similar to those of the President. During the 1980s, the litmus test for judicial appointments was support for the conservative cause on race matters as drawn from the Constitution and not case precedence. The conservative slap in the face to black America was the appointment of Clarence Thomas, a black man, to the Supreme Court.

Thomas, an ultra-right wing conservative, sees the world through the eyes of the white framers of the Constitution, rather than those of black America. Former President George Bush said, "Clarence Thomas was the most qualified candidate in the country who knew what it was to be poor." In a *Washington Post* article (April 18, 1994) Columnist Jack Anderson disagreed with George Bush on both counts. According to Anderson, "Thomas's writings and decisions denote someone who disdains the downtrodden and is callous about protecting civil liberties." Thomas's court opinions supporting the beating of handcuffed prisoners, gender discrimination in selecting juries, and denial of immigration rights to black Haitian refugees, show him to be a judicial activist whose legal interpretations parallel the views of the drafters of the Constitution.

Supreme Court decisions are based on the Constitution. But, since the original intent of the Constitution was to enslave blacks and deny them their humanity, fairness for blacks is impossible. To change conditions and make them sympathetic to black goals of empowerment and wealth, would be to drastically change the intent of the framers. If judges rely on original intent, blacks would have no rights.

According to Eric Black, there were serious disagreements among the framers on many issues, but on the specific issue of slavery the framers' original intent was crystal clear: The framers intended to approve and codify the subordination and exploitation of blacks into law.[6] They intended to reward slave holders and give them extra representation and power in Congress. And, they intended to make it unconstitutional for anyone to attempt to harbor or assist a black slave. Seemingly, these intentions were very strong forces underlying the Constitution.

It is likely that blacks would have continued their battle for constitutional rights in the 19th century had they not been discouraged by the Supreme Court's unrelenting pattern of biased interpretations of black peoples' rights under Emancipation and the 14th Amendment. A critical examination of court rulings and the legal status of black Americans prior to the 1954 Brown decision should make even the heartiest optimist wonder why blacks would try to seek protection from any court, especially the Supreme Court. Over the last century and a half, various court rulings followed a circular course, from indifference to hostility, to benignity. The Supreme Court stood silent while lower courts emasculated the 14th and 15th Amendments. There were few, if any, favorable rulings for blacks during the first 160 years of the Court's existence.

The Supreme Court's Dred Scott Decision in 1857 reflected the prevailing attitude towards the legal rights of blacks. Although it had taken 11 years for the case to reach the Supreme Court, the ruling was swift and sure. The Dred Scott Decision stated emphatically that neither free or enslaved blacks were considered to be citizens and hence, could not sue for their freedom. Representing the majority opinion, Supreme Court Justice Taney wrote: "Blacks are inferior beings and as property, they lack citizenship and have no rights that a white man is bound to respect."[7]

Following the Civil War, Congress, for partisan reasons, modified the Constitution to eliminate the most egregious wrongs against blacks. In the late 1860s, Congress enacted the 13th, 14th and 15th Amendments. These Constitutional amendments were specifically enacted to abolish slavery, grant blacks citizenship with equal protection, and establish voting rights for blacks. However, the Supreme Court emasculated the 14th and 15th Amendments with a succession of unfavorable court rulings that restored Southerners' control over blacks.

The Court's aggressive and negative rulings against blacks accelerated after Emancipation. In 1883, the Court voided the Civil Rights Act of 1875 and refused to strike down discrimination by individual citizens. In 1896, the Supreme Court further reinforced its notion that blacks were not to be respected, when it gave its blessings to the Jim Crow system of separate-but-equal in the case of *Plessy vs. Ferguson*. The separate-but-equal doctrine hung a cloak of respectability around 60 more years of unbridled discrimination against blacks.

The succession of anti-black Supreme Court rulings and the Compromise of 1877 obliterated the purposes of the 13th, 14th and 15th Amendments for newly freed slaves. In the Compromise of 1877, the Northern champions of the black cause compromised to accept the Southern race system.[8] The Southern conservatives and wealthy class then experienced little difficulty in persuading the Supreme Court to ignore other Constitutional revisions on behalf of blacks.

Following the Civil War, history repeated itself. Southern whites again had control of the land, but had neither money nor labor. For the second time, black labor was commandeered and used to develop the Southern economic and social structure. The Southern states passed highly discriminatory Black Codes to keep blacks in a position of servitude. The Codes, a mandate for slavery, gave white Southerners a manageable and inexpensive labor force. The Codes and subsequent laws and ordinances, as indicated in the Appendix, made it illegal for blacks to engage in normal social behavior, such as owning a dog, looking out of the same window that whites looked out of, raising and selling agricultural products, crossing a state line and being on the street after dark.

The nature of these Black Codes effectively nullified the 13th Amendment and permitted local law enforcement agencies to arrest blacks and place them in involuntary servitude as "criminals who had been duly convicted." It was common for local sheriffs to provide Southern planters with imprisoned blacks for free labor. Blacks were forbidden to work without written contracts. They were also forbidden to learn to read and write. Though they could not read legal contracts, they were bound, and in all too many instances, were arrested for having breached or broken the terms of their sharecropping agreements.[9]

The 13th Amendment contained an exception clause that cleared the way for nearly a century of involuntary black servitude, because blacks had no income alternatives. Although the government had promised compensation to slaves upon Emancipation, blacks never received the promised 40 acres of land, tools or the mule. Abandoned without resources, most black freedmen had little recourse but to accept the white planter's terms.

In some Southern states, advertisements invited blacks to voluntarily reenter slavery for the benefit of the South, the old white masters, and the nation. Just as the socio-political context nullified the effectiveness of the 13th Amendment for blacks, it also made the 14th Amendment a dead letter for blacks. The equal protection clause was written into the Constitution as part of the 14th Amendment in 1868. But it wasn't until 1954 that this language was interpreted to make it unconstitutional to overtly and explicitly discriminate against blacks.

The court interpreted the 13th, 14th, and 15th Amendments broadly and applied them to many situations unrelated to blacks. By the turn of the century, the court used the new Constitutional amendments primarily to protect the wealth of major corporations. In 1886, the Supreme Court used the 14th Amendment on equal protection and due process to abolish 230 state laws that regulated corporations. Corporate legal counselors argued that corporations were "persons" and their money was property protected by the due process clause of the 14th Amendment.

Of the 14th Amendment cases brought before the Supreme Court between 1890 and 1901, only 19 dealt with blacks, versus 288 with corporations.[10] The court showed favor to the corporations, but it ruled against blacks in all 19 cases. The court refused to hear the majority of cases involving blacks who were openly disenfranchised, exploited, terrorized and lynched by the powerful and wealthy. Between 1882 and 1892 approximately 2,600 blacks were lynched.

Obstacle # 3

Absence of Group Economics and Capitalism —The practice of perceiving and acting on issues and events from a social rather than a capitalistic perspective is a major impediment to black empowerment. An old adage says, "When in Rome, do as the Romans do." Blacks are in America and America is a capitalist nation. Thus, blacks will have to adopt the American capitalistic approach if they are to build their economic strength. The founding fathers intended this nation to be an experiment in capitalism.

Dr. William E.B. Dubois, the preeminent black scholar, once described the concept to a black audience in Atlanta. He said: "Capitalism is like having three ears of corn: You eat one, you sell one, and you save one for seed for next year's planting."[11] Using Dubois' definition as a measuring device, blacks have yet to practice capitalism. Black people are neither producers nor savers. Primarily, blacks are consumers.

Blacks spend 95 percent of their annual disposable income with businesses located within white communities. Of the five percent that remains within black communities, another three percent is spent with non-black owned businesses. It is difficult, if not impossible, for black communities to maintain a reasonable quality of life and be economically competitive when only two percent of their annual disposable income remains within black communities.[12]

Conditions in black communities are made worse by the fact that too many black business owners believe in developing their business but not the black community. They are shortsighted in valuing temporary business development above long-term community development. *USA Today* reported on April 11, 1994 that of approximately $9 billion that went to black 8(a) businesses from government setaside contracts, nearly all of the black businesses were located in white communities. The tax revenue and jobs from these government contracts went into white rather than black communities, but supporters of the programs explained that they fostered "minority businesses" not community development.

With black consumers and black businesses spending 95 percent of their income in white communities, whites live comfortably off double incomes, reaping 100 percent of their own and 95 percent of blacks' income. Essentially, black consumers and business owners have joined whites in boycotting black communities. Their failure to practice group economics further impoverishes black communities.

Obstacle #4

Pursuing Myths and Elusive Dreams —To achieve economic power, blacks as a group must redesign civil rights traditions. Blacks are out of sync with the times and are still chasing civil rights. The process of rethinking our civil rights tradition begins with reexamining America's race problem from the perspective of black economic and political empowerment. The section below explores myths or dreams that are to their detriment.

Myth No. 1: Integration

Real integration is a dream that will never come true for blacks. Even if it did, it would not change the nature of black life in America. The reality of integration is that the integrating group loses all self-determination, since all plans and goals must be processed through and approved by the dominant society into which the minority group is integrating. Integration is a detriment to blacks, because the larger white society will neither allow blacks to assimilate nor give them assistance to alter the negative marginal conditions in which they must live.

Black businesses and individuals situated in and wholly dependent on the continued acceptance and goodwill of white communities are vulnerable and powerless. They cannot change anything in the white communities or businesses because they are only guests. Integrated blacks' conditions are made more precarious by the reasoning that they have little, if any, support within the white community and they cannot depend upon receiving support from the black community whose powers were weakened by those who abandoned the community to integrate. Similarly, it is difficult for the nonintegrated black masses to identify with the integrated few. Therefore, both the integrated and the non-integrated are rendered powerless by their social divisions.

Power flows from the group, the trunk of the tree, not in reverse from the individual or limb to the trunk. So, as long as the black masses remain powerless then every black individual remains powerless and vulnerable, even if they or their businesses are "integrated."

The integration process has major political significance in large urban areas where blacks are in control of government apparatus. When blacks are the majority population and are the controllers of government, the last things they should be concerned about are integration and minority development. It is self-destructive to continue to behave as a powerless minority seeking integration when one's group is the dominant majority population.

While urban revitalization plans should be built around economically and politically empowering cities' black masses, black elected officials are reading outdated development strategies that suggest the best way to help blacks is to re-attract whites into the cities. Such development philosophies are racist and shortsighted. It confirms the belief in white superiority and black inferiority, that blacks cannot govern and progress without white involvement. Integration will be a no-win situation for black people until they have sufficient racial power, wealth, competitiveness, and respect. At that point, integration will become just one of a number of options open to them.

In summary, once blacks gain power parity, they will have the option of integrating or separating. Currently, they have no such choices. Integration requires blacks to give up their culture, values and all that is identifiably black. The integration process is divisive and detrimental to blacks' self-empowerment goal, because it dilutes and fragments their numerical strength, placing them further in the minority in a nation whose political principle is that the majority rules. Black people are the only group of people — ethnic or racial — that has consistently sought to integrate and continues to seek integration, though white society has repeatedly rejected them.

Once blacks began to integrate, they abandoned their businesses, schools and communities; they also lost disposable capital that is now redirected to white communities; they even lost their middle-class black role models, who followed whites to the suburbs. The loss of black capital and role models has left black communities across the nation impoverished and without leadership. And, worst of all, under integration black people have had to shape their goals, values and behavior around white America's standards, though whites' approval likely will not reap financial or political gains for black people.

Myth No. 2: Equal Opportunity for All

Black America devotes a significant amount of time and energy chasing the myth of equal opportunity, which was the forerunner of the dream of racial integration. Both the myth and the dream are improbables. Inequality of power and wealth will naturally exist, so long as human greed and competition motivate human behavior.

On the other hand, the myth of equality does perform an invaluable service for those who hold a disproportionate share of the wealth, power and material resources. This myth not only keeps blacks distracted from learning how to increase their share, but it keeps blacks believing that at least their children or their children's children will have a fair chance at the brass ring. The greatest service that the myth of equality provides for the dominant power holders is the idea that, if blacks are not successful achieving a fair share of power, wealth, and material resources, it is their own fault.

Integration and equal opportunity are grounded in the belief that dominant white society will voluntarily share power with blacks. Power is rarely shared, especially between competitive groups. Power holders have no desire for equality. James R. Kluegel and Eliot R. Smith, in the research for *Beliefs About Equality*, showed that whites resist changes regarding racial inequalities, because they tend to classify inequalities that relate to the black underclass as "non-issues."[13]

Many whites do not believe that structural limitations impede blacks. Some even believe that, if individuals would coexist with their social peers, and stop trying to integrate, inequality would not be an issue. Everyone would then be in common groupings, they reason. Whites will accept blacks as equals only when blacks have acquired parity of wealth and power. Pursuing the concept of equality rather than the basis of equality—which is wealth and power—is a quagmire that bogs blacks down and wastes their time and efforts.

Conservative logic holds that if all people acknowledge that America is race neutral, then blacks have achieved their long-sought "equality" without whites ever having to redistribute resources and power to blacks. Through the 1980s, conservatives checkmated blacks on preferential policies and quotas by arguing that America is a color-blind society and all governmental policies should be race neutral. The only way America will ever be color-blind is if everyone literally lost their sight. Conservatives have learned to use black rhetoric against blacks. They argue that any decision that is race conscious violates the 14th Amendment and is therefore unconstitutional. However, without preferential treatment, or affirmative action for blacks, structural racism will continue to advantage whites. This is the way the power holders want it to be. If the white power holders had wanted blacks to have equality, they would not have kept them outside and beneath mainstream society for nearly 400 years.

Myth No. 3: Eradicating Poverty

The way an individual or group perceives itself is a critical determinant of their drive and goals. Though blacks bear a disproportionate burden of poverty, it is a self-limiting exercise in futility for them to overly identify with poverty programs and policies. Poverty is a given in life. Affluence is poverty's fixed extreme. Both poverty and affluence are horizontal, social and economic characteristics that inflict themselves on all racial and ethnic groups regardless of geographic locations.

Blacks ought to be realistic in their approach to poverty and poverty politics. Although poverty is a relative state among groups of humans, it is a given fact of life. It cannot be eradicated. Poor people's marches and government-sponsored poverty programs cannot eradicate poverty. And, even if government policies and programs could eliminate poverty, the conservative, wealthy elite would not allow it to do so. Due to limited black resources, it would be far more productive to view poverty as a vertical characteristic and concentrate efforts not on eradicating it, but on providing as many blacks as possible with the education, wealth and power-building tools they need to lift themselves out of poverty.

Myth No. 4: Cultural Diversity

Cultural pluralism and diversity have become very popular buzz words, yet the American melting pot has proven to be an optical illusion. Cultural diversity is a term used to equate blacks with other groups, though they are not. As a recent newspaper article reported: "The demands of immigrant groups and others diluted and eventually trivialized the very special claims of blacks for national attention."[14] Blacks are models for ethnic, racial or gender groups, yes. However, a multi-cultural or cultural diversity ethic that equates all subculture grievances with those of blacks belittles and neutralizes blacks' efforts to resolve their unique dilemma.

Cultural diversity gives the dominant society unrestricted entry to black culture, while socially and economically excluding blacks from white culture. Black culture is allowed to assimilate, though blacks cannot. For every ethnic group, except blacks, cultural diversity has advantages. Main streets throughout America reflect the nation's cultural diversity by featuring Chinese, Japanese, Mexican, Italian, Greek, French, East Indian, Vietnamese and Cambodian restaurants. These groups have the option to assimilate into the mainstream with their culture intact. They establish other businesses, economies and their own communities. Blacks don't have the benefit of an identifiable culture of their very own. A mishmash of African heritage, "soul" and black history is offered as black culture. Cultural diversity or pluralism would be advantageous to them if all things were equal, but they are not.

Myth No. 5: Black Ethnicity

Contrary to the popular rhetoric of social engineers, political pundits and politicians, blacks are not ethnics. Ethnicity is the sharing of a common language, religion, culture, and set of racial characteristics. But, blacks in this country are an amalgamated racial group. They share the English language, but belong to every religious group, have no clear-cut culture and have a racially mixed family tree. Therefore, the concept of ethnicity does not aptly describe blacks and should not be used to merge black interests with those of other groups.

There are those with specious motives who attempt to classify blacks as an ethnic group in order to blame them for not having reached parity with other ethnic groups. The movement to classify blacks as ethnics is political sleight-of-hand that springs from modern conservatives' attempts to promote their so-called color-blind political strategies. If blacks permit themselves to be classified as an ethnic group, blacks will suffer a major political loss.

Leslie McLemore, of John Hopkins University, defined an ethnic group as those "who differ culturally from the dominant population, but share enough characteristics with the main population to be acceptable after a period of time."[15] Apparently non-black ethnics are viewed as allies of the majority white community, because they share common characteristics, non-black skin, immigrant backgrounds, absence of the slavery legacy. Blacks have shared American culture for nearly 400 years and have yet to be "melted" into the mythical melting pot. Classifying blacks as an ethnic group sets them up for a new round of "benign neglect."

Myth No. 6: Sexism Is Equal to Racism

The form, degree, and intent of discrimination against blacks and women has always been vastly different and, therefore, should not be treated equally. Blacks were legally subordinated and exploited as producers of wealth and human comfort for a society that denied them the rights to enjoy the fruits of their labor. Contrarily, women as a protected class, enjoyed the fruits of every black worker's labor, but were denied the luxury of laboring with blacks to produce such fruits. Therefore, sexism is more a class issue and a class struggle.

Equating discrimination against women to discrimination against blacks is like comparing a headache with cancer. Being a woman in the mainstream society may have its challenges, but it can in no manner be compared to being black in America. Yet, in the 1970s, the two struggles were linked.

As one insightful writer noted, "The class category of women was placed in the same category as blacks, not only as being oppressed, but as suffering the same degree of segregation, exploitation and discrimination as blacks. The constitutional violations of the rights of women to equal citizenship were equated with constitutional violations of the rights of blacks."[16] Nothing could be further from the truth. Through such social devices as families, marriages and racial segregation, white women have had access to the fruits of white males' wealth and power. Blacks have not.

From a racial perspective, white women always had the advantage of enjoying the fruits of racial discrimination and the option of categorically discriminating against blacks. Blacks have never had a counter option of discriminating collectively against women. The women's movement supplanted the black civil rights movement more than a generation ago and has generated a demand for woman power and sisterhood that now serves as a major impediment to black family unity and racial solidarity. It is no accident that every time blacks are on the verge of receiving relief from their oppressive conditions, the women's issue emerges.

Both conservatives and liberals support the issue to dilute entitlements to blacks. The first attempt by women to press their own cause, to the detriment of blacks, occurred in 1870. Women tried to push Congress to write them into the Constitution under the 13th, 14th and 15th Amendments, which were specifically enacted to ensure that the freed slaves had equal rights under the law. Shortly after Emancipation, Congress passed the 15th Amendment, that ensured equal voting rights for all citizens regardless of race, color, or previous condition of servitude. Women's attempts to have gender included in the Amendment failed.

Reasonable congressmen felt that the Civil War had not been fought over the status of women, but for the freedom of five million black slaves. Women were not included in the 1860s constitutional amendments because they had never been excluded from society. The original Constitution did not make reference to or exclude gender. Supreme Court Justice Joseph Bradley wrote in an 1873 editorial, that "Man is, or should be, woman's protector and defender."[17] And, throughout history, social customs have assigned women to a special, privileged and protected class. Therefore, women didn't need a special amendment.

Some women's suffrage groups openly criticized Congress for its exclusion of women from the 15th Amendment. One prominent white feminist, Elizabeth Cady Stanton, used strong racist and elitist arguments against placing the enfranchisement of black males above the concerns of white women. According to author Eric Foner, Stanton said, "Think of Sambo . . . who [does] not know the difference between a Monarchy and a Republic, who never read the Declaration of Independence, making laws for Lydia Maria Child, Lucretia Mott, or Fanny Kemble."[18]

The feminist attacks attempted to drive wedges between black women and black men. Stanton spoke out in support of voting rights for white members of the sisterhood. "The black women," she contended, "would be better off as the slave of an educated white man, than of a degraded, ignorant black one."[19]

Racism is different from sexism in both intent and effect, as Sojourner Truth, a black activist heroine and feminist, aptly noted during a women's convention in 1851. After listening to white males discuss white women as a protected class, she dramatically rose to her feet and said: "That man over there says that women need to be helped into carriages and lifted over ditches. Nobody ever helps me into carriages. And ain't I a woman? I would work as much and eat as much as a man, when I could get it, and bear the lash as well. And ain't I a woman? I have borne 13 children and seen 'em most all sold off to slavery, and when I cried out with my mother's grief, none but Jesus heard me!"[20]

Sojourner Truth's point was that she suffered, not because she was a woman, but because she was black. Had she not been black, she would have been in the same protected class with white females. Apparently, Sojourner's effort to draw the distinction between race and gender fell on deaf ears and continues to be intentionally misinterpreted. Feminists continue to compete against blacks.

The issue of gender protection under the Constitution arose again in 1964 when a Southern congressman insisted that women be included in an amendment to the Civil Rights Act. However, equality of the sexes was a lesser concern than undermining the bill's power to help blacks. Racist conservatives rose up in support of the amendment. Representative George William Andrews of Alabama said: "Unless the amendment is adopted, the white women of this country would be drastically discriminated against in favor of a Negro woman."[21]

This attempt to derail the Civil Rights Movement succeeded. The amendment easily passed, signalling the start of a trend by liberal politicians and organizations to push blacks even further onto the back burner by equating other categories of people, who considered themselves equally aggrieved, to blacks. The rights movement soon expanded to include not only women, but Hispanics, Asians, Jews, the handicapped, gays, senior citizens, immigrants, drug users, migrant workers, the mentally ill and illegal aliens. But the biggest push went for women, since even a racist white male knew that promoting benefits for women would be little more than redistributing wealth to his white mother, sister, daughter, or wife. Thus, the wealth and power would not leave the white race.

Myth No. 7: Black Feminism

The popular feminist movement has injured relationships between black women and black men. "The sophisticated use of racism and capitalism has placed . . . black women in a position of being a major competitor of black men for jobs, education, housing, and other services and necessary resources," said Haki R. Madhubuti, in his book *Black Men: Obsolete, Single, Dangerous?* Madhubuti explained the conflict between black men and black women saying, "Black women did not place themselves in this delicate position as a ward of the system. They have been maneuvered and strategically used for the benefit of the white majority just as the black man has."

Although their gains have not been quite as spectacular as those of white females, black females have improved their historical advantage over black males. Black women have always been more acceptable to the dominant white society. As with white feminism, black feminism has always been present, but has been fairly low key. Black women have always been able to find work when black males could not. They were more preferable, because they were less threatening.[22] Black women are also beneficial for government reporting purposes, since a black female counts both as a female and as a black.

In 1954, the income of black women surpassed black males and the income gap has continued to widen. Black women could work, go to school, socialize and breed with whites when black males could not. Slavery intentionally placed black women in matriarchal roles in order to dominate black men. Not only did such role reversals weaken the black family structure, they also placed the black female in closer physical and symbolic proximity to the white male.

White males' power position afforded them sexual access to black females. A white male with a black female mistress was an acceptable part of Southern life and was often part of the rites of manhood for young white males. Black males, who were forced into a status below the black female, were totally powerless to protect black females.

Today, the rise of the "black sisterhood" has the potential to be a divisive and destructive social phenomenon that could impede black self-empowerment. The black sisterhood here refers to black women who have indirectly joined with white males and white females to further depress black males. Using black females to subordinate black males places the race where it was centuries ago. In slavery, female slaves were typically field "drivers" who set the work pace and tasks for male slaves. Though many worked alongside of the male slaves, they were usually given the easier, management jobs, supervising children's crews and trash gangs.

Within the household, black females were typically the surrogate overseers of the entire yard staffs as well as the slave holders' young children. The black females' advice was sought and accepted in family and household matters. Up until the civil rights period, the black females' domestic authority was exceeded only by the white master and mistress.

Black males as a class were never granted the full social and economic options to play out the male role as head of the black family and household. More than a third of black males today are unemployed, poorly educated, on parole, probation or in prison, and have a life expectancy that is 20 years shorter than a white female and 10 years shorter than a black female. Black males are an endangered species. That has been the case historically. They were enslaved on a ratio of 2 to 1 for every black female. As far back as the 1840s, certain Southern states enacted an annual $5 per capita tax on free black males in order to punish them for simply being black, male and free.[23]

Racism historically has been a male-to-male phenomenon — a device to strengthen one male's group at the expense of the other. Debates about sexism thwarts meaningful discussions about racism, further divides a weakened race and underscores the weakened condition of the black male. Blacks are already the lowest among the ranking of racial and ethnic groups in America, if not the world. Some black women often fail to understand that if sex discrimination disappears, the white female will again simply join the white male on the veranda of the plantation house or in the suburbs and black women will once again serve the mint juleps.

Obstacle #5

Criminalizing Blacks—The criminalizing of blacks, especially black males, is a major obstacle to black empowerment for at least three reasons: 1) American society has long linked crime to blacks, especially young, black males; 2) blacks have been forced to live in marginal social conditions that produce pathological, survival behavior; and 3) black communities lack an accountability mechanism that could establish, reward, and punish behavior that is detrimental to them. Since the late 1960s, blacks have been so overexposed to black crime within their communities, that they now accept it as normal black behavior.

National public policies and institutions began centuries ago to produce and perpetuate the laws, racial images, and myths that imprisoned blacks within the concepts of crime and violence. For blacks, criminal justice has never been blind. White society criminalized black behavior out of fears and financial self-interest. According to Leonard Curry, the author of *The Free Black In Urban America, 1800-1850,* blacks were arrested for activities that would not have been a crime for whites, such as strolling in certain neighborhoods and looking suspicious. Sometimes blacks were imprisoned for even less specific crimes, such as "violating various city ordinances" and "playing games with whites." In some instances, no crimes were committed. White planters would commit blacks to prison "just for safe keeping." All of these incarcerations showed up in the records as black crimes against society.

An abusive use of the legal system to criminalize blacks primarily occurred in urban areas where the white power structure had fewer options for controlling and using blacks. As far back as 1826, in Massachusetts, free blacks were less than one percent of the population, but nearly 17 percent of the prisoners. In Pennsylvania, blacks were two percent of the population, but nearly 34 percent of the prisoners; and in New Jersey, blacks were also only two percent of the population, but nearly 50 percent of the prisoners.[24] Today, blacks still make up 35 to 50 percent of the state or federal penal total population. Approximately 37 percent of America's black male population is either in jail or on parole or probation. The criminalizing phenomena has destroyed black individuals, families and communities.

The criminalizing of blacks does not excuse blacks who are engaging in criminal activities from being held accountable for their behavior. But the black communities should hold them accountable, not only the majority white society that fosters the conditions that encourages blacks to commit criminal acts. Many blacks have in the past and will continue to commit petty blue-collar crimes in the future. But all behavior is caused whether it is perceived as being good or bad. It should be noted, therefore, that black crime markedly increased at the same time and in direct proportion to blacks' becoming obsolete and expendable as a labor class in the early 1960s. As black wealth, income, employment, business, educational and male role model opportunities diminished throughout the country, black criminal activities increased.

If American justice were to ever be color blind, crime would have to be redefined and fairly enforced. For instance, white law breakers would not be treated any differently for their white-collar crimes than blue-collar criminals. The term white-collar crime was coined in 1940, and referred to illegal acts carried out by respectable members of the community or persons of high status in the course of their occupations.[25] And, white-collar crimes are usually nonviolent offenses carried out by respectable people to gain money, property, or personal benefits through deceit. John Farley stated in his book, *Sociology*, that white-collar crimes cost the society from $40 to $200 billion a year (not including the savings and loan thefts). This is eight times the cost of all common, blue collar crimes. Yet, our prisons are 99 percent filled with blue-collar criminals who are predominantly black. [26]

With so many more expensive white-collar crimes being committed, why are there not more white-collar prisoners? Because most white-collar crimes are committed primarily by whites, and crime statistics are skewed towards reporting blue-collar crimes. White-collar crimes go to civil rather than criminal courts, and are typically excluded from crime reports. When crimes such as inside stock trading, toxic waste dumping, embezzlement, bribery, income tax evasion, expense account padding, larceny, computer fraud, money laundering, extortion, blackmail, counterfeiting, government contract manipulations, and saving and loan thefts are included in the crime reports, the typical criminal turns out to be wealthy and white. In terms of acts of violence, personal injuries and deaths, a California public health official stated that medical quackery causes more deaths in the United States every year than all [blue collar] crimes of violence.[27] Yet, few quacks ever go to jail, and none have ever been sentenced to the electric chair for medical malpractice. Even in the rare cases where individuals are arrested and convicted for white collar crimes, they receive light sentences and are frequently sent to resort prisons.

Criminals should be arrested and prosecuted, regardless of the color of the collar or color of the skin. Whites do not commit as many blue-collar crimes. Their privileged status, contacts, options, and wealth gives them greater access to basic necessities and resources of the society, without their having to commit criminal acts. Until black America breaks the shackles of black criminality, either actual and imagined, it will be very difficult, if not impossible, for them to achieve economic and political self-sufficiency and self-empowerment.

Conclusion

The greatest impediment to black empowerment and economic justice has been the Constitution, which institutionalized the relative social and economic status of blacks and whites and codified racism in America. After using the Constitution to expropriate black labor, create a racial ordering of acceptability and foster a wealth and power imbalance between blacks and whites, the government and the court system are now using the Constitution to impede any effort to correct the disparities. The government and the courts now allege that any preferential treatment for blacks would be unconstitutional reverse discrimination. The Constitution ought to be just as supportive or tolerant of affirmative action, setasides and preferential treatment for blacks as it has been for whites. Indeed, in all their wisdom, the drafters of the Constitution had to have known that discrimination against blacks was in fact preferential treatment for whites.

4

Why Whites Chose to Enslave Blacks

"What is my disease? Tell me! Who can name my crime? Is it only that I am black and not white?"[1]

*T*he impact of black enslavement remains clearly visible in the protracted living conditions in black communities across the nation. As discussed later in Chapter Six, the financial impact was and continues to be unbelievably beneficial to whites and others around the world. Over the years, social scientists have written volumes of material depicting slavery and its impact on both black and white Americans. They have described in minute details blacks' struggles and the failures of race relations. What they have neglected to answer is the core question: why were blacks, above all other population groups, singled out for and successfully kept in slavery for such a protracted period of time?

Since black enslavement was such a unique experience, black Americans need to thoroughly understand why they were chosen to serve as slaves. By clearly understanding the strategies and decisions whites and others used to conquer and use them as fodder for domestic and global economies, blacks will be better able to prevent such abuse from ever happening to them again. In addition, blacks will be able to better articulate why white America should never again minimize the impact of black enslavement and Jim Crowism and never again equate other so-called minority grievances with the afflictions that it has heaped upon blacks.

The practice of human enslavement is a phenomenon of mankind that extends back to prehistoric times. However, the enslavement of black people in America has been so totally unique in its role, scope, and consequences that historians, politicians, and social scientists have referred to American slavery as a "peculiar" institution. These observers of human behavior considered black enslavement peculiar because it defied all accepted religious precepts and secular standards of normative behavior. It did not comply with traditional justifications for human enslavement. Moreover, black slavery did not end in the traditional manner.

The white slave holders did not voluntarily free blacks. Nor did the slaves successfully rise up in revolt to free themselves. It took a four-year Civil War, costing nearly a half million lives, with whites fighting against other whites, and still the Southern white's economic and psychological dependence on black people could not be totally broken. No other human enslavement has engendered such intense emotional attachments, conflicts, hatreds and wealth for as many nations as did black enslavement.

Was there something that was uniquely different about black people that caused nearly the entire world to support and profit from their enslavement? The answer to this question is critical towards helping blacks to better understand the dynamics of slavery and its impact on current and future events. If blacks were enslaved simply because of skin color, then slavery was beyond the control of blacks.

On the other hand, if weaknesses or other conditions made blacks targets, then blacks must study those conditions and ensure that they are never again so vulnerable. Blacks cannot yet afford to put slavery behind them, as numerous black and white leaders suggest. Black enslavement must be a constant reminder of the ramifications of a lack of collective unity, strength and self-determination.

Mankind's Historical Enslavement

Historically, human enslavement, like other human activities, was purposeful. In both ancient and modern enslavement, humans were rarely randomly enslaved. The enslaver or master normally enslaved individuals or groups as a result of personal debt, religious differences, or as imprisonment stemming from war. Besides being a form of social punishment, slavery was enforced to comfort the master and provide free labor. Since ancient times, wars and religious conflicts have followed mankind's development and produced a constant flow of slaves and masters. Arabs enslaved the Mongolians, who in turn enslaved the Chinese and the Russians. The Hebrews enslaved and were enslaved by the Egyptians. Victorious Roman and Greek armies conquered the Mediterranean area and made slaves of nations and men regardless of race, ethnicity, or color. Human enslavement became so common that even the poorest people became slave masters.

The commonness of human enslavement caused the Roman society and the Catholic church to establish policies and laws to provide parameters for the practice of bonding human beings. Under the old Roman slave laws, slavery was accepted as a temporary condition that could befall any person. Therefore, Roman laws focused on protecting the slave's humanity and basic rights during the temporary enslavement. The Catholic church intervened on behalf of slaves to assure that they maintained rights such as the right to purchase freedom, protect their property, testify in court and marry.

Due to the Catholic church's strong influence in Latin American societies, some slaves were able to win their freedom in court, with compensation from cruel slave masters. The church intervened primarily to provide the slaves with escape hatches from slavery. The slave could work off or pay off his indebtedness to his creditor or assimilate into and become loyal to the society of his military captors. In addition, the slave could disavow his own religion and accept the religious affiliation of the master. In ancient times, the Catholic church and Roman law gave the enslaved some options.

The Uniqueness of Black Slavery

America's enslavement of blacks was unique in nearly every respect from previously known instances of human enslavement or serfdom. Some of the characteristics and factors surrounding American slavery are listed below:

- The sheer number of people enslaved was unprecedented. An estimated 15 million to 60 million blacks were captured in Africa for enslavement. More than 35 million died en route to various ports, with approximately 15 million actually reaching the slave markets. The incompleteness of records makes it impossible to give an exact number, but Robert R. Kuczynski, a leading authority, estimated that a minimum of 15 million were shipped.[2] Hundreds of millions of the originally enslaved Africans' offspring served as slaves or lived as subordinated, exploited human beings for hundreds of years.

• The racist enslavement of blacks was introduced into the world at the same time that individual freedom for whites was blooming. Serfdom and servitude were disappearing in Europe. The Catholic and Protestant religions were undergoing reform and increased liberalization. And, secular philosophies were embroiled in the intricacies of liberty, freedom, and equality of mankind. European rulers responded by liberating and even financing the migrations of their subjects to the New World, including many of those who were then living in poor houses and prisons.

• Black slavery was, purely and simply, racial and economic exploitation, that caused economic revolutions and entrenched disparities between blacks and whites. Economically poor, nonindustrialized nations of Europe, like Spain, Portugal, Germany, and England, commercialized human exploitation and suffering for the primary purpose of looting gold, silver and precious commodities in Africa and the New World. Old forms of mercantilism were converted to new capitalism. Banking, currency, and marketing reforms were created. Africa became a warren for the commercial hunting of strong ebony bodies. Subsequently, skin color became a sign of degradation for its wearer and a sign of wealth for its owner.

• All manner of nations and religious orders used secular reasoning and religious precepts to promote the belief that people with black skin owed an unpaid debt to people with pale skin — a debt that could only be paid through perpetual bondage. The source of black indebtedness did not result from military or religious retaliation, because recorded history emphatically shows that West African blacks never left their African continent to go to war with another nation. There was no known organized effort of blacks to impose their religions on any white societies and there is no recorded balance of payments that were due to European nations as a result of any trade relations with black Africa. The same could not be said for any of the European nations, which routinely sent armies to engage in warfare, promote Christian religions and conduct exploitative trade with other nations.

• Enslaved blacks were integrated or scattered throughout the world as a minority group. Slave holding nations outside of the African continent maintained a majority white population or a white power structure that kept the society's racial balance weighted against blacks. Prior to black slavery, a slave was rarely removed from his homeland. The scattering or forced integration of blacks as slaves within various foreign nations fixed the image of blacks as poor, powerless creatures who were to be pitied and even despised, but always used. At the same time, it portrayed whites as the great conquerors, masters, and lords of the jungle who had subdued the Dark Continent and its primitive inhabitants.

• Lastly, black enslavement was the first instance in history that had worldwide collaborative, race-oriented support for slave trading. Prior to the 15th century, slavery was more of a one-to-one phenomenon: warrior to warrior, nation to nation. Never had there been a situation where all white nations of Europe were collectively against blacks on the African continent. At different times in history, Arabs, Spanish, Portuguese, Italians, English, Dutch, French, Jews, Egyptians, and Russians had individually fought and enslaved each other. There had been continuing religious crusades and forms of religious proselytizing that caused wars between Christians and Moslems, Moslems and Jews, Catholics and Protestants, and pagans and Christians. Black slavery drew the notice of all religious orders, Christian and non-Christian alike. Yet, religious leaders supported and justified black enslavement.

The Religious Crusade for Black Enslavement

The systematic enslavement of people of African descent occurred, to a large degree, from a religious crusade conducted by organized religions. According to *Webster's Dictionary*, a crusade is defined as: "Any vigorous, aggressive movement for the defense or advancement of an idea or cause." There have been few causes that were comparable to or generated more consternation and world benefit than institutionalizing black slavery.

For more than four centuries, various religious denominations vigorously orchestrated and justified black enslavement policies, activities, and financial gains. Christian and non-Christian religions varied in their intensity of support, but they all used religious precepts to support secular governments' slave profiteering.

The Moslem Religion

There is little doubt that the first and oldest religious enslavers of black Africans were Arab Moslems. A scarcity of early credible data makes it difficult to pinpoint when the Moslems began to intrude into Africa in pursuit of wealth and slaves. But, based upon writings that are available, there is little doubt that the Moslem religion was heavily involved and a committed enslaver of people of African descent.

They began regular military invasions into East and West Africa around 700 A.D. By 1000 A.D, Moslems routinely combined their commercial trade with spreading the Islamic faith in black African communities. Medieval Moslems considered black Africans to be primitive and especially suited for enslavement. Around the 10th century, Arabs conducted regular military and religious expansions throughout the Mediterranean area. They used these invasions to seize wealth and black slaves.

David Brian Davis, in his book, *Slavery And Human Progress*, indicated that Moslems from the Middle East have enslaved and sold into North African slave markets no less than one million black Africans every 100 years, for the past 1,000 years. This practice represents no less than 10 million blacks enslaved and exploited by one group alone. Ironically, most black African countries converted to the Islamic faith during the 14th century. The Arabs' continuous enslavement of blacks, therefore, must be driven by factors other than blacks' religious faith.[3]

The Jewish Religion

During Biblical times, the Hebrews owned slaves and were slaves. The degree of Jewish involvement in the modern black slave trading and exploitation of blacks is heatedly debated. *The Washington Post* cited extensive research by Jewish historians who claimed that Jews were involved in nearly every aspect of black slavery, including as slave traders, financiers of slavery, and Confederate War supporters.[4] The Post article also claimed that Jews owned slave vessels, textile mills and tobacco plantations.

Though the data were taken from scholarly research done by Jews, Jewish organizations dispute many of the researchers' conclusions. In his book, *The Crisis of the Negro Intellectual,* Harold Cruse took a neutral position on the issue of Jewish involvement in black slavery. "Jews, as individuals, were no different from other individual whites. They were pro-slavery, antislavery, slave traders, pro-Union, pro-Confederate, and so forth."[5]

Other observers acknowledge that certain Sephardic Jews did participate in black slavery by financing a limited amount of the slave trading ventures in South America and the Caribbean islands. But, Cruse went on to say that American Jewry as a whole, never took a position, pro or con, on the slavery issue. "The oldest Jewish fraternal organization in America, the B'Nai B'Rith, established in 1843," wrote Cruse, "never involved itself in the moral crusade of the abolitionists." With the exception of the recent writings of Jewish authors, there had been little publicized information that the Jewish religion, as a whole, was for or against black slavery.

The Catholic Church

The Catholic church's support of black slavery was second only to the Moslem Arabs. The Catholic order not only justified black slavery, but was a major owner of slaves. In 1488, Pope Innocent VIII accepted a gift of one hundred Moorish slaves from Ferdinand of Spain and then distributed the slaves to various cardinals and nobles. By 1502, the Catholic church worked closely with the Portuguese government which had authorized the Christianizing of black slaves before sending them to its colonies.

A Spanish priest, Bartolome de Las Casas, in 1514, sought and obtained royal permission for each Spanish settler to bring 12 black slaves into the colonies. He wanted to use blacks to relieve the suffering of Indians, provide an abundant supply of free labor, and lure more Europeans into the Caribbean colonies. Why a Catholic missionary would subject blacks to the pains of slavery to relieve the suffering of Indians, and provide lifetime comfort to Europeans was answered by historian Norman Hodges, who said: "Bartolome de Las Casas had seen black slaves in Europe and considered them more suitable for bondage than Indians."[6]

Over the next century, in both Latin and North America, the Catholic church continued to support the systematic enslavement and subordination of blacks by Europeans and Indians. Manuel de Nobrega, a Jesuit priest, demonstrated his true feeling about Indians vis-a-vis blacks in Brazil. Upon arriving in Brazil in 1557, he publicly denounced the enslavement of Indians, but allowed black slavery to exist even within his own religious order.

More than 50 years later, in the year 1610, a Latin American Catholic priest named Father Sandoval, questioned the moral rightness of black enslavement and wrote to church functionaries in Europe inquiring as to whether the capture, transport, and enslavement of African blacks were legal activities sanctioned by church doctrine. In a letter dated March 12, 1610, Father Sandoval got his answer from Brother Luis Brandon, who responded:

> "Your Reverence writes me that you would like to know whether the Negroes who are sent to your parts have been legally captured. To this I reply that I think your Reverence should have no scruples on this point. We have been here ourselves for 40 years and there have been among us very learned Fathers. Never did they consider the trade as illicit. Therefore, we and the Fathers of Brazil buy these slaves for our services without any scruples . . ."[7]

The coup de grace of the Catholic church's support for black enslavement in Hispanic America occurred in 1612. In that year, Peter Claver, a Spanish Jesuit, went to Colombia to be the "official Friend of the Negro slaves" among the hierarchy of the Catholic church. During his 40-year stay in Latin America, he demonstrated this official friendship, not by opposing black enslavement or compensating slaves for their labor, but by baptizing about 300,000 black slaves in order to save their souls.[8] While he baptized the toiling slaves, the gold, silver and other wealth created by their labor continued to flow into the coffers of Europe and the Vatican.

More than three centuries later, while visiting Jamaica in the summer of 1992, Pope John Paul II apologized for the Catholic church's role in promoting and supporting black slavery. Possibly, the Pope's apology comforted black suffering somewhere in the world. Many blacks saw the Pope's apology as a verbal bandage on a festering cancer. The Pope's apology for a moral wrong was a good first step, but black slavery was more than a moral wrong. It was an economic wrong that still needs to be corrected. The cure must meet the cause. The Catholic church did not benefit morally from black slavery. It benefited financially. The Pope and the Catholic church owe the descendants of black slaves the wealth, social status, and humanity — the inheritance — that was stolen from them.

The Protestant and Baptist Religions

The Protestant religions in America have always reflected the values and mores of the dominant white society. Beginning in 1619, the protestant denominations accepted and supported secular decisions to enslave and exploit blacks as a separate labor class for the betterment of the developing white nation. The church was a cultural center and promoted white unity, while dividing blacks between the pagans and the Christians, the domestics and the field workers, the docile and the unruly. Protestant ministers finessed the theological teachings of the oneness of man by dividing theory into the present and the hereafter. They taught that in the present world blacks were inferior beings. Faithful slaves were to accept their lot in life, be obedient to their white masters and their souls would find equality with whites in the next world.

Following the French and Indian War, Quakers became increasingly sensitive about their socioeconomic relationship with slavery, but did not openly demand an end to slavery until much later, when they resolved to neither buy nor sell slaves. Protestants, in general, stayed loyal to the secular public policy of black enslavement, even though a few sects felt black slavery was morally wrong. Since the wealth produced by slavery was primarily in the South, they saw slavery as an economic issue. The Protestant and Baptist churches practiced the philosophy that the enslavement and exploitation of blacks were part of the South and its religious norms. The moral questions of slavery and race were either ignored or justified by the use of Biblical references that were included in the King James version of the Bible that was written after England officially approved black slave trading in 1618.

For the Southern churchgoers and ministers, the Christian principles of the Bible were intertwined with the higher calling to protect the privilege and superior class of whites in the South. "Christianity became an intolerable doctrine unless translated into Southern Christianity, and in the 1840s, Southern Baptist and Methodist congregations seceded from the national groups and formed Southern denominations whose ministers and teachings would not question the rightness of the Southern course and would call God and the Bible to the defense of human slavery."[9]

Secular white society felt black slavery was indispensable to their way of life and insisted that, since God had marked blacks as "Noah's curse of Ham," the church's primary duty was to offer theological justifications for the existence of the peculiar institution. And, they did until the 1800s, when the religious justification was replaced by a biological and genetic justification.

Something Peculiar

Modern black slavery in the United States was often referred to as a peculiar institution because it was unusual in every sense. *Webster's Dictionary* defines peculiar as "something unusual or belonging exclusively to a person or thing." Black slavery, which was diametrically different from ancient or Roman slavery, was the most extensive and harshest subjugation imposed upon any race of people ever. It was an economic practice that was exclusively or peculiarly aimed at black people.

A number of conservatives argue that blacks were not singled out for slavery because they were black. Moreover, it is argued that blacks were not mistreated by the white slave masters and that slavery was not profitable, and that blacks gained as much from the slavery experience as the white master. Thomas Sowell, a black conservative economist, in his book, *The Economics and Politics of Race,* put forth a claim that the progeny of black slaves around the world are much better off, compared to blacks in Africa, because of the slavery experience.

Sowell further posits that black slaves were treated no differently from any other enslaved group in history. His weak assumptions allow him to conclude that blacks, therefore, have no grounds to complain about their historical treatment in America.[10] When 20 to 35 million blacks were outright killed and another 15 million were physically enslaved, psychologically abused, academically impaired, and economically impoverished for nearly 400 years, what other group of human beings does Sowell believe would have a greater right to complain?

TABLE 2 Comparative Analysis of Ancient Enslavement and Colonial Black Enslavement	
ANCIENT ENSLAVEMENT	**COLONIAL BLACK ENSLAVEMENT**
Slaves' basic rights were honored.	Black slaves had no rights.
The Catholic church accepted slaves as humans and intervened on their behalf.	Most religions supported black slavery and intervened on behalf of the slave holders, offering Biblical justification.
Slavery was viewed as a temporary and unfortunate social condition.	Black slavery was permanent and inherited.
Governments did not use their powers to exploit any racial group for private wealth and power.	European nations and colonial powers conspired to manipulate and enslave blacks in order to develop the New World and colonize Africa.
Slave ownership was viewed as status symbol and a measure of the slave holder's existing wealth and power.	Slave holding was used as an essential component of capitalism; it empowered even the poorest white to acquire wealth.
Slaves were mainly debtors, prisoners of war or victims of religious persecution.	Black enslavement did not result from financial indebtedness, war or religious persecution. Blacks were enslaved because they were black.
Inferiority stigmas were never permanently assigned to either the slave or his racial or ethnic group.	The skin color of the black slaves was sensationalized and made into a badge of degradation and permanent inferiority.
There was no preference for any particular race to serve as slaves.	Colonial slavery initially targeted Indians and indentured white servants, then blacks.
Slaveholders allowed slaves to retain their racial identity and dignity.	The blacks were psycho-socially conditioned to despise themselves; racial disunity was rewarded.
Slavery provided personal wealth and limited benefits directly to individual slave holders.	Slavery provided wealth for nations and institutions; empowered an industrial revolution and brought modern capitalism to Europe.

The Comparative Analysis of Ancient Enslavement and Colonial Black Enslavement, **Table 2,** outlines many of the essential principles, customs, practices and beliefs upon which slavery in America was founded. The table also highlights the extent to which the old slavery system was modified in order to perpetually hold blacks in bondage. The comparison underscores the reason that black slavery was known as the peculiar institution. Still, the question that remains unanswered is why European immigrants, who were allegedly fleeing poverty, hard work, religious persecution, governmental abuse, and economic serfdom, would so readily subject blacks to the same conditions that they were seeking to escape via coming to America.

The policies and practices of ancient and colonial slavery were as different as day and night. Since most of the slaves in ancient time were of European and Middle-Eastern origin, the commonality of skin color between slave and master could account for the leniency in ancient slavery.

White slavery ended after the Mameluke Rebellion of the 14th century, in which the Mamelukes, white prisoners enslaved by Arabs who were attempting to establish a world empire, revolted. According to Chancellor Williams, ". . . [T]he murderous onslaughts of the white slaves against their erstwhile masters so shocked the white world that the general enslavement of whites ended forever." After the Mameluke Rebellion, black Africa became the "exclusive hunting ground for slaves."[11] And since the 15th century, slavery has been primarily confined to blacks, perhaps because blacks failed to demonstrate, as the Mamelukes had, that enslavement was totally unacceptable to black people.

Why Indians Were Not Enslaved

Since a favored device for minimizing slavery and its impact on blacks is to counter that "Indians were treated even worse", it is important that a comparison be made of the differences or similarities in the treatment of blacks and Indians by the dominant white society. Historical and contemporary facts show that blacks were treated differently and worse in most respects. These differences concern degrees of degradation, cultural acceptance, government assistance and reparations.

As examples, during the two-and-a-half centuries that blacks were enslaved and being worked to death, Indians were free to move about and resettle. They carried weapons and defended themselves. The government established Indian Bureaus that built and financed a national system of tuition-free schools and required that Indian children attend. The bureaus provided them with food, clothing, housing, and farming tools. They were given back millions of acres of land upon which they could construct homes, farms, or businesses and never pay any form of taxes. They were never stripped of their culture, religion or sense of history. They were free to marry someone from any race or ethnic group. Many states, such as South Carolina and North Carolina encouraged marriages between white males and Indian women.

Indians contributed to the development of the nation through a non-personal loss of title to millions of acres of land, that millions of their people died trying to hold on to. But Indians had an option that blacks never had. They never carried the social and psychological burdens of having been enslaved. All of the five civilized Indian nations were black slave owners and slave traders. Worse, all of these Indian nations supported and fought on the side of the South in the Civil War in fear of losing their black slaves.

Unlike American Indians, blacks had few, if any, options. As slaves, blacks' freedom and liberty were taken from them. They were confined by laws and chains, could not carry weapons and were the primary targets of hostile Indians. There has never been a government agency established solely to provide them assistance. It was unlawful to teach a black to read and write even nearly a century after Indians were attending free schools. When schools were finally built, they were separate and unequal. Blacks were forced to finance their own schools and pay tuition to non-black schools. They were denied the right to acquire free land or, to this day, purchase land in certain areas.

Blacks have received no reparations for their centuries of personal physical abuse and stolen labor. They sought 40 acres and a mule, but received neither. They were released from centuries of servitude penniless, naked, ignorant, hungry and landless. They were legally defined by quantities of blood and every state enacted laws that forbade blacks to marry and commit sexual unions across racial lines. It was a capital offense for a black man to approach a white women. Blacks were separated from their culture, history, religion and family. Lastly, blacks continue to bear the scars and legacies of their inhumane and unique experience in American society.

Still, the great difference in the treatment of blacks and Indians does not answer the question, "Why were blacks selected for slavery over the

TABLE 3
Comparison of Enslavement Factors for Whites, Indians and Blacks

Reasons to Enslave	Reasons Not to Enslave
INDENTURED WHITES	
Constituted an available labor pool.	Perceived to be a member of same "master" race as the slave owner.
Voluntarily contracted into servitude.	Had rights and entitlements, including "freedom pay" at the end of the contract.
AMERICAN INDIANS	
Were not white; considered "heathens."	Respected by colonists as a conquered nation, not as individual slaves.
Were ill-educated, poorly organized and had no wealth or technology.	Escapees were familiar with wilderness; blended in with non-enslaved Indians.
SUB-SAHARAN AFRICANS/BLACKS	
Called "Negroes," blacks were not considered citizens of a country.	None
Skin color and features made them highly visible and prevented escapes.	None
Their mother country did not seek retribution on the colonists.	None
Tribal chiefs routinely enslaved and sold their fellow blacks to foreign traders.	None
African agriculural work patterns made blacks more suitable to agrarian plantations.	None
Africans demonstrated a greater willingness to adjust to slavery than Indians or white indentured servants.	None

American Indian?" Both blacks and Indians had a darker skin color than the white Europeans and both practiced non-institutionalized forms of religion, lacked firearms and were accessible for enslavement. The same factors that dissuaded Europeans from enslaving Indians in Latin and Central America also dissuaded European settlers from enslaving the Indian population in North America. Settlers, being on native Americans' land, were at a significant strategic disadvantage.

The American Indians were fierce warriors, whose behavior the white man could not predict and they rightly feared retribution from free tribesmen. Moreover, from an economic standpoint, enslaving American Indians was not a good investment. A runaway Indian slave could skillfully find safety and blend into the wilderness. As with the white indentured servant, the strong disadvantages made Indians unsuitable for slavery.

Although Indians were conquered, the white conqueror had a certain degree of respect for Indian culture. A basic principle of American Indian culture was a willingness to fight and die rather than be enslaved. They also had an inclination to exact revenge upon their enemies. This determination and strength impressed the white settlers.

Out of respect for them, many whites learned the American Indian languages and cultures. There was considerable cross cultural contact, with white settlers often boasting of being blood brothers or having Indian blood in their veins. The nation further honored the Indians by enshrining their likeness on American coins and institutionalizing their cultural contributions. Dominant white society's respect for the Indian was so great that an Indian image symbolized the nation before it was replaced by "Uncle Sam."

The white settlers had no such respect for African people or culture. They did not respect Africa, African languages, religions or black color. **Table 3** compares the pros and cons of indentured white servants, Indians and African blacks. Apparently, there were fewer advantages for enslaving whites than any other race. In fact, the analysis indicates that the darker the skin color, the more attractive the group was for bondage. Slave holders and traders quite likely used this criteria in making decisions about who best to enslave. They decided that enslavement of powerless blacks carried with it far more pros than cons. Backed by European religions, laws and social customs, a national public policy in America developed that identified blacks as the chosen people.

Undoubtedly, much of the disrespect that many whites hold for people of African descent stemmed from black people's compromising disposi-

tion and willingness to accept endless abuse and enslavement. Their unlimited compassion, patience, fears, concern for others and physical endurance were signs of mental weakness.

Not all blacks were submissive, but for those bold enough to bolt from
the plantations, their dark skin color was a highly visible target in a rural
or urban setting, making it nearly impossible for an escapee to hide and
elude capture for very long. Most blacks who did escape successfully
were unfamiliar with the surrounding wilderness and consequently had to
seek shelter in an urban environment in the Northern states or Canada.
Federal and state governments enacted fugitive slave laws that required
white citizens, bounty hunters and Indians to recapture black slaves for
rewards.

All of the other racial and ethnic groups rank above blacks in acceptability in America. It is likely that blacks would not be so vilely disre-
spected if they had fought harder against enslavement. African blacks
who did protest enslavement did so silently, jumping to their deaths from
slave ships, rather than fighting to the death. Groups that were willing to
fight to the death were considered difficult to control or defeat in battle,
and worse, were not wise investments, because slave masters could not
control, defeat or trust them.

There is no available documentation that indicates that white slave
holders ever seriously considered importing Asians or Hispanics into
America as slaves. By the 1660s, European settlers had turned almost
exclusively to blacks for their slaves. It is clear that there were conditions or characteristics associated with each ethnic or racial group that
either encouraged or discouraged enslavement.

A Global Ranking of Oppression Based on Skin Color

Although European oppression of other peoples was widespread and
occurred on a global scale, it had differences based on skin color. The
oppression of blacks has always been uniquely different, in kind, intensity and scope, from discrimination against Asians, Hispanics or Indian
groups around the world. **Table 4** lists some of the differences.

The table illustrates the apparent criteria and ranking factors used to
oppress peoples of different color as well as the benefits and results of
each group's enslavement. Those people closest in color appearance to
whites were oppressed less. These color gradations and other physical

TABLE 4		
A Global Racial Ordering of Colonial Oppression		
Continent	**Population Characteristics**	**Techniques Employed**
ASIA	Large complex civilization of yellow-skinned people.	Colonial powers imposed a numerically small superstructure upon existing civilization. Good rulers were allowed to maintain a great deal of power. This technique enabled the colonial powers to exploit the people and the land; and allowed Asian culture, language, and family structure to remain intact.
NORTH AMERICA	Thin, separate populations of browned-skinned people called Indians.	Colonial powers confiscated land; killed and forced natives onto less desirable land called reservations. This allowed colonial powers to exploit the land and pass ownership and wealth to their heirs. Native American culture and heritage remained intact and were enshrined into the U.S. coinage and national culture.
AFRICA	Separate pockets of black-skinned people.	Colonial powers imposed total control by colonizing, exploiting land, people and resources for centuries. Colonial powers executed mass displacement of people and accumulation of wealth; their actions destroyed families, culture, history, and sense of community by exporting blacks for global slavery.

characteristics have been reflected in America's immigration policies and laws since 1790 and help to explain why some cultures are more acceptable to whites than others. Though Japanese and Chinese, for instance, did face some discrimination at certain periods of history, they are generally more acceptable than blacks, especially in some of the more racist and oppressive countries of the world, such as South Africa.

African blacks have suffered from two kinds of peculiar institutions: American slavery and international colonial oppression. Many societies established their customs and treatment of blacks based on the patterns set by the European enslavers. Consequently, blacks have been subordinated to the lowest level in every nation and society. The socio-psychological impact of centuries of slavery, abuse, international colonization and exploitation is cumulative, but the full impact is yet to be determined, beyond the human devastation that is visible in black communities and countries around the world.

The psychological and sociological implications of centuries of enslavement of blacks and international colonization of black countries are mind-boggling. Blacks were raped of their wealth, culture, language, religion, human capital and humanity, and not permitted to bond for four centuries. Blacks now have little, if any, foundation for rebuilding and competing in a New World order that demands sophisticated skills, tools, technology, wealth-power and group unity. Blacks have been assigned to the lowest level of ethnic acceptability in America. This could explain why other racial and ethnic groups have been able to outperform them. Other groups do not carry the psychological, sociological and political burdens that blacks bear.

Strategies of Oppression

R. A. Schermerhorn, in an article entitled, *"Power as a Primary Concept in the Study of Minorities,"* explained how blacks suffered a double dose of white oppression and exploitation.[12] He hypothesized that the use of power over a less powerful group takes three forms: 1) the group with the greater power annihilates the powerless group or drives them out of the territory; 2) the more powerful group dominates the other group from a distance; or 3) the more powerful group brings the weaker group within its own geographic boundaries and efficiently controls it.

European whites have used all of these forms of power, in varying degrees, around the world. For example, the first form was used on American Indians to confiscate their lands; the second form is presently used by European nations to control the natural wealth of Africa; and the third form was used to control and exploit black labor in America.

These control methods have secured white Europeans' power over populations and natural resources, limiting the subordinate groups' access to dominant society. Generally, the colonization and oppression of non-black people were not as severe or prolonged as it was for darker-skinned people. For instance, no other racial or ethnic group was forc-

TABLE 5				
The Ranking of Harshness in the Trading of Black Slaves *				
Trader's Country of Origin	Harshness Rating	Trader's Skin Color	Duration Rating	Black Assimilation Policy
England	1	White	5	Forbidden
France	2	White	6	Forbidden
Dutch	3	White	4	Forbidden
Spain	4	Swarthy	3	Forbidden
Portugal	5	Swarthy	2	Permitted
Arab Nations	6	Darker	1	Permitted

* Ranking Key: 1 = The harshest slave trading customs; also 1 = the longest period of involvement in slave trading. Thus, traders from England were the harshest and those from Arab Nations have had the longest period of involvement.

ibly separated from their indigenous culture and country. The first blacks entered America in a questionable status aboard a Dutch warship, but shortly thereafter, specific social sanctions were imposed against them by the colony of Maryland. Once the subordinate status of blacks was established, the plantation society incrementally fine-tuned the slavery system.

Ranking of Slave Trading Nations

Nearly every European nation at one time or another participated in the slave trading business. The most prominent enslavers were the Arabs, English, Portuguese, Dutch, Spanish, and French. History indicates that though slave trading was a cold, impersonal and inhumane business, some slave trading nations established a reputation for being harsher or more lenient than other nations in their policies, practices and general treatment of the enslaved.

There were interesting correlations between the nationality and skin color of the slave traders and the social practices between them and their slaves. For instance, the greater the difference between a slave's skin color and the trader's skin color, the harsher the treatment was and miscegenation or sexual contact between the two was less likely to occur. On the other hand, the more similar in skin tone the two were, the more likely miscegenation would occur. Interestingly, those nations that were the farthest away from Africa geographically were harsher than those in closer proximity.

As indicated in **Table 5,** Arabs were rumored to be the most lenient towards black slaves, yet they have practiced slave trading longer than any other nation. Arabs continue the practice of enslaving and selling black Africans.[13]

Black Resistance Against Enslavement

Many West African blacks resisted enslavement, though they were confronted by the collective military and economic might of Portugal, Spain, Germany, England and Arab nations. Of the estimated 35-to-50 million blacks captured for shipment out of Africa, two-thirds never reached the slave markets. Most were killed resisting their captors or succumbed to the inhumane conditions of the slave ships. Some committed suicide. Contrary to the image of a happy slave, many physically mutilated themselves in order to reduce their market value or killed their own offspring to spare them the ordeal of enslavement; others died from new diseases, overwork and unhealthy living conditions; some were killed by other slaves or whites for the most trivial of reasons.

Slave rebellions tended to be less drastic. For instance, some rebel slaves simply impeded the work process by breaking work tools, feigning illness, running away and refusing to work. Some sought their freedom and revenge by setting fires to plantation buildings and the masters' houses. There were so many incidents of poisoning that many states passed laws prohibiting blacks from working in and around drug stores or supplies. Though it was a capital offense for blacks to defend themselves or strike a white person, there were about 150 to 200 organized slave rebellions.

Unlike the Indians or the Mamelukes, blacks eventually accepted slavery and complied with societal laws that forbade self-defense, insurrection and attempts to escape. They acquiesced then appealed to white conscience and morality in hopes of getting whites to end slavery.

Even today Blacks use the same technique, trying to overcome the legacies of white racism, abuse and exploitation. It is clear that new methods must be employed. Most black appeals to the moral conscience of white society have fallen on deaf ears. John Locke, a prominent philosopher, summarized many whites' feelings about the plight of blacks when he said that an abused or enslaved man had the moral obligation to take up arms in defense of his own freedom, even if it meant his death. In short, it is not white society's responsibility to be both the exploiter and savior of black people.

Conclusion

The enslavement of Africans gave this nation its class structure and labor base and strongly influenced its political and economic ideologies. And the residual effects of slavery flourished even while America searched for its own moral soul, personal freedoms and economic independence. Slavery in America was unique in the history of enslavement, because it was based on skin color. There were many reasons that whites decided to choose blacks to serve as their slaves and, still led by these notions of race, whites today perpetuate the slavery pathology. Thus, racist beliefs continue to fester within the cultural and social fabric of American society, shackling blacks as they grope towards more effective ways of improving their living conditions and economic status.

5

Why Blacks Cannot Emulate Ethnic Immigrants

"Where is blackness in the rainbow?"
C. Anderson

During the last three decades, it has become "politically correct" to dump blacks and their racial problems into broad categories such as ethnic issues, special interest and minority groups. It is also popular now to view the grievances of all groups as equal in all respects. Placing blacks into an aggregation of dissimilar groups and equating their circumstance with other minorities is little more than political sleight-of-hand, an illusion of equality in a so-called color blind American society.

America is far from being color-blind and equality exists only in the minds of those who pretend that inequality is equality. It is disingenuous to equate black Americans' conditions with any other ethnic, religious or so-called disadvantaged minority. Blacks have a unique history in this country in that their status was predetermined by the dominant society's national public policy on the use of black Americans.

Grouping blacks with lesser aggrieved groups, in effect, mutes and obscures the legitimate grievances of blacks, while veiling the moral, legal, and financial responsibility the dominant society has to correct the suffering of 36 million black Americans. Declarations that the country is now color-blind are misstatements that resolve nothing. The color-blind myth simply maintains the status quo, thereby keeping blacks noncompetitive and marginal. If four centuries of slavery and Jim Crowism have taught blacks anything about race relations, it is that as long as people can see, color will be a factor.

Both by nature and nurture, humans are motivated to be self-centered and to place their self-interest above all others. Self-interest leads to competition among individuals and groups for material and social gains. Carl N. Degler reasoned that in a fluid and competitive social structure, all devices are used or called upon to assist in the gaining and maintenance of status, power and economic advancement.[1] Dominant white society has a long history of masking the reasons that it would not correct the debilitating conditions that it has imposed on black people. Dan Lacy, an historian, criticized the hypocrisy of the dominant society's attitude towards blacks, saying:

> "Whites denounce blacks as lazy and lacking ambition while they resent black competition. They are angered by taxation for welfare and other social programs, but are equally angered by equal opportunity and affirmative action job policies for blacks. They mock the lower academic achievement of black children, then assign the best teachers, materials and financial resources to white schools in the suburbs."[2]

Whenever blacks attempt to change their circumstances by demanding assistance from the various levels of government, whites predictably ask the question: "Why can't blacks be self-sufficient like the Jews, Italians or other ethnic groups and help themselves, rather than going to the government for assistance?" Some blacks, those who lack competitive skills and income opportunities, ask government and white society for public assistance because they prefer public aid to stealing what they need. Most blacks are demanding compensation or reparations from the government for the centuries of expropriated labor and the legacies of slavery and Jim Crowism that continue to place European whites, Hispanics and Asians over them.

Blacks are too socially and economically handicapped to effectively compete in an integrated society with advantaged racial and ethnic groups or other protected minorities, such as women and the disabled. To classify and equate blacks with these groups is not only a dishonest, do-nothing approach, it also portends serious future social disturbances. America has maintained a racial and ethnic ranking of preference (**See Table 6**) that places European whites, Asians, Hispanics and Indians over American blacks. These preferred groups have a double advantage over blacks. They have a higher social acceptability and they were never mistreated by dominant white society or government the way 16 generations of blacks have been treated. This double advantage makes it clear why it is inappropriate and misleading to lump blacks into a minority category along with preferred and protected groups.

Black Americans cannot emulate European, Asian and Hispanic ethnics, because social barriers have never permitted blacks to access the assimilation process, which is reserved for non-black ethnics. How can marginally existing blacks walk an ethnic path towards self-improvement when they are not treated like an ethnic group? And, even if they were so treated, both the government and the majority society would continue to allow an unending flow of new ethnic immigrants to preempt blacks in the assimilation process. How fair is it to ask blacks to emulate other groups when nearly 100 percent of blacks' ancestors were in America before nearly 100 percent of the ancestors of today's Jewish, Italian, German, French, Japanese, Chinese, Irish and Hispanics?

Yet, these more recently arrived ethnic groups have been assimilated and blacks have not. It was white society's willingness to offer assimilation to everybody but blacks that has placed the greatest burden on blacks and forced them to now seek alternative routes, outside of mainstream white society, to gain economic and political power. Had dominant society had any real intentions of assimilating blacks, it would have done so before it assimilated the other groups. Or, at worst, white society would have assimilated blacks immediately after the Civil War, when blacks were first freed.

In addition, it is not possible for blacks to emulate immigrant groups, because those groups have always had options to help them rise from one social class to another after they arrived in America. Immigrants were never burdened with the experiences or the legacy of slavery and Jim Crowism. They came to America with hope and a belief that the situation here would be better than in their country of origin. Centuries of immigrants have entered this nation believing that it was the land of unlimited opportunity, where a person was free to achieve and go as high as his skill and God-given talents would take him.

As Asians and Hispanics find places in the economy, they are allowed to move upward on social and occupational ladders, says historian Andrew Hacker, in his book, *Two Nations: Black and White, Separate, Hostile, Unequal*.[3] Blacks have had no such options. Sixteen generations of blacks have been denied such a reality. Blacks continue to dream of integration as they spend their time and resources fighting for basic civil rights and the first-class citizenship that every ethnic immigrant has when he enters this nation.

On the other hand, ethnic immigrants and other minorities have directly profited from the marginal success of the black Civil Rights Movement that opened doors in the areas of employment, academics, and housing. The black movement, in its various efforts to establish affirmative action, eliminate discrimination and seek economic parity, has drawn most of the fire from a disapproving, reluctant white society. When forced to make a civil rights accommodation, whites have hired women, Asian and Hispanic ethnics and the handicapped, ahead of blacks. These other groups have achieved significant advances over the past two decades, piggybacking on the civil rights legislation blacks fought long and hard to win. Blacks' socioeconomic push was effectively neutralized when they became "minorities."

The definition of minority continues to expand and to become more amorphous. Today, almost everyone is a minority in some way. Anything that applies to every group has no real meaning for any group. However, the term minority holds major political advantage for those who wish to maintain a status quo. Blacks are further undermined when included in a minority category because none of the other so-called minorities were statutorily deprived by the government of their humanity or their right to enjoy the fruits of their own labor.

Blacks: Immigrants or Not?

Historians often refer to American Indians as the nation's only indigenous or non-immigrant population group. This notion is false. If American Indians are America's only non-immigrants, then that would make blacks immigrants, which they are not. The ancestors of American Indians migrated to North America across the Bering Straits from Asia. Black Americans did not immigrate to America. They were transported to America against their will. Inherent in the term immigrant is the element of choice in the selection of a new home in a new nation.

Many ethnic immigrants come to America fully equipped with the economic know-how and business acumen that they developed in their home countries. As required by U.S. immigration policies, many are well educated and have professional trades. They have business experience and access to products and industries in their mother country around which they can build businesses in this country. They have boundless hope and competitive motivation to succeed in this land of opportunity.

Their business contacts and products may be related to importing ethnic foods, arts and craft products, or exporting American products to their home countries. Most black businessmen have limited business experience and few cultural products to market. For the most part, they do not have family, friends or other natural business contacts in Africa. European, Asian and Hispanic immigrants come here with contacts in their countries of origin, which they often use for commercializing their culture into business opportunities in America.

Few legal immigrants in modern times have come to America impoverished. Many are people of material and social substance at home, particularly those that came as political refugees, forced to leave behind businesses and careers when sudden crisis hit. Even if they are forced to start over, they are equipped to do so. Many enjoyed assistance from the U.S. Government through legislated refugee programs for groups such as the Cubans, Vietnamese, Cambodians, Hungarians and Koreans. Others received assistance and aid from the Central Intelligence Agency (CIA) and the U.S. State Department when they arrived.

The immigration process encourages ethnics to develop and control their communities. While blacks are seeking to build their businesses around the integration process, ethnic immigrants are more nationalistic in their practices. They do not buy into the melting pot myth. Understanding the principles of the way this country's economy works, they seek to create specialized niche economies around their culture within the larger framework of the national economy. Immigrants are not opposed to venturing into other racial or ethnic communities to take advantage of wealth building opportunities. But, they keep their own community relatively closed to outsiders.

This is true in the Little Italys, China Towns and Little Havanas in this country. In Miami, Florida, for example, Cubans control the number of non-Cuban business going into their communities of Little Havana and Hialeah. Unlike blacks, ethnic immigrants practice a business home rule that says, "I got my neighborhood. Now I will get yours." They demon-strated their home rule philosophy and influence in 1992 when Cuban residents boldly blocked Iranian businessmen from opening stores in their communities, solely because the entering business owners were not Cu-ban.

As the major business owners in black neighborhoods in the Miami area, Cubans own most of the bars, liquor stores, grocery stores, auto-mobile parts stores, banks and gas stations in black neighborhoods. Cu-ban business owners take capital out of black neighborhoods, but will not allow non-Cuban businesses to set up and take capital out of their com-munities. Clearly they understand the power dynamics of group econom-ics. Blacks do not.

Culture-Based Ethnic Businesses

Many of the early immigrant groups established "cultural niches" or turf control over certain public sector jobs, businesses and vocations. When these groups cornered niches, they then had avenues for providing employment, business, and political opportunities to incoming members of their group. Control of these social and economic areas promoted intra-group dependency. They provided opportunities to attract capital, market their culture, maintain a community economy and exact ethnic economic accountability. Black communities do not own or control socioeconomic centers within their communities. Douglas Glasgow, a sociologist, pointed out many of the traditional examples of ethnic economic centers, in his book, *The Black Underclass*. He wrote:

"The Italians sought and ruled the shipyards, docks, unions, ethnic restaurants, and fire departments; Jews took over the garment and jewelry industries, banking and lending industries, major professions and entertainment. The Irish dominated the alcoholic manufacturing, distilling and distribution industries, police departments and bars; Asians established ethnic-oriented communities, restaurants, cleaners, stores, and supply houses." [4]

Blacks were not permitted to establish culture-based businesses. Prior to Emancipation, the North and South enacted laws and ordinances that prohibited blacks from owning businesses that competed with whites. Even after Emancipation, that remained the case. Blacks were prohibited by the legal and social sanctions that withheld capital, market opportunities, access to resources and education from establishing businesses. Even in raising tobacco, cotton, and various livestock, where blacks had unquestionable skill, they were generally forbidden to raise and sell their products in competition with whites.

The horse racing industry is another example. After the Civil War and until the first decade of the 20th century, black jockeys dominated the horse racing industry. Although they were skilled jockeys and horse trainers, blacks were not allowed to develop any businesses based upon their experience around the tracks. By the second decade of the 20th century, horse racing had become a major sport and wealth building business. Black jockeys and trainers were replaced by white trainers and Hispanic jockeys.

Blacks were not allowed to compete with whites at any level of life. No other racial or ethnic immigrants have been confronted with such systematic opposition to their personal freedom, economic independence, and right to earn a living.

Blacks Lack a Sense of Unity

Another reason that blacks cannot emulate ethnics is their lack of group unity or sense of community. Racial integration, black peoples' long standing objective, is the antithesis of group togetherness. Integration fragments blacks into even smaller groups and scatters them among the majority white society. This scattering has destroyed the cohesion of black communities.

Upper and middle class blacks live in small enclaves, as powerless minorities, among white majorities all across the nation. They are isolated, without a bond to their racial roots and typically see themselves as disunited, weakened people. Although it raises a great deal of emotional conflict, successfully integrated blacks invariably find comfort and security in being white in most respects except color. There are few emotional bridges back into the black communities, so they identify with and support the power and material resources of the white communities.

Government and dominant white society have historically rewarded blacks who identified with the larger white community and placed their welfare above that of the black community. For selling out their own community, blacks were often rewarded with special positions, money, or meritorious manumission.

There has been no similar legal or reward system to encourage members of Asian or Hispanic groups to turn against members of their own race. Contrarily, they have received rewards for maintaining a strong sense of community and ethnic identity. Cultural unity and community cohesiveness have been the key to their survival. They came with extended families intact. They came with the freedom to send back for loved ones they had left behind.

They engaged in trade, moving goods and currency back and forth. They were generally free to practice their cultures in this country, guard their traditions, school their children in their own languages, practice their respective religions, and in every other way, live as free citizens. Not one of those freedoms was historically available to blacks, certainly not during slavery.

Ethnic immigrants have good reasons to have a completely different frame of reference about America than do blacks. Ethnics enjoy the support — economic, social and otherwise — of the dominant white society. The government has been a great deliverer of jobs, wealth and relocation assistance to ethnic immigrants, to which the recent North American Free Trade Agreement (NAFTA) with Mexico will attest.

Contrary to the moral of the Horatio Alger story, that every individual and group should pull themselves up by their own boot straps, immigrants have historically received governmental assistance. In the Southwest, illegal immigrants from Mexico, who never paid taxes, have no difficulty securing welfare, social security benefits, education, or medical care. More than 50 percent of the babies born in some hospitals in Southern California in 1993, were born to illegal Mexican aliens.

Free access to public services and benefits without having to pay centuries of dues, shapes the way immigrants see America. Ethnics do not view discrimination in the same way black people do. An immigrant may be more willing than blacks to sweep the streets and polish door knobs, because he would have little reason not to believe that his future will be better, if not for himself, then for his children. Blacks have no such optimism. They have spent centuries sweeping, walking and living on the streets and they realize that a brighter future for themselves and their children is questionable.

Skin Color

Skin color is the single most important factor that prevents blacks from emulating ethnic immigrants, because it defines their role, status, and limits their access to resources. The skin color and physical attributes of non-black ethnic immigrants is much closer to that of whites. White ethnics and Asians are more acceptable to the dominant white society than are blacks.

The long history of American race relations seems to point to one fact; that blacks' high visibility has made them a convenient target for many of the social conflicts and insecurities of each white ethnic group that has reached these shores.[5] Ethnic immigrants learn early, and one of the last things they forget, is to avoid contact with America's black pariah. Other groups can blend in or assimilate into the dominant culture. Blacks' skin color does not permit them to blend.

Blackness Phobia

For centuries, the concept of blackness has held intense meaning for whites. The black color has the ability to distort, dominate, or totally obliterate whiteness, or the absence of color. The concept threatens whites' ingrained values of culture, race dominance, blood lines and genetic purity. White society's fear of blackness, power and potency necessitated legal definitions that tracked the flow of black blood. The fear of blackness made it important that society rigidly define who and what was black. Once defined, neither black persons nor their blood, were permitted to assimilate into mainstream society or white veins. Even a small quantity, one drop of black blood, could dominate white blood, and determine a person's race.

Across the nation, laws were enacted defining who was black. These laws established strict standards for whiteness, declaring that one-fourth, one-sixteenth, or even "one drop" of black blood made a person black, while conversely, no amount of white blood in the human body could dominate a single drop of black blood. No other ethnic population in the nation, including those with visibly non-white biological features, have ever been so rigidly defined. The One Drop Rule was once used as a standard by the U.S. Census.

James F. Davis, in his book, *Who Is Black: One Nation's Definition*, lamented how blacks are held to a different blood lineage definition than members of any other racial or ethnic group. For example, Indians, who are typically held to be worse off than blacks, were never held to the same degrading standards as blacks. Persons of one-fourth or less American Indian ancestry were not generally defined as Indians unless it was their choice. Either way, they were acceptable to the larger society and could assimilate. The same seems to have applied to immigrants from the Far East and the Pacific Islands.

There are no statutory efforts in America to determine which persons were one-eighth Hungarian, Russian, Japanese, Mexican, Turkish, Canadian or members of any other immigrant groups. The quantity of blood, or the one drop of blood rule, targeted blacks. As James F. Davis said, "Americans do not insist that an American with a small fraction of Polish ancestry be classified as a Pole, or that someone with a single remote Greek ancestor be designated as Greek, or that someone with any trace of Jewish lineage is Jewish and nothing else." [6]

The blood rule was practiced to keep the offspring of mixed marriages from "passing." Passing is the practice of a light-skinned black person living as a white or person of another race. Again, when non-blacks decide to assimilate into the larger culture they are rarely restricted, ostracized or confronted, with charges of "passing." Mixed ethnics, especially second generations, are free to be whatever ethnic or racial group they declare themselves to be.

Harold Cruse says, "Blacks have never had the option of being anything more than what dominant white society would let them be or wanted them to be."[7] The groups to which blacks are equated, under the broad minority category, all have options. They can change their names, language, culture, country of residence, nationality, sexual preference, and religious affiliation. Since the basis of discriminating against blacks is skin color, blacks will have options only when they learn how to change their color. But, on the other hand, that would create the problems of passing.

The Psychological and Economic Baggage of "Passing"

Dark-skinned blacks reacted to light or mixed blacks' passing with feelings of abandonment and anger. Many felt offended that a mixed black would reject or choose to live as someone other than a black person. Whites took offense because the passing black had beaten their blood monitoring practices and was unlawfully enjoying the fruits of white society. On the other hand, dark-skinned blacks passed during slavery, in reverse. Darker black slaves who ran away, passed by pretending that they were freeborn or freed blacks. The darker skinned blacks dressed and acted as if they had natural rights to freedom.

Immigration Laws

Immigration laws create and maintain a racial, ethnic, religious, and color balance in America. Color gradation has been an important ranking factor. The darker the skin color, the lower the immigration quota. Blacks had the darkest skin color with a racial quota of zero. A writer for the Virginia Gazette, as far back as the 1700s, alluded to the foolishness of such an order of acceptability:

> "If Negroes are to be slaves on account of his color, the next step will be to enslave every mulatto in the Kingdom, then all the Portuguese, next the French, then the brown complexioned Englishmen, and so on until there be only one free man left, which will be the man of the palest complexion in the three kingdoms."[8]

During the century that followed, quotas kept free blacks out of the country. With the exception of the English, the codes restricted new immigrants from any one country to two percent of the number of the individual's nationality residing in the continental United States, as determined by the Census of 1890. Immigration laws passed in the 1880s and 1890s were based on the census figures of 1790. Blacks were slaves and not considered citizens. Thus, with the exception of a few blacks from the Caribbean islands, blacks were excluded.

Almost 30 years later, in 1924, the United States Immigration and Naturalization Service upheld the zero immigration quota for blacks and they were officially shut out of the United States until the late 1960s. The quota remained zero until 1965, when black African nations began to receive their independence from colonial rule, and had to be officially recognized. One can only suppose that as these nations ascend in power and wealth, the American immigration quotas for their citizens will rise accordingly.

Black Patriotism

Ironically, no other racial or ethnic group in America has demonstrated the long-term patriotism of blacks. Blacks are the only non-white people to have fought in defense of America in every military conflict since the country's beginning. Blacks have fought in armed conflicts against the mother countries of most of the ethnic immigrants now in America. For nearly four centuries, blacks were the first to die in support of the principles of the nation. Yet, they are excluded while foreign immigrants arrive daily at the doors of this great nation, and are welcomed.

The Ethics of Hard Work

It is common to hear Japanese, Chinese and Germans being cited as model hard workers. Before blacks became obsolete as common labor in the 1960s, they were the models for doing the hardest, dirtiest, most dangerous and backbreaking work. Ironically, conservatives and government are suggesting that emulating these recent immigrants and their hard work is the cure for blacks protracted poverty and high unemployment.

Recommending more hard work for a race of ex-slaves is similar to curing an alcoholic by suggesting that the drunk do more drinking. Having never been compensated for centuries of past labor is the bigger part of the problem, not whether black people are willing to work hard.

If blacks were unwilling to work hard, it would be understandable after 400 years of no pay to low pay. Which ethnic immigrants in America have worked harder than the black slaves? Certainly the Japanese, Chinese, and Germans did not work harder in America than black slaves. If the Japanese, Chinese and the Germans were the hardest workers, would it not have made more sense for colonial white society to have enslaved the Japanese, Chinese, or Germans, rather than blacks who were allegedly lazy and unwilling to work? Why would supposedly bright businessmen spend 250 years traveling half way around the world to kidnap 35 to 50 million innocent, but lazy blacks, then knowingly bring them to America to do work that other ethnic groups could do better?

Even in instances where these ethnic groups worked hard, they did it with the consciousness of paid free men. The indentured servants from India, the Chinese coolies, though they were mistreated, were still free and paid for their labor. They had the option to quit and return home to their homelands any time they so desired. The sweatshops in New York City were reprehensible, but the Chinese workers were free and paid. They were not property. No one owned, beat, or killed them and their families for not working.

The Japanese are often held up as labor models for blacks, but blacks were never treated as well as the Japanese, even though blacks fought with the American military troops against the Japanese in World War II. If blacks had been treated as well as the Japanese, perhaps then, they too could be held up as great respecters of hard work.

The United States Government paid $20,000 in reparations to each Japanese American who was forced to live in internment camps during the four years of World War II. For their three to four years of internment, the Japanese Americans were compensated nearly 42 years later. Not only did the United States government award reparations to each relocated Japanese, it gave the Japanese community a national apology.

Granted, the reparations, made after years of court battles, and after most of those entitled to them were already dead, can in no way compensate for what was lost. Still, it was a debt acknowledged and paid. Blacks, on the other hand, after four centuries of lost humanity, life and wealth, have received nothing.

The Myth of Hard Work

The moral value of work was promoted under the aegis of Puritan ethics that most early colonial settlers preached about, but did not practice. The intense labor demands of the New World required most settlers to work. But, contrary to the moral myth, they tried to avoid work by forcing others to do it for them, while they took the credit and the profits. White society was especially adept at avoiding certain kinds of work when blacks were present. Since hard labor in and of itself did not convey nor confer dignity, they did not want blacks to see them doing lowly work. Arduous work carried a low status and was routinely avoided by whites, who preferred being seen in a management capacity.[9]

The white Southerner's disdain for hard work was commonly accepted in and around immigration ports. Stanley Lebergott in his book, *The Americans: An Economic Record* supported the common impression that if anyone was lazy it was more likely the enslaver rather than the enslaved.

Modern day conservatives continue to believe that the answer to black America's problem is more diligence and hard work. In his book, *The Economics and Politics of Race*, conservative black economist Thomas Sowell is eloquent in his admiration of immigrants' willingness to work long and hard to get ahead. However, he condemns blacks on the assumption that blacks developed poor work habits and a "resistance to work" that had developed under slavery." Thomas Sowell believes the lazy slave myth, though the term lazy slave is an oxymoron. A lazy slave would have had a very difficult time surviving under the inhuman conditions of American slavery. Sowell apparently feels that black people had an obligation to produce for the their overseers. Why blacks should have felt such an obligation is unclear.

Stripping people of the fruits of their labor takes away the primary motive for them to work. Absent personal compensation, what were the incentives for slaves to work harder? Would they have been emancipated or received compensations or reparations for doing so? Would the slaves have gotten better food, shelter, clothing, education or pensions in an early retirement? Would the race's stolen humanity, wealth, and cultural heritage have been returned? Or did the slaves know the answers to these questions and realize that the cold, hard truth was that most slave holders preferred to work slaves to death in their prime to avoid the expense of taking care of them in their old age?

Who was lazy? The white slave masters bragged about building a wealthy aristocracy that could devote its time to a leisure life in the study of art, philosophy and the finer things in life. The Earl of Egmont in 1740 quoted a Carolina merchant who sought to avoid work. He said: "Where there are Negroes, a white man despises to work, saying, 'What? Will you have me as a slave and work, like a Negro?'"

Winthrop D. Jordan, author of *White Over Black*, supported the white slave holders' need for black laborers, stating that it was impossible for white men to work the fields, because "the labor was so severe that hundreds of Negroes yearly lost their lives through hard work."[10] Even the paid white servants did not perform the extremely hard work when blacks were available. The white masters prided themselves on being a leisure class and only doing gentlemen's work. If the five million black slaves were lazy, they took their example from the best teachers.

What immigrants came to America for the purpose of hard work? In the formative years of this nation, most immigrants coming to America were vagrants, criminals, hustlers, adventurers and others seeking to strike it rich quick. America was advertised as the place of unlimited land, natural resources and a slave underclass. The hard work myth for immigrants contradicted the inscription on the Statue of Liberty, which says, "Give me your tired . . . yearning to be free." Tired immigrants did not leave their native lands around the world to come to America so they could work even harder. They could have worked hard wherever they were. They came to America to be free of undue hard labor. They came seeking opportunities to accumulate the fruits of their relatively easy labor here. They came to enjoy labor-saving devices. And, they came, escaping from underclass status in their own countries, to a place with a ready-made underclass — black people. At last, they knew they would not be on the bottom rung.[11]

Who's Who in Racial and Ethnic Rankings

If blacks are at the bottom, who is at the middle and the top in the racial and ethnic ranking system of this country? The major elements in determining one's ranking are race, skin color, country of origin, ethnicity and religious denomination. The higher your ranking, the more you are welcomed and preferred to live as a citizen in this nation. America was established as an English-speaking, Anglo-Saxon Protestant nation.

Wealth and power were concentrated at the top of the scale in the hands of White Anglo-Saxon Protestants (WASPs) and decreased in accord with the darkness of a person's skin color. The racial and ethnic ordering as shown in **Table 6** is a comparative analysis of the allocation of benefits, access to resources, immigration policies and foreign affairs relationships. There has always been an open immigration policy with certain allied WASP nations.

It was not possible for the United States to remain an English-only nation. However, government policies kept the American population and power close to the original founders in culture and other respects. The highest positions of wealth and power are held by white Anglo-Saxon Protestants, Catholics and Jews. These groups have well entrenched social positions characterized by a predominance in economic and political power and buttressed with a strong cohesive group solidarity. Since the founding of the nation, power and wealth have remained concentrated in the hands of the WASP.

America was an English colony that adopted English culture and forms of government. The English are at the top of the ranking as indicated in **Table 6**. They accorded blacks the lowest acceptable status and the national public policy has maintained a nearly 100 percent shutout of people of African descent. Consequently, even if America has humanitarian concerns about the social conditions in Ethiopia, Somalia, Sudan, Haiti, or black South Africa, America will not provide a place in this country for many seeking permanent refuge. Their skin color makes them unacceptable.

TABLE 6
The U.S. Government's Preferential Ordering of Immigrants
According to Official Quotas Set in 1924

Nationality	Skin Color	Religion	Immigration Quota
English	White	Protestant	Open
Irish/N. Europe	White	Protestant	34,007
Western Europe	White	Protestant	28,567
Eastern Europe	White	Protestant	51,227
Southern Europe	White	Catholic	3,845
Middle East	White	Jewish/Muslim	124
Far East	Yellow	Buddhist/Other	100
Hispanic	Brown	Catholic/Other	Restricted
African	Black	Combinations	Closed

Sources: Sixty-Eighth Congress, Session I documents and the U.S. Department of Justice Immigration Records; Interpretation of data by Howard Zinn, author of "People History of the United States." [12]

The Irish, the other part of the British kingdom, were also reputed to dislike blacks. According to John Garraty, author of *The American Nation: A History of the United States*, "The Irish disliked the blacks, with whom they had to compete for low level work in some large urban areas when first entering the country. One Irish leader, Daniel O'Connell, admitted that the American Irish were among the worst enemies of the colored race." The Irish had their share of problems in the emerging American hierarchy. In fact, for a time, only the blacks and the American Indians were beneath them.[13]

The pattern that emerged was a direct correlation between the relative power of a foreign nation and the status of its immigrants in America. When America was a developing nation, for instance, England was powerful and wealthy. Immigration data reflects this pattern. The English settlers held positions of power in the new country and their people in

Europe had unlimited immigration rights into this country. Other less powerful nations like France and Germany were allowed fewer immigrants,
based upon the descending importance of their home countries in the
world order. Powerful countries and their citizens were respected.

Blacks and Ethnic Immigrants
Compete for Resources

A continuing flow of immigrants, decade after decade, from 1607 to
the present day, came believing that America abounded with freedom
and wealth. Common sense dictates that had they anticipated they would
face the kind of life most black people face, immigration would have
ceased immediately after the first boatload arrived. The flow of immigrants never ceased, because they were never treated like blacks.

As a matter of fact, ethnic and racial immigrants historically have been
a wedge between whites and blacks, giving whites an alternative to in-
teracting with blacks. Each time in history, either before or after a war,
when the American economy was expanding and could have offered
material economic benefits to blacks, a new influx of immigrants or refugees arrived, to fill the void and "further exiled blacks from fruitful participation in the national life," according to historian Dan Lacy.[14]

A major myth is that there has been competition between blacks and
ethnic groups. There has been no such competition. European ethnics
simply bumped blacks from whatever they were interested in getting,
because they were higher in the order of social preference. After they
finished competing for jobs, housing or union control, blacks then applied
for anything that was available. If racial customs did not exclude blacks,
they optimistically waited until jobs or housing were passed down through
the ethnic hierarchy, extending from English down to Jewish.

As competition for resources increase and blacks become more frustrated, conflicts for power, resources or even basic rights are developing
between blacks and all ethnic and racial groups who rank higher than
blacks in the order of preference. If blacks' marginal level of subsis-
tence does not improve, they will become the common denominator in
every social clash. Since the 1980s, blacks have clashed with Arabs in
Cleveland and Detroit. In the early 1990s, New York and Boston were
outraged over the slaying of blacks by Jews and ethnic whites. Violent
confrontations between blacks and Koreans, Vietnamese, Laotian, and
Cambodian merchants have arisen across the country in cities like Phila-

delphia, Washington, D.C. and Los Angeles.

The continuous conflicts in Miami between blacks and Cubans have ignited four major riots since 1973. In some instances, blacks were angered by a single offensive act. At other times, the riot was a response to what blacks perceived as a pattern of offensive acts. Centuries of unjust racial subordination to immigrants has generated a smoldering tension between blacks and those who came to the community from foreign nations higher in the preference order than blacks.

Today there is little cooperation, political or otherwise, between blacks and minority groups. For the most part, ethnic minorities do not support black causes. They have been getting a free ride at black peoples' expense on civil rights and minority programs. As members of loosely formed political "coalitions," they are mostly quiet while blacks agitate; but they are quick to stake their claim on affirmative action benefits won by blacks.

From Los Angeles, California to Miami, Florida, conflicts arise between blacks and ethnic groups as they seek their share of power and wealth in the mainstream beyond the shadow of blacks. In the 1990 mayoral election in Chicago, Hispanic leaders leapfrogged between white and black factions, offering support wherever there seemed to be the most to gain for their Hispanic communities. David Dinkins, the first black mayor of New York City, lost his reelection bid in 1993 along the lines of racial issues. All the ethnic blocks, except Puerto Ricans, voted against Dinkins.

Burgeoning Hispanic-Black Conflicts

In the 1990 Census data, 85 percent of those listed as Hispanic also classified themselves as Caucasians. This ethnic group is the fastest growing population that is challenging blacks for numerical and political dominance as a minority, which it is not. Hispanics have enjoyed the benefits of having it both ways. First, they criticize white society for its disproportionate share of wealth and power, then they classify themselves as Caucasians. These groups classify themselves as Caucasians for social purposes, then as minorities to qualify for governmental programs.

The question then is no longer "Who is white?" It is "Who is permitted to be classified as white?" Hacker in his analysis of 1990 Census data, indicated that most Asians, Middle Easterners and Hispanics by culture and color are allowed to enter and move up the class system. They are permitted the option of calling themselves "white" for benefit purposes.[15]

Thus, a common front is being formed, with blacks the only excluded group.

Hispanics reap great advantages and receive benefits under minority programs by calling themselves minorities. Although first generation Hispanics do experience some cultural discrimination, they have not suffered historical, statutory injuries by the government within the continental United States. Their higher ethnic acceptability among whites deflects benefits and resources that should be directed to blacks.

Besides having gotten themselves included under the minority label, what is the justification for the U.S. supporting a never-ending influx of Hispanics from Mexico, Central America, Latin America and the Caribbean Islands? How can Hispanics, whose ancestors have previously benefited from black enslavement, equate themselves to blacks, who are still suffering through the worst human holocaust in the history of mankind?

More specifically, why would the government continue to perpetuate a wrong by comparing a fluid, ever-changing Hispanic and Asian immigrant population with a static black population? Hispanic and Asian populations qualify to receive services to help minorities to assimilate and advance into mainstream society. The static black population remains intact until the next generation of immigrants arrive, needing minority assistance.

The Department of Commerce *Money Income of Households, Families, and Persons in the United States: 1991* report indicated why most Hispanic and Asian ethnics should not be grouped with blacks. **Table 7** shows that from the Civil Rights Movement of the 1960s to the 1990s, whites, Hispanics, and Asians have maintained a constant income advantage over blacks, with no appreciable closing of the gap. For a comparative example, the median household income for 1991 was $18,807 for blacks, $22,691 for Hispanics, $31,569 for whites, and $36,449 for Asians.

How can Asians and blacks be considered equal in a minority assistance or affirmative action program, when Asians have not been historically enslaved or statutorily deprived and have median household incomes that double that of blacks? This kind of economic injustice troubles blacks and serves as a major cause of ethnic clashes.

When examining population figures, similar concerns should be raised about comparing the conditions of blacks to Hispanics. Blacks were being handicapped centuries before the present Hispanic population arrived in the United States. In 1840, when there were four million blacks in

America, there was no record of any significant number of Hispanics.

By 1862, the annexation of Texas, California and other territories in the southwest increased the Hispanic population to approximately 4,000 as compared to five million black slaves and freedmen. By the turn of the

TABLE 7 Median Household Income by Race and Hispanic Origin: 1967-1991		
Race	1967	1991
Asian	Not available	$36,449
White	$27,949	$31,569
Hispanic	Not available	$22,691
Black	$16,228	$18,807
All Households	$26,801	$30,126
		Source: U.S. Department of Commerce

century, Hispanic immigration combined with high birthrates had increased the Hispanic population by approximately 2,500 percent; the black birth rate increased by nearly 100 percent.

The 1900 Census data reported a population of 100,000 Hispanics and nine million blacks. Over the following 90 years, the birthrates of the two groups remained relatively equal. Yet, the 1990 Census showed an incredible increase in the Hispanic population, that was growing at a rate that was nine times faster than the black population. How could the Hispanic population close the gap between themselves and blacks in such a short period of time? The answer is in the annual immigration influx of nearly two million Hispanics, by both legal and illegal means. This amounts to a continuous, never-ending flow of Hispanics into this country, all of whom enter the social order at a higher rank than blacks.

Conclusion

Blacks are not immigrants and cannot emulate them. Their circumstances spring from different experiences and options. Blacks have been a part of this country from its inception. They have never received recognition or benefits commensurate with their labor and wealth contributions to the development of this now rich and powerful nation. The difference in the treatment accorded Asian, Hispanic and European ethnics makes it quite clear that contributions of hard, uncompensated labor, patriotism and cultural gifts have little to do with who is permitted to assimilate and enjoy the fruits of American society.

Dominant society remains insensitive and ignorant of the great insult to injury it has committed by allowing a string of immigrants across the centuries to receive the first-class citizenship status that has been denied black Americans, who have served as builders, laborers and military veterans. Blacks are insulted when members of ethnic and racial groups come to America from countries that were formerly U.S. enemies. Indians, Asians, Hispanics and nearly every conceivable European ethnic group has engaged in some form of declared war against Americans. Blacks are the only racial or ethnic group that has fought in every major conflict on the side of white America.

The insults are further compounded when white society provides new immigrants refugee aid and family assistance, while begrudging it to blacks. More insults are added on as whites then label the newcomers "minorities," accord them equal claims to the country's affirmative action programs; sell them homes in neighborhoods where blacks remain excluded; make business loans to them that are denied to blacks, and praise them for their strong sense of cultural unity —the same unity that white society fears and seeks to destroy when exhibited by blacks.

6

White Bridges to Wealth and Power

"The strength of the powerless is its knowledge of the powerful."[1]

S ince the beginning of time, Africa has been generally recognized as the richest continent on earth. It was blessed by both God and nature with a richness of soil, natural resources and human spirit. Biblical and secular records proclaim Africa as the birthplace of all mankind. As admonished, mankind was fruitful and multiplied, leaving Africa with additional historical and cultural richness. With so much richness and heritage, one must wonder why Africa remained the most poorly developed country on earth and why generations of blacks around the world are so totally impoverished and powerless.

If blacks are to change their marginal conditions, they must know the secret to other racial and ethnic groups' wealth and power. Blacks need to know what devices Europeans used to acquire and establish control of wealth, especially since just a few centuries ago, Europe was an impoverished continent. Moreover, if blacks are to achieve self-empowerment, they must be able to see the parallel between Europe and the United States. They must know not only the socioeconomic development of Europe, but also what specific factors stifled the development of Africa.

Modern-day black impoverishment and powerlessness began neither in the urban ghettos nor rural cotton fields of America. Nor were they elements of West African culture. These racial conditions began in the interior of West Africa and can be directly linked to the geopolitical practices of European whites and Arabs centuries ago. Historical records clearly evidence that European wealth was extracted from Africa and the Americas using black labor as the primary instrument.

It would be difficult, if not impossible, to precisely pinpoint when European whites began to exploit Africa and blacks, because it appears to have started by chance, then escalated into an international practice founded on a racial ideology and broad sense of a white community. Religious, ethnic and national differences within the broad Caucasian family became subordinate to the collective economic exploitation of blacks during the Middle Ages. The economic exploitation of Africa and blacks began in the minds of Europeans and Arabs who placed greed and profit above the value of human life. Their collective greed and machinations have left blacks a legacy of suffering and a black holocaust that has yet to end.

The Beginning of the Great Wealth Displacement

If a marked displacement of Africa's wealth into European treasuries is any indicator, then it can be speculated that the major extractive period began during the 14th and 15th centuries. During this time, the entire European continent was riddled with poverty, famine, feudalism, and diseases. The entire continent was in an economic depression, especially Western Europe. Europe's economy was also weakened by the steady loss of precious metals to Asian nations, who would accept only gold in payment for trade purchases.

While Europe was enduring stagnating socioeconomic depressions, West Africa was known for its flourishing empires, major regional trading centers and for producing some of the world's finest artifacts. Nations throughout the Mediterranean area were drawn to these West African trading centers by rumors of massive wealth. Three large empires, Ghana, Mali, and Songhay, drew European, Moorish and Arabian traders into West Africa's great trading cities, such as Gao and Timbuktu. Arabian and Moorish traders routinely sought West African cash crops and natural resources, especially gold, silver, ivory and salt.[2]

Arab traders' interest in West Africa was more than routine trade. Their

Exhibit 1.

TIME LINE: 1400 - 1600

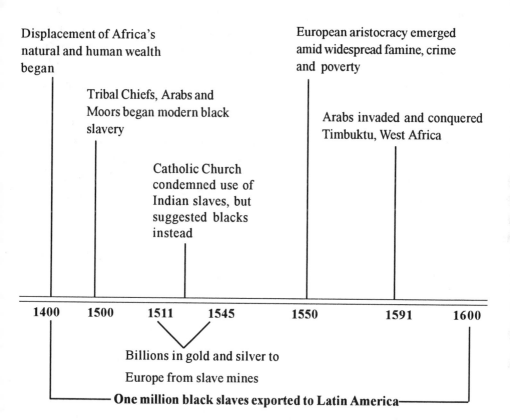

Displacement of Africa's natural and human wealth began

Tribal Chiefs, Arabs and Moors began modern black slavery

Catholic Church condemned use of Indian slaves, but suggested blacks instead

European aristocracy emerged amid widespread famine, crime and poverty

Arabs invaded and conquered Timbuktu, West Africa

| 1400 | 1500 | 1511 | 1545 | 1550 | 1591 | 1600 |

Billions in gold and silver to Europe from slave mines

One million black slaves exported to Latin America

aggressiveness reflected their interest in controlling and profiting from the wealth of West Africa. Though they controlled most African seaports, especially along the length of the Red Sea, Arabs felt threatened by inland black unity and empire building. The Arabs sought greater access to African wealth through intermarriage, concubinage, trade and religious proselytizing missions advocating one religious brotherhood.[3]

The Arabs fabricated a trading language, Swahili, to facilitate trade. Often they exerted religious pressure and continually fostered holy wars that weakened the great West African empires. Arabs labelled black Africans pagans, then pressured them to disavow their own West African culture and practice of ancestor worship and to accept instead Arabic culture based in the Islamic religion. This cultural and religious conversion undermined blacks' African heritage and broad sense of a black community. Moreover, the religious conversion to the Islamic faith gave Arabs nearly unrestricted access to West African societies and wealth.[4]

Religion and Color Unite Racial Exploiters

The removing of wealth from Africa was not completely confined to Arab and Moorish traders. They were later joined by traders from Portugal and Spain, who established trading ports around the coast of West Africa, an area commonly known as the Ivory Coast. These groups built their trade around their naval strength and rarely traveled to inland markets. In 1441, the first Africans were kidnapped and taken to Lisbon, Portugal for the specific purpose of enslavement. Contrary to many reports, the first Africans kidnaped and taken to Portugal were not West African blacks. They were Berbers, an Arabic-speaking, light-skinned people who practiced the Moslem religion and belonged to the Caucasoid race.

The Portuguese returned the Berbers to their desert homes after they had extensively questioned them about black West Africa's alleged wealth. This incident probably represented the first steps in developing a plan to capture and trade slaves and to establish slavery as an international business rather than a trading custom.[5]

Since color was the decisive factor in slavery, it was important to know who was and was not a member of the black race. Moors were not classified as members of the black race. In northwest Africa, the offspring of blacks, white Berbers and Arabs became known as Moors.[6] They lived along the Mediterranean Sea, north of the Sahara Desert. Few identified with West African blacks, who lived south of the Sahara. However, the few Moors who were black, with the aid of some Islamic converts, pushed the doors to West Africa's natural and human capital wide open.

The Arab and Moor merchants were the few traders who could safely venture into the interior trading markets. Most traders dared not leave the coastal port cities. Norman Coombs, in his book, *The Black Experience,* expressed the belief that though many Mediterranean and European nations were more advanced than West Africa in military weaponry, science and technology, the formidableness of Africa's interior and the reputed fighting skill of the black warriors dissuaded the more militarist nations from attempting to take West Africa's wealth by force. Instead, they chose to gain access through trade activities.

By the late 16th century, West Africa had lost its reputation of invincibility. Her great empires had been weakened by divisive internal forces, which diminished the sense of West African nationhood or togetherness and left its natural and human capital resources unprotected. Tragically, West African leaders failed to take protective measures to guard their natural and human resources from the wealth-seeking self-interests of foreign traders.

Black-on-Black Enslavement

Black West Africans' sense of community was narrowly and divisively based on tribal origins rather than on the commonality of black skin color and collective racial destiny. Tribal and extended family commitments rarely extended beyond the village compound. West African societies that practiced tribalism had a narrow group identity, much racial detachment and intergroup animosities. The practice of black-on-black enslavement made them vulnerable to united ethnocentric groups, who were seeking wealth and power at any cost. Weakened from within, West Africa had little basis for developing a broad community capable of uniting against a common enemy.

This tribalism provided the wedge that Arab traders eventually used to divide and conquer nearly every tribe in West and Central Africa. African tribal chiefs ignored the greediness of foreign traders, who sought increased access to African wealth. Divided and preoccupied with old tribal differences, many West African societies saw little wrong in enslaving and selling blacks from other tribes into slavery.

Having escaped Portuguese slavery based upon their lighter skin color, the Berbers joined the Arabs and became the first modern people to create a continuing commercial demand for a large number of black slaves. Historian David Brian Davis indicated in his book, *Slavery and Human Progress,* that Arabs enslaved and exported into the Middle East at least one million black slaves every 100 years from 800 A.D. to modern times. This practice continues at unknown levels today.[7]

The Rationale for Black-on-Black Enslavement

West African tribal chiefs had a long history of exchanging slaves with Arab traders. Eventually, they expanded the practice to European traders. An important trading custom of the tribal chiefs was to insist that all foreign traders purchase some of the chiefs' personal slaves in order to demonstrate an "act of good faith in bargaining."

Other historians, such as Norman Coombs, August Meier and Elliott Rudwick, posit that tribal chiefs could have included this slave-purchasing

Exhibit 2.

TIME LINE: 1605 - 1625

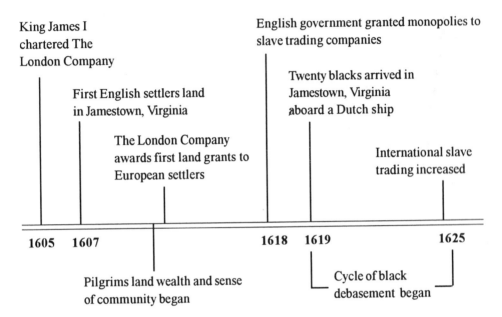

King James I
chartered The
London Company

English government granted monopolies to
slave trading companies

First English settlers land
in Jamestown, Virginia

Twenty blacks arrived in
Jamestown, Virginia
aboard a Dutch ship

The London Company
awards first land grants to
European settlers

International slave
trading increased

1605   1607   1618   1619   1625

Pilgrims land wealth and sense
of community began

Cycle of black
debasement began

ritual in their trading practices for the purposes of impressing Arab and Moor
traders with their toughness as well as their absolute control over their subjects and resources.[8] If this in fact was their motive, then they succeeded.
The Arab and European traders became convinced that, if tribal chiefs could
procure slaves, the trade would be profitable and they had no reason to ex-
pect reprisal from any black nations. A massive slave trading operation developed, and according to an article in *The Washington Post*, the Arabs
were still engaged in the slave trading of blacks in 1993.[9]

The Doctrine of Unequal Exchange

While Africa's human capital was being displaced through slavery, so too
were its natural and mineral wealth. Arab, Moor, Spanish, and Portuguese
merchants traded low value, fabricated items, such as pig iron, brass rings,
religious artifacts, household gadgets, and used firearms, for Africa's highly
valued commodities, such as gold, silver, quality leather, long cotton, art
objects, black slaves and ivory.[10] European-manufactured items were primarily for decorative purposes or tribal warfare. African commodities, on

the other hand, were internationally used to undergird major economies and currencies. This imbalance, described by Thomas Sowell, a black economist, as the doctrine of "unequal exchange," allowed natural and mineral wealth to be transferred from Africa in a steady flow.

Massive displacement of Africa's human capital and natural resources weakened West Africa's social and economic institutions. The doctrine of unequal exchange depleted Africa's resources, but the wealth and revenue generated from commerce with Africa revived Europe's sagging economies. With surplus funds in their treasuries, European nations strengthened their military and commerce communities.

By the 17th century, European nations had formed a competitive sense of racial togetherness within the European family. In addition, they shared a common desire to possess more, if not all, of Africa's wealth. As a result, Europeans established trading routes and outposts along the coast of West and South Africa. Foreign traders boldly ventured into the interior in search of natural resources and human "black gold." Exploiting tribalism to divide and conquer, traders supplied the chiefs with weaponry and other compensation for killing or enslaving other Africans. The traders succeeded in gaining control of much of the African continent.

The self-destructive attitudes of the tribal chiefs has yet to be fully explained or understood. But historian Norman Coombs offered one explanation as to why the chiefs so willingly traded their valuable resources to European and Arab traders. According to Coombs, African tribal chiefs willingly participated in such questionable trade practices because West African economies were subsistence-based and therefore people were satisfied with the status quo and saw no need to accumulate wealth and power.

True or not, white traders took advantage of the tribal chiefs' generosities. This self-destructive tribalism, self-enslavement and lack of concern for wealth were interpreted by Europeans as signs of inferiority. They believed these "uncivilized, childlike heathens" neither appreciated nor deserved their God-given wealth. Consequently, whites rationalized that it was their moral duty to take and utilize Africa's wealth and put blacks to productive work as slaves.

By the latter part of the 15th century, West Africa's great trading markets had been closed down by Arab invaders and its great university centers were under the control of Arab scholars. The interference of Arabs and Europeans into the government, educational and religious affairs of West Africa caused the economic conditions of Africa and Europe to reverse. Africa grew poorer while Europe grew richer and more powerful.

Europe: From Weakness to Strength

It was no mere coincidence that in the latter part of the 15th century, Europe began recovering from centuries of poverty, while Africa was increasingly exploited of its mineral wealth and human capital. As millions of Africans were being kidnapped and sold into slavery around the world, slavery became a simple mechanism by which the wealth of Africa and blacks could be transferred to Europe. Displacement of African wealth was so massive during the 1500s and 1600s that socioeconomic and political upheavals resulted.

Northwestern European nations won the competition against Southern European nations to determine which would become the major slave-trading region. Southern European banks were the first to feel the effects of the influx of new European wealth. Banking and commerce activity in Western Europe caused a lending and investing revolution that resulted in the relocation of the international banking center from the Mediterranean area to Western Europe. The old mercantile economic principles eventually evolved into the basic economic principles of modern capitalism and political doctrines.

With their newly acquired wealth, the major goal of European nations was to accumulate large amounts of gold and other precious metals. Most European nations needed to replenish their depleted gold reserves. Further, Europeans wanted access to raw materials, especially gold and silver, because of their unusual value and rarity. The amount of gold and silver owned by developing European nations was a measure of their newfound prosperity. The new mercantile merchants fostered and promoted a new capitalistic principle — in order for one person to gain wealth another must lose wealth.

Slavery represented a viable means by which one might be enriched at the expense of others. Western Europeans entered slave trading in the 16th century and applied the new capitalistic principles to old trading practices. Achieving maximum return on investments became the rule. Under Roman laws, slaves had certain rights. But under English laws, slaves were treated as property with no rights. Black slaves were reduced to a level of chattel, equal to property or any other tool. To achieve maximum return on their investments, black slaves were to be worked to death during their prime years in order to recapture the investment as early as possible, because old black slaves had no value. In 1664, an English Puritan reportedly called slave trading the worst kind of thievery in the world.

Africa: Drained of Resources and Human Capital

Through the centuries, Europeans espoused ethnocentric doctrines that encouraged a total and complete exploitation of Africa's natural resources and human capital. By the late 1800s, massive and concerted exploitation had taken its toll. The wealth power gap between European nations and African nations had widened so much that European nations were no longer fearful of Africa and felt that they could invade and exploit her at will.

In 1885, European nations met at a conference in Berlin and without notifying any African nations, drew lines on a map to divide the African continent among themselves. Shortly thereafter, European nations established colonies throughout Africa. They colonized 90 percent of the African continent and controlled nearly 100 percent of its wealth. Only Liberia, an American colony, and Ethiopia were uncolonized at that time.

In the mid-1960s, some black African nations were restored to independence, but not because white European nations had developed a moral conscience or no longer needed to exploit Africa and its people. Instead, European nations freed the African nations, because they had acquired most of their wealth and power and now felt that they could control those nations just as effectively from the outside.

Columbus Searches for Gold, Finds Slaves

Natural resource wealth that Europeans acquired from Africa whetted their appetite for the finer things of life. Most European nations wanted gold and silver, because these metals were needed for coins, but moreover, they represented the new mark of wealth. These precious metals were more useful than land, because they could buy anything anywhere. Thoughts of gold, jewels and spices from foreign lands stimulated investment in trade, as merchant and gentry classes pressed their governments to secure new markets.

Competing monarchies in Spain, France, Portugal and England were willing to gamble lives and newfound wealth on finding more precious metals and spices in new worlds. Adventurers, such as Christopher Columbus, accepted the challenges from his financial backers and made several fortune-hunting trips to the New World. On his second trip, Columbus promised the Spanish Crown that in return for financial help he would bring them "as much gold as they need . . . and as many slaves as they asked."[11] Seventeen ships and hundreds of men were provided for his second voyage to the New World. To further encourage his success, the Crown "promised Columbus 10 percent of the profits, a governorship over any new lands, and fame."[12]

Columbus and his military contingency arrived in the Caribbean islands and made inquiries about the location of gold. After only a few pieces of gold were found, Columbus expanded his search to all of the islands, traveling as far as Haiti. He used his military advantage to conscript the peaceful, unarmed Arawak Indians into his massive gold search. As the search became futile, angry Europeans took out their frustrations on the defenseless Indians. Many were killed and mutilated. Other Arawaks were driven to commit suicide. Within two years, nearly half of the 250,000 Indians in Haiti were dead. By the year 1515, there were 50,000 Arawak Indians; by 1550, only 500 remained. Howard Zinn said that, "A report in 1650, showed that none of the original Arawaks or their decedents were left."[13]

Failing to find a significant amount of gold, Columbus attempted to at least keep his promise to the Crown regarding slaves. He selected 500 of the strongest male and female Indians and shipped them back to Europe for servitude. But, nearly all of them died in route or shortly thereafter, due to climate and temperature differences between their Caribbean homeland and the European continent. Now, like the elusive Bahamian gold, an entire race of Arawak Indians does not exist.

The Americas Become an Extension of Africa

Following Columbus' explorations to the New World, a new sense of European nationalism developed. European nations competitively explored South and Central America and the Caribbean islands in search of gold and other precious metals. When these resources were discovered, small contingencies of European whites colonized the areas in hopes of producing wealth in the name of their motherland. But, European whites were allegedly physically incapable of doing the laborious work and the Indians had been killed off. As a result, black slaves became the chosen tools for producing wealth in the Caribbean and throughout the Americas.

Black slaves were needed in the plantation fields of the Caribbean, the tobacco fields of the Piedmont and the mines of South America. It was the massive influx and dominance of black slaves in mining and agricultural production that directly linked black enslavement to Europe's increased wealth, power and industrialization.

Organized religions joined hands with governments in the race to capture wealth in the New Worlds. They merged, searching for lost souls and lost gold. In the early 1500s, high officials in the Catholic Church designated African blacks as the primary instrument of mining wealth for whites in South and Central America, because Indians were being killed off by the rigorous labor and European diseases. Blacks were perceived as being physically more durable and expendable. Portuguese and Spanish slave traders moved into high gear, buying, selling and shuttling black slaves across the Atlantic Ocean.

More than 90 percent of Africa's kidnapped blacks were shipped to South America and the Caribbean islands. Between 1600 and 1800, black slaves outnumbered the white Europeans entering the Americas. Up until 1820, blacks outnumbered Europeans transported across the Atlantic by a ratio of 3 to 1. Most were settled in Brazil, giving it the largest black population outside of the African continent.

These black slaves and their descendants were Brazil's dominant population until the great mass of European white immigrants arrived in the 1880s, long after slavery had been terminated and European wealth and power had been amassed. These new white immigrants arrived to reap the "fruits" created by forced black labor. A century later, the descendants of Brazil's black slaves are still excluded from enjoying the fruits and are so impoverished that death squads murder the hordes of black street children who scavenge for food.

Wealth Production in the Americas

Portuguese and Spanish colonization of the Americas represented the first systematic and concerted practice by European nations to use African blacks as the main instrument for accruing wealth. From the 1500s to the 1880s, their long-distance trade policies and practices were based on profits from Africa and her dark peoples. The high profits caused black enslavement to be known as the "Golden Harvest." The economies of South and Central America and the Caribbean islands were based on products made by Africans. Black labor spawned numerous cottage industries that provided Europe with a constant flow of sugar, tobacco, molasses, vinegar, rum and precious metals. These products significantly changed Europeans' consumer appetites and demands.

Black slaves produced a phenomenal amount of wealth for slave traders, settlers and European nations. In the South American and West Indian markets, slaves drew an average sale price of $500 in the 17th-18th centuries. When this figure is multiplied by the 10-to-15 million black slaves that historian Howard Zinn estimated were transported to the Americas, the revenue from onetime only sales would amount to more than a trillion dollars in today's currency. African slaves were typically sold at least twice before reaching their final destination. As a matter of practice, most of the black slaves brought into the Caribbean markets typically were "seasoned," then resold into slave markets in South, Central and North America at much higher prices and profits.

By the 16th century, European powers sought mineral wealth in Africa and Latin America, using what they perceived to be the best possible mining equipment — black slave labor. Mines in Peru, Bolivia and Brazil initially used local Indian labor, but these groups proved to be especially susceptible when confronted by various European diseases, hard work and rigorous discipline. A royal ordinance in 1503 officially sanctioned introducing black slaves into the Spanish colonies to replace the Indians.[14]

Between 1501 to 1700, nearly four million black slaves were exported to Latin America and the profits of their labor filled various European treasuries. By 1660, slaves in Latin American mines had exported $536 million ducats to Spanish treasuries.[15] At today's value, these gold and silver ducats would be worth hundreds of billions of dollars. Near the end of the 17th century, Europe's holdings of gold had increased by 20 percent and its total stock of silver tripled. France had also amassed an abundance of new precious metals from Brazilian mines.[16]

The wealth-power produced by black slave trading in the Americas intensified competition between European nations. Spain became one of the world's wealthiest and most powerful nations when it pushed Portugal out of the slave trade and mining in Latin America. Between 1550 and 1600, the amount of silver shipped into Spanish treasuries quadrupled. Kings Philip III and IV used the revenues to militarily protect and acquire more slaves.

Much of Spain's new wealth was passed onto neighboring nations in order to repay Italian and German merchants who had financed many of Spain's trade wars in the Americas. Although Spanish, Portuguese and other European nations disagreed over who should possess wealth produced by slaves in the Americas, there was little, if any, disagreement over which racial group would be the labor force used to produce the wealth.

Europe Developed a Broad Sense of Community

England established North America as a colony populated by white-skinned people, preferably of English ethnicity. The English, proud and puffy people, enjoyed boasting of their heritage and bloodlines. King James, the ruling monarch, had offered to share the wealth of the new colonies with all who sought to settle and be loyal to the English Crown. But, the New World wealth was to be kept within the English ethnic family first and the broader European family, second. A doctrine of racial and ethnic exclusivity simplified the process of establishing a broad sense of community in the strange New World. As the sense of community took root, a foundation was laid for European whites to survive and prosper through expropriated Indian land and black labor.

European whites' fears of the large number of black slaves intensified their desire to maintain a broad sense of a white community. But in their efforts to maintain a white numerical dominance, they abandoned being an English-only country and recruited other white European ethnics. The inclusion of other ethnics did not conflict with the original doctrine of exclusivity. Rather than a nation for Englishmen only, America's mandate was broadened to a nation for "whites only."

The three primary sources of white wealth were inherited wealth, land ownership and expropriated black labor. The first major bequest of white wealth was passed across the Atlantic Ocean, from Europe to the white settlers, during the colonial period. This wealth from the English Crown promoted colonial settlements. British royalty made direct awards of large land grants to royal favorites, territorial governors and land companies. Royal land grants often encompassed millions of acres.

King James issued the first license to establish colonies in North America to the London and Plymouth trading companies, a group of merchant capitalists who sought to improve foreign trade and increase the country's stock of gold.[17] These chartered companies organized immigrant groups who were interested in seeking wealth in America. They financially sponsored the first white settlers, who could not otherwise afford to come to America and were typically impoverished vagrants, criminals or adventurers. English immigrants were generally directed by government-licensed trade companies to "search for all manner of mines of gold, silver and copper" in America.

The London Company established its first colony of white settlers in Jamestown, Virginia in 1607. And, contrary to popular myth, few early European settlers immigrated to America for the primary purpose of seeking religious or political freedoms. Most came to the New World for the same reason that most immigrants come to America — for economic opportunities. The London Trade Company promised the immigrants monetary dividends from any gold or precious metals they found. But, like their predecessor, Columbus, they found no gold. Fewer than half survived the first year. Of 6,000 new settlers who arrived between 1620 and 1622, two-thirds were

Exhibit 3.

TIME LINE: 1634 - 1667

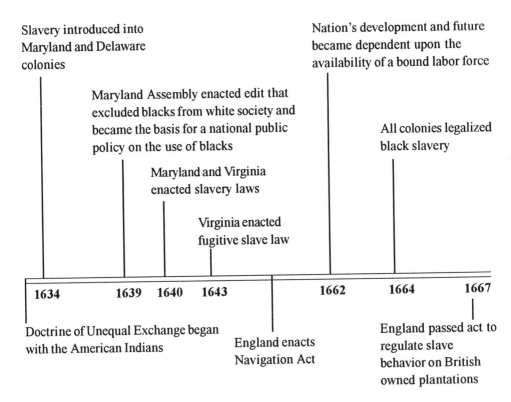

Slavery introduced into
Maryland and Delaware
colonies

Nation's development and future
became dependent upon the
availability of a bound labor force

Maryland Assembly enacted edit that
excluded blacks from white society and
became the basis for a national public
policy on the use of blacks

All colonies legalized
black slavery

Maryland and Virginia
enacted slavery laws

Virginia enacted
fugitive slave law

1634   1639   1640   1643   1662   1664   1667

Doctrine of Unequal Exchange began
with the American Indians

England enacts
Navigation Act

England passed act to
regulate slave
behavior on British
owned plantations

dead before 1625. Friendly Indians rescued the remainder and taught them
how to survive in the harsh wilderness.

European settlers repaid the Indians' kindness by establishing trade relations based on the doctrine of unequal exchange. As discussed earlier, this
exploitative trading practice had been successfully used by European traders
on tribal chiefs in West Africa. And, like Africans, the Indians traded valuable items, such as furs, gold, land, tobacco and food, for less valuable items,
such as Bibles, blankets, trinkets and rum. The Indians' usefulness to the
settlers was short-lived. The settlers were good students and quickly learned
how to survive in the wilderness. As the Indians became less valuable than
their land and natural resources, the whites killed, enslaved or drove them
from their homelands.

Wealth Power Struggle Fomented Nationalism

England's new wealth and power gave rise to a sense of ethnic identity and nationalism among the settlers. This nationalism evolved from a real or imagined new cultural unity— a strong sense of "we" against "them." The "thems" were other nations that England sought to subjugate, namely Indians and Africans. The "wes" were fellow Englishmen, who colonized the "thems" across the globe.

To protect the "wes," England strengthened its maritime control over long-distance Atlantic trading routes. It enacted the Navigation Act of 1651, which in effect, declared a form of economic warfare on other European nations by requiring that goods imported from any European nation or any English colony be shipped only on British vessels. The Act also prohibited the colonies from either developing manufacturing industries or purchasing processed goods from any nation other than those under the control of the British Crown.

In addition, the Navigation Act gave England the power to establish a monopoly in both the slave trade and the marketing of slave-produced products with the colonies. The English government's control of colonial trade virtually guaranteed English industries a monopoly over raw materials and cash crops. This rendered the American settlers entirely dependent upon England to provide them with raw materials, consumer products, slaves and military protection. England's monopoly so restricted and taxed the colonists that they grew belligerent and eventually became "thems" rather than "wes" and revolted in order to win their independence.

Racism and the Appetite for More Wealth

Wealth created by slaves in the New World stimulated cultural changes within Europe. For example, when Europe began to prosper from the wealth exploited through its colonial settlements, wealthy merchants and aristocracies were created. Their leisure life-style and consumer demands prompted a new cultural movement. The aristocracy and middle class discussed new philosophies of religion, science, politics and business. Their neo-cultural values justified imperialism, capitalism and racism. Europeans espoused the belief that they were a superior race that had a mission to civilize so-called inferior races.[18]

This ethnocentric view was sustained by a broad sense of unity and community founded upon skin color, Judeo-Christian religions, an espoused work ethic, and a belief in the organized exercise of authority. Europeans' theft of other peoples' lands was justified by their Christian piety. They believed that God had given land to all mankind to be cultivated. So, their belief in their own racial superiority supplied the foundation and justification for their seeking to colonize and exploit the world.

Throughout the 1700s, European nations competed for the control of territory and resources in the New World and exercised varying degrees of harshness towards the local inhabitants. As European settlers established colonial governments to supervise the displacement of wealth from the oppressed countries to the mother countries in Europe, the welfare of the exploited was of secondary importance. The calculating cruelty of colonization in Sir William Blackstone's statement, that "the King can do no wrong" was a necessary and fundamental principle of the English Constitution. This political phrase clearly indicated the way Europeans felt about their role in exploiting slaves and Indians in the new lands.

The English also buttressed their religious justification for colonization with a legal system based on the concepts of individual and private property rights. In response to criticism of English colonization, an unknown Englishman wrote in 1622 that "it is lawful to take a land which none useth and make use of it." This Englishman undoubtedly was referring to an old English legal concept, the Rights of Discovery, which was in part based upon European legal doctrines, racial arrogance and military superiority. It gave white European colonists the right to practice "finders keepers" with any land or resources that they "discovered." With the cultural and legal backing of the Rights of Discovery, European whites believed that they had a license to steal.

In his book, *A People's History of the United States,* Howard Zinn expanded on the way white settlers felt about their claims to Rights of Discovery. Zinn wrote:

> "The governor of Massachusetts Bay Colony, John Winthrop, created the excuse to take Indian land by declaring the area legally a 'vacuum.' The Indians had not 'subdued' the land, and therefore had only a 'natural' right to it, but not a 'civil right.' A 'natural right' did not have legal standing." [19]

Native American culture had not generally prepared Indians to protect themselves from the land-expropriating practices of the white settlers. White society's legal concept of private ownership of property and resources was an unfamiliar concept to Indians who, like African blacks, were communal. Shared rights and responsibilities for the land and its resources was the basis of their culture and survival. Conflicts between European and Indian culture were resolved at the expense of scores of Indians. When the first white settlers arrived in the 1500s, about 2 million Indians possessed the two billion acres that is now the continental United States.

Today, about 800,000 Indians reside on some 200 reservations, a land mass of about two percent of the original amount of land that they possessed when the pilgrims arrived in 1607. Moreover, the lands that were set aside as reservations for American Indians were some of the worst lands in the nation for sustaining agricultural products, livestock and human life. Due to white society's oversight and later discoveries of precious metals and resources, these reservations occasionally did produce wealth.

Stolen Land: The Second Greatest Wealth Producer

Land ownership was second only to slave labor as a source of white wealth and power in America. Without the approval of the Indians, The London Company, an officially chartered immigration agency, sought to lure immigrants to America by substituting land grants of 100 acres to each colonial settler in lieu of the potential gold dividends. Other English chartering companies and colonial assemblies followed suit by offering land grants to newly arriving European immigrants.

The practice of awarding land to the head of each established household was effectively used to entice European immigrants to America. These land awards represented windfall wealth that insured economic opportunity and provided them with the basic tool for earning a living. It also generated a sense of togetherness among European immigrants in a new land. "The typical colonial family only needed two acres of land per capita to produce sufficient food to survive," says Stanley Lebergott, in his book, *The Americans: An Economic Record.* Lebergott further stated that "the greed of the European immigrants changed the use of Indian land from limited substance to widespread cash crop farming, from religious inspiration to land speculation for capital gains."

The land grants to assist colonial settlers served as one of the earliest forms of affirmative action in America. The grants gave immigrants a basic level of wealth, which they could leverage to purchase additional acreage, household, farming equipment or bring black labor onto the land. This whites-only affirmative action program allowed three-fourths of America's colonial families to own their own farms.

Land grants alone were not the only government-backed benefit given to white settlers. After all, a new nation of aristocrats and a privileged class could not be built simply on the basis of land ownership. Without an available pool of labor, land had little value. It had to be cleared and brought to production. To achieve a maximum return from the land, the white settlers needed two things: cash crops and goods for European and local markets as well as

Exhibit 4.

Land Distribution

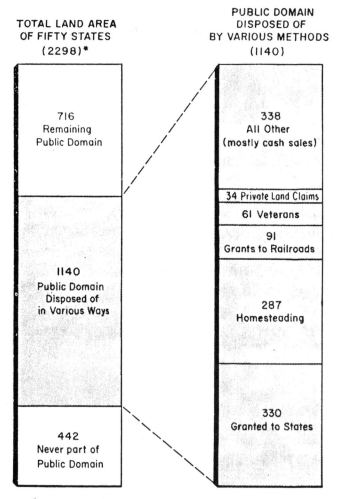

Figures in millions of acres.

PUBLIC DOMAIN AND ITS DISPOSAL

Most land in the United States was once public domain. Half of the entire national area was once public domain but has been disposed of. States were granted a large portion of it; other large areas were sold or homesteaded, but a variety of disposal methods were employed.

a well-disciplined, available non-compensated and permanent labor supply. The free white labor force would not satisfy these criteria because it was scarce and expensive. Few European immigrants were willing to "till the soil" for another when free or cheap land was available to any white who wanted to homestead. If European serfdom had taught the Pilgrims anything, it had taught them that it was essential to own one's own land and strictly avoid being bound to another's land.

Shortly before the Revolutionary War, wealth had accumulated in the colonies and the settlers were some of the richest people in the world. Less than two percent of the American immigrant population had zero or negative net worth. England's tariffs and economic acts that sought to redistribute the colonies' wealth to the mother country triggered a backlash of independence. After the war, the new congressional government established its own devices for transferring wealth to preferential groups. Westward expansion added new wealth-building opportunities through land and slave ownership. The Northwest Ordinance of 1787 opened this new territory for homesteading. The government sold the land at public auction for $1 per acre.[20]

To insure that the land would not end up in the wrong hands, Congress in 1790 passed the first national Naturalization Law, which specified that America would open its doors to "white immigrants only." Local governments enacted anti-mobility and anti-contracting laws that forbade blacks to either own or even step foot onto land in the new territory. Thus, government land policies had a double benefit for whites. It gave them an opportunity to gain land and it laid the foundation for a permanent wealth gap between them and blacks.

Slaves Forced France to "Sell" Louisiana Territory

In 1802, just as America was on the verge of being squeezed out of the international cotton market, black slave insurrections in the Caribbean islands gave America a land windfall. Slaves successfully revolted against their French oppressors. A self-taught Haitian slave named Toussaint L'Ouverture led a slave revolt that, with the help of yellow fever, defeated a 20,000-strong French army. Without a doubt, the Haitian Revolt took advantage of the only time during the colonization of the New World that white slave holders dropped their guard enough to allow slaves to break free and take control.

Napoleon sent a French military expeditionary force to recapture Haiti, but the French troops were beaten, thereby forcing France to sign a peace treaty granting the slaves their freedom and Haiti its independence. The broader international white community operated from a policy that a "threat to black slavery anywhere is a threat to black slavery everywhere," but neither the United States nor any other country bothered to assist France.

France's defeat at the hands of the slave army destroyed Napoleon's dream of building a French settlement at the mouth of the Mississippi River at the current site of the city of New Orleans and set the stage for the United States to purchase the Louisiana Territory for a mere $15 million, less than 5 cents per acre. The purchase of the Louisiana Territory, which extended from the Mississippi River to the Pacific Ocean, doubled the size of the United States.

Ironically, the Haitian Revolt provided additional land for raising cotton, which justified the expansion of black slavery. Shortly thereafter, old planters and new immigrants joined the land rush to acquire huge tracts of the new free land. They echoed the national slogan for pursuing wealth: "Open more land and buy more Negroes."[21] European whites were given ownership to the land and black slaves were given the obligation of picking the cotton for the next 150 years.

Spain Follows France's Lead, "Sells" Florida

During the early 1800s, Florida was the only part of southeastern North America that did not belong to the United States. Though the U.S. government had made numerous offers, Spain refused to sell Florida. As Spanish territory and not apart of the United States, Florida was a natural attraction for displaced Indians and runaway slaves. Escaped slaves took refuge in Florida and established geopolitical relations with the Indians. Slaves and their mulatto offspring were often given high village positions as chiefs, interpreters, military advisors and scouts, all of which aroused southern white slave holders, who saw this as a lure to slaves seeking freedom. [22]

White planters and slave holders encouraged General Andrew Jackson—who was noted for grabbing Indian land for his friends and personal ownership — to use his military forces to remove from Florida the Indians and escaped slaves. General Jackson complied, publicly arguing that Florida was a sanctuary for escaped slaves and marauding Indians who presented a menace to white society. Florida, according to Jackson, was essential to the defense of the United States. In 1814, having established his public premise for taking military troops into the Spanish territory, Jackson intentionally triggered the first of three Seminole Wars.

Jackson also burned Indian villages, seized Spanish forts and blew up Fort Negro on the Chattahoochee River in North Florida, killing more than 200 women and children. His military incursions into Florida created a political problem for Spain, which in 1819, agreed to give Florida to the United States in 1821. In appreciation, a grateful U.S. government appointed Jackson Florida's first governor. Jackson assumed the governorship then reverted back to his earlier practice of making money for himself and his friends by expropriating Indian land and black labor. He advised his friends to purchase Florida land and black slaves before the prices rose.[23]

An Indian treaty was signed in 1819 and most of the Indians and free blacks were forced out of Florida. Jackson kept his promise to make free or cheap land available in Florida for cotton and sugar production. But some defiant Indians and black slaves dismissed the treaty and continued to fight for their land ownership rights for another 20 years. The Third Seminole War ended in the 1840s, when Oceola, the Seminole chief, died in captivity and John Horse, the highest ranking black-Indian leader, after nearly 50 years of battles, ceased fighting without ever having been defeated or captured.[24] When finally concluded, the Seminole Wars had cost the U.S. government 1,500 soldiers and $20 million dollars in military expenditures.

In 1970, the U.S. Indian Claims Commission awarded more than $12 million in land reparations to the remainder of the Florida Seminole Tribe. The government also offered an apology. Notably, however, the contributions made by black Floridian ancestors were left out of the history books and their offspring were left out of the apology as well as the reparations. Blacks have yet to receive any monetary reparations or historical recognition for their role in bringing Florida into the Union.

Blacks, Cotton and the Annexation of the Southwest

The United States went to war with Mexico in 1846 largely to satisfy slave holders' interests in acquiring the fertile Texas plains for raising cotton. Mexican authorities offered a limited amount of free land to groups of white land squatters, but were not willing to sell land to cotton planters. By the 1830s, more than 20,000 whites had moved into the Texas Territory with more than 2,000 black slaves.

Mexican authorities outlawed slavery, but white slave holders evaded the law by "freeing" their slaves, then forcing them to sign lifetime contracts as indentured servants. The Mexican government responded by seeking to block any further white immigration into the territory. The 20,000 whites already in the territory responded by declaring squatters rights on Mexican land, then publicly declaring such lands to be free and independent from Mexico.

Exhibit 5.

TIME LINE: 1705 - 1760

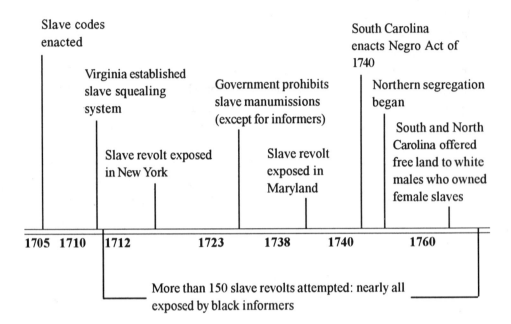

Slave codes enacted

Virginia established slave squealing system

Slave revolt exposed in New York

Government prohibits slave manumissions (except for informers)

Slave revolt exposed in Maryland

South Carolina enacts Negro Act of 1740

Northern segregation began

South and North Carolina offered free land to white males who owned female slaves

1705 1710 1712   1723   1738   1740   1760

More than 150 slave revolts attempted: nearly all exposed by black informers

Large Mexican armies attacked the American planters at the Alamo to recover Mexico's land. After the fall of the Alamo in the late 1840s, the President of the United States declared war against Mexico to justify annexing the territory for slave holders. Stanley Lebergott, the writer, quoted President Tyler, who said, "The war with Mexico gave the United States a monopoly of the cotton plant and thus secured to us a power of boundless extent in the affairs of the world . . . The monopoly . . . was the great and important concern . . . [It] places all other nations at our feet; an embargo [on cotton exportation during] . . . a single year produced in Europe a greater amount of suffering than a 50-year war."

The U.S. won the brief war and Texas entered the Union as a slave state. Abolitionist William Lloyd Garrison called the war an "invasion . . . waged solely for the despicable and horrible purpose of extending and perpetuating American slavery."[25] On January 21, 1848, Frederick Douglas, a former slave, wrote about the war in his Rochester newspaper, *The North Star.* He said:

"Mexico seems a doomed victim to Anglo Saxon love of dominion of land."

1862: The Homestead Act

The Homestead Act of 1862 represented America's last great land policy. It was enacted on the eve of the Civil War and provided that anyone living on land for five years while making some improvements could acquire a free title to 160 acres. This act remained in effect until 1900 and provided 400,000 to 600,000 white families with homes and farms. Of all the public land that this act passed into private hands, not more than 11-to-17 percent was settled by homesteaders. By 1900, most of the land had gone to speculators, who thus acquired the claims to rich western lands, timber and mineral rights without having to bid or compete for the wealth.

Blacks were unable to acquire any of this last-time giveaway of land wealth. Many were interested but had their lives threatened by whites and decided not to pursue the free land. The acquisition policy of the Homestead Act was that anyone who "tended the land should not have to pay for it." But again, hypocrisy reigned. No one had spent more time tending land than blacks. Certainly not European immigrants. Yet, even free blacks were not allowed to participate in the famous land rush in the West.

Both free and enslaved blacks were forced to delay their land ownership dreams and await the freedom that the Civil War would bring. Blacks were legally freed by the Emancipation Proclamation, but the end of their servitude did not result in receiving the compensation that was given to white indentured servants. At the end of their servitude, white indentured servants typically received a small parcel of land as well as a suit of clothing, farming tools, crop seeds, livestock, some money and sometimes guns. These were the minimum tools needed to earn a living and protect one's family.

Emancipation set blacks free as ignorant, penniless, defenseless, landless, powerless and noncompetitive human beings. Nearly five million blacks were made wards of the public, dependent upon handouts, welfare or whatever they could steal in order to survive. No attempts were made to correct the centuries of social engineering to which black slaves had been exposed.

They had no homes or friends in either the North or South. When they asked for a little help or a hand up, President Andrew Johnson in 1866, with Southern states' encouragement, slapped them in their sullen, black faces by vetoing a congressional bill that would have given black slaves a mere "40 acres and a mule" as compensation for 250 years of bondage.

Southern Slave Holders: The Leisure Class

Until recent times, Southerners sought to build and maintain a nonworking class of aristocrats that prided itself on a life-style of unearned leisure that resulted from black labor. The Southerners' view of blacks and work was based on their definition of work and their exploitation of natural resources. Sitting on the verandas or under the old oak trees became a way of life. It was as much a Southern reality as a Southern mystique.

The South's leisure degenerated into laziness. Blacks were the working class. Whites were the management class that enjoyed seasonal light work. Successful planters bragged about not having to do dirty, hard "nigger work." In accordance with the national anti-black public policy (see Chapter Seven), blacks remained the working class while whites took credit for being the management or brains behind black labor.

White Indentured Servants: Temporary Labor Only

The dream of living in a world with unlimited free land and economic opportunities appealed to impoverished whites still living in Europe. Many whites were willing to sell or contract their labor to white land owners for an opportunity to live and work in the New World. For the cost of transportation from Europe, many whites signed indentured servitude contracts. A typical contract lasted for seven-years, but actually it rarely lasted beyond the servant's 21st birthday.

Unlike slaves, white servants retained some personal rights, (for example, the right to sue, testify in court, etc.) and at the end of their period of servitude, they received monetary compensation and basic necessities for establishing a homestead and earning a living. Disgruntled indentured servants occasionally renegotiated their contracts in order to receive better provisions, or they simply broke the contracts by fleeing and establishing their own homestead on the frontier land that was available and free to any white person.

The instability of the white servant labor force killed the indentured servant system. By the mid-1600s, it became clear that indentured white servants were not meeting the plantation owners' labor and production needs. Moreover, the land owners could not impose complete physical and psychological control over white indentured servants. Therefore, the land owners could not maximize profits.

Since the land owners had abandoned using captured Indians as slaves, whites found that black slavery, which was flourishing in the Caribbean and

South America, was the most viable labor alternative. Furthermore, England had recognized the enormous economic potential in supplying slaves to the plantations. Though England had hoped to keep North America as an English nation, labor demands in the North American colonies persuaded England to organize the Royal African Company in 1672 in order to supply and coordinate her slave trading activities in the New World.

With the labor question resolved, the expropriation of Indian land to European whites had to occur as quickly as possible. Between 1607 and 1887, European whites acquired nearly every valuable square foot of Indian land via theft, legal discrimination, an occasional purchase, and the violation of more than 371 Indian treaties. The American government's redistribution of Indian land amounted to preferential treatment or affirmative action for white settlers, especially when combined with the government's facilitation of black slavery.

Moreover, to increase land utilization, some states, like North and South Carolina, granted free land to white settlers simply for owning slaves. In 1663, these states offered 20 acres of land to every white male who owned a black female slave. Such land awards encouraged miscegenation practices between white male slave owners and black female slaves. This practice also increased the slave owners' slave holdings and raised the black female to a higher, more acceptable level over the black male slave.

The dream of owning freedom and land, which drew white settlers to America and liberated them from feudal oppression in Europe, was black peoples' worst nightmare. It smothered blacks' dreams by shackling them into endless human exploitation.

Black Labor: The Greatest Source of White Wealth

Before discussing more recent ways that whites have created bridges to wealth and power, it would be beneficial to take one final look at the economic impact that black slavery had and continues to have on economies in America and worldwide. A close examination of financial data reveals why whites have been so adamant about keeping blacks as a permanent underclass of laborers. The world saw Blacks and their labor as sources of wealth — black gold.

England was the king of slave trading nations. Not only was it the dominant slave trader, but was also the primary beneficiary of wealth produced by slaves in the Americas and Caribbean islands. As discussed earlier in Chapter Four, the English system was the harshest and undoubtedly the most profitable of the six major slave trading nations. For example, by 1795, Liverpool, England alone had more than 100 ships carrying slaves. This fleet of ships accounted for 50 percent of Europe's slave trade.

Overall, during the 1700s, slave trading revenues expanded England's foreign trade by more than 700 percent and annual slave trade revenues averaged nearly $5 million, which in today's dollars would be nearly $50 billion annually.[26] Slave trading and the related commercial activities were so lucrative that these activities alone elevated England from a poor nation to the single-most powerful nation in the world.

By 1860, annual sales of slave-produced cotton generated more than $30 billion for England. Meanwhile, English textile mills were still annually manufacturing increasing levels of cotton goods for retail sales. England's trading relationships with American slave plantations were so profitable that England viewed the prospect of an American Civil War to free black slaves as a significant threat to its national interest. England was well aware that growth in the English economy and the establishment of its industrial infrastructure was founded upon slave-produced products.

In fact, in 1844, England announced in the *Report of Foreign Nations* that

Exhibit 6.

TIME LINE: 1775 - 1800

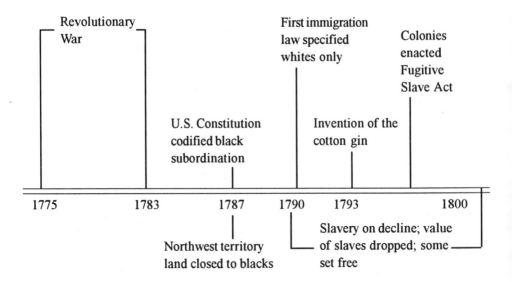

TABLE 8			
Comparison of Slave, Land and Cotton Prices			
Year	Avg. Prime Slave Prices	Per Acre Public Land Prices	Per Pound Price of Cotton
1800	$600	$1.00	$0.15
1810	$900	$1.50	$0.24
1820	$1,050	$1.40	$0.29
1830	$800	$1.00	$0.11
1840	$1,200	$1.50	$0.15
1850	$700	$1.50	$0.08
1860	$1,600	$2.25	$0.10
1862	$1,800	$2.50	$0.13

Sources: "Cotton Is King" by Elliot; "The American Nation" by Garraty and "Without Consent or Contract" by Fogel. [27]

"since 1808, $4 billion of fixed capital has been invested in preparation for cotton goods that were wholly dependent upon slave labor." England was not willing to lose that large financial investment or the steady flow of wealth from black labor without a fight. In an effort to maintain the institution of slavery that had benefited the English nation for more than two and half centuries, England offered to intervene in American domestic affairs in order to prolong slavery. In addition, many within England's private business sector contributed financially to pro-slavery organizations in America.

Wealth Produced in the Southern States

Contrary to popular myths, prior to the Civil War the South was not poverty stricken, but held the greatest concentration of per capita wealth in the nation. Each of the nearly five million slaves represented not only a labor device for income, but also a commodity — a negotiable instrument. Slaves constituted a medium of monetary exchange that could be bartered or accepted as collateral when currency or other valuables were in short supply.

A white person with a slave never lacked economic opportunity, since his "human capital" could always be transformed into other forms of wealth, if necessary. Ironically, before the invention of the cotton gin, slavery was on the decline. The value of slaves had dropped to an average of $400 to $500 for a prime field hand. At this low market value, some northern slave holders were "setting blacks free" in an attempt to cut their losses. More than 30,000 were freed around 1790. But within a decade, prices began to rise and track cotton prices. A half century later, on the eve of the Civil War, a prime slave was typically valued at $1,600 to $1,800.

Land ownership, whites' second great source of wealth, did not surpass slave ownership as the primary form of wealth accumulation until well after the Civil War. The profitability of black slaves as a wealth-producing commodity was so great that anything short of a civil war would have had little, if any, effect on the slavery system. The $7 billion capital investments in black slaves in 1860 exceeded all other business investments in the North, South, and the federal budget combined.

The value of a black slave, had a direct correlation to cotton prices. From year to year, as the price of slaves went up or down, so did the price of cotton. Slaves' values dictated the market value of cotton, and cotton set the value of slaves. This direct relationship existed from the latter part of the 17th century to the mid-18th century. Furthermore, the prices and values varied very little from region to region within the country. Slaves were walking credit cards. Any white who owned a slave could always earn money by either selling the slave's labor or selling the slave. Both the slave and his labor carried value.

Consequently, non-slave owners were decidedly poorer than those who owned slaves, and since nearly all of black slaves were in the South, the nation's wealth was in the South. According to Robert W. Fogel, in his book, *Without Consent of Contract*, in 1860, two out of three males with a $100,000 personal net worth lived in the South and owned slaves. The wealth accumulation of the typical cotton belt farm was four times greater than that of the usual Northern farmer, and was 91 times greater than that of the typical urban common laborer. A comparison of Northern and Southern farms indicates that wealth was disproportionately skewed to the South. On average, the large Southern plantation owners who used slave gang systems had 18 times more wealth than a Northern farmer, and nearly 400 times more wealth than the average Northern urban laborer.

Robert W. Fogel claimed that a "poor Southerner who owned nothing more than two black slaves had assets comparable to the average Northerner with all of his personal property, livestock, modest savings, and real estate."[28]

White wealth created through slavery benefited not only the actual plantation owners, but also numerous businesses in the community. Many Southern entrepreneurs acquired wealth by providing support services and goods to slave holders. Some Southern businesses could survive by providing services and goods ranging from household effects and farm tools to the leather slave restraints sold exclusively to plantations. This demand was significant enough that nearly 20 percent of the manufacturing firms that serviced slave plantations were located in the South prior to the Civil War.

Farms and small town businesses sustained themselves by buying and selling slave produced products. Businesses supporting plantations generated massive amounts of capital, which was circulated throughout the communities. The multiplying effect helped establish and sustain Southern seaport towns like Charleston, Savannah, Norfolk and New Orleans.

After the slaves were emancipated, those who had founded their livelihood in exploiting free black labor feared the potential financial consequences. Former plantation owners, merchants, bankers, shippers, clerks and, in fact, the entire Southern community had a vested financial interest in maintaining a large and cheap supply of labor.

Reconstruction failed to provide the former slaves with any measurable economic start. The denial of 40 acres and a mule ensured that these former slaves would never comprise a part of the American ownership class. Moreover, the larger white communities restricted blacks from producing and marketing products that competed with white businessmen or farmers. Cultural customs and laws forced the newly emancipated blacks to conform to the historical image of blacks as common laborers.

Although blacks were skilled and well-experienced agricultural planters and livestock breeders, they had no farm tools, livestock, money or land upon which to earn a living. And the larger community had no intentions of allowing black labor to escape their control. Most blacks in desperation were compelled by white hostility to return to the plantations, either for pitiful wages or as sharecroppers, where they were soon bound to the masters' land almost as firmly as they had been in bondage," said historian Norman Hodges.[29]

The Northern States also Thrived off of Black Labor

As in the South, the Northern economy also thrived off of the labor of black people through profits from businesses connected to the slavery industry. And contrary to popular beliefs, most Northerners were not opposed to black slavery. A few abolitionists opposed slavery on moral grounds, but the greater preponderance of Northerners, directly if not indirectly, supported slavery by enjoying the fruits of it by eating the food, wearing the cotton, and drinking the rum that black labor produced.

New England, the home of the Quakers and antislavery forces, had three times as many textile mills as the entire South. These mills manufactured, processed, retailed, and generally thrived off of slavery-produced cotton. The first cotton mill in the U.S. was built at Beverly, Massachusetts, around 1808. By 1817, slaves were annually producing more than 126 million pounds of cotton that had a value of approximately $15 million, for processing in Northern textile mills alone.

Numerous historians, including Stanley Lebergott, E.N. Elliott and Robert Fogel, documented the high productivity of slaves and the products and wealth they produced for Northern as well as Southern businesses. By 1850, more than 1,000 cotton factories operated in the United States. Northern mills processed one-quarter of all slave-produced cotton. This cotton provided clothes, fabric, jobs, income, wealth, taxes, and other benefits to populations throughout the North. So while Northern antislavery forces opposed slavery on moral grounds, it was apparent from the kinds of businesses that were supporting the Northern economy that nearly every Northerner benefited from slavery.

Black slaves produced the raw products for the markets and in turn were a market for the finished products. The textile and leather industries tailored a major portion of their consumer items towards a captured market — the slavery institution. New England textile mills used long strand cotton to make fine fabrics for whites, while the short strand cotton was used to produce the cheapest and coarsest cloth for blacks. The cloth, referred to as "black cloth" or "nigger cloth," was the lowest grade material that the textile industries could use to produce clothing for five million slaves and free blacks.

The shoe industry was equally discriminating in its quality. Like the textile industry, the Northeast shoe industry produced two different grades of footwear for the South. It produced fine shoes for the white market which were carefully crafted, expensive leather boots. The manufacturing outlets also designed cheap, rough footwear, such as sandals and brogans for black slaves and freed blacks with marginal incomes. Judging from public records, there is little doubt that the textile and bootery industries were extremely profitable businesses during slavery. So much so, that a few of the original companies were still in existence a hundred years after slavery ended.

The high economic value of exploiting black labor would not let slavery die a timely death. Many Southern slave holders cautioned Northern abolitionists and businessmen not to hurt their own business opportunities by advocating freedom for blacks. For example, in 1787, John Rutledge of South Carolina argued that it was counterproductive for the Northern states to oppose slavery because they would benefit by transporting the products of slave labor.[30] In subsequent years, as Rutledge predicted, Northern shipbuilders amassed fortunes building commercial vessels that hauled slaves and durable goods to the Caribbean islands, European and other ports around the world.[31]

Nearly a third of England's well-known maritime fleet was constructed by these northeastern ship builders. But the industries' benefits did not end there. Major insurance and bonding companies also developed around the shipping industry. They issued policies to cover slave-produced goods from most major ports. At the behest of industrialists and shipbuilders, Northern states invested in the construction of water canals and railroads to speed slave-produced products across the nation.

Though the North pretended opposition to the roots of slavery, the North drew its very existence from the South and its "peculiar institution." The financial benefits of slavery effectively muted the voices of most Northerners. When forced to make a choice between making wealth and making policies to free five million lowly black slaves, whites in the North, like the South, placed a greater value on accumulating wealth and power. Of those who sympathized with black slaves, probably few associated the price of black suffering with the quality of life that whites were privileged to lead as free citizens.

Abolitionists and other antislavery groups did not relate the slave products to the production of wealth, consumer products, and life's comforts. Elliott, a writer and lawyer, in his pre-Civil War writings summed up the moral issue and the ineffectiveness of religious organizations in abolishing slavery. In 1853 he wrote that "religious antislavery forces were ineffective because nine-tenths of the cotton consumed in the Christian world was produced by black slaves." He charged that all who enjoyed the fruits of black enslavement were co-conspirators.[32] Without black labor there would have been few products to market or taxes for government. Black people and their labor was first and foremost an economic issue, not a moral issue. This is just as true in the 20th century as it was in the 17th, 18th and 19th centuries.

In all probability, had the antislavery forces made ending slavery an economic issue in need of an immediate conclusion, instead of a moral issue that would change as men's hearts changed, slavery would not have lasted for 250 years. As an economic issue, the abolitionists could have directly embargoed or boycotted products produced by slave labor, just as the colonists had

Exhibit 7.

TIME LINE: 1801 - 1849

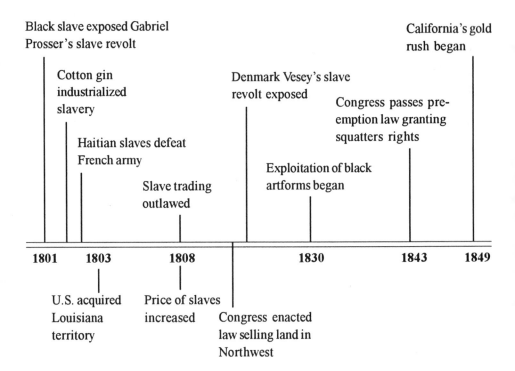

Black slave exposed Gabriel
Prosser's slave revolt

California's gold
rush began

Cotton gin
industrialized
slavery

Denmark Vesey's slave
revolt exposed

Congress passes pre-
emption law granting
squatters rights

Haitian slaves defeat
French army

Slave trading
outlawed

Exploitation of black
artforms began

| 1801 | 1803 | 1808 | 1830 | 1843 | 1849 |

U.S. acquired
Louisiana
territory

Price of slaves
increased

Congress enacted
law selling land in
Northwest

boycotted products from England in order to get their own freedom during
the Revolutionary War.

Creative Slavery Profiteers

During the off-seasons, or when a slave owner had more labor force than
work, he would rent out slave crews on a "mobile basis" to surrounding farms.
According to several historians, it was quite a common sight to see large
slave gangs moving on the roads early in the morning or late in the evenings
between plantations or farms. These slave gangs were often rented to other
planters or to local factory operators.[33] Fairer minded slave holders would
even allow slaves to contract out their services in day labor, and retain a
portion of their own earnings. The few slaves fortunate enough to have such
masters were often able to save enough to eventually purchase their own
freedom. Other smaller businessmen earned sizable incomes by auctioning

or breeding black slaves.

Auctioneers established offices in major slave entry points and seaport towns such as Charleston, Norfolk, and Baltimore. The typical auction fee was a commission of 2.5 percent of the total sale cost of each slave. If we assume that each of the five million slaves was sold at least once, then a 2.5 percent auctioneer's commission paid on the average price per slave of $1,000 would have produced a billion dollar industry. After the United States banned slave trading in 1808, the top prices of prime slaves gradually rose as high as $1,800.

Slave traders and investors sought alternative ways of meeting the nation's growing demand for slaves. Between 1810 and 1864, a larger commercially profitable domestic slave trading industry was established between the old slave states and the newer states entering the Union. Slave breeding emerged as a profitable industry. In 1810, a full one-third of the profits of plantation owners in the older regions of the South resulted from breeding slaves for sale in the interstate slave trade.[34]

White males used their power to manipulate the sexuality of black males for economic gain. They used them to breed with their own slaves or leased them out for stud service. Most large plantations had a stable of black slaves to perform stud services, which brought in money from neighboring farms.

Every newborn black baby represented hundreds of dollars in capital gain to the slave holder. Black studs, like prize bulls, brought the top dollar in slave trading. Similarly, black females were advertised and sold for their reproductive potential, especially teenage females. Even older black females had higher value, if they had successfully given birth to a child. According to one commentator, "A fair price for a healthy 30-year-old Negro woman with a child was 1/4 more than that of a non-breeding woman."[35]

Blacks and Indians Denied Access to Gold

In a financial sense, Black slaves had the midas touch. Their labor in Virginia's tobacco fields created the first gold rush. Their labor and cotton created the second gold rush in the fields of the East and Mid-West.

As a result of the war with Mexico over Texas and slavery, California was acquired from Mexico through the Treaty of *Guadelaupe* Hidalgo. Almost immediately afterward, in 1849, a natural resource — gold — was discovered in California. This discovery of gold ignited a massive influx of wealth seekers from around the world. Within four years of the big discovery, more than $200 million worth of gold had reportedly been extracted.

National race-based economic preferences and immigration policies emerged and were adopted in the California gold fields. The two groups who had contributed the most towards the building of the new nation — Indians, with their land, and blacks, with their labor — were systematically excluded from participating in the gold rush.

In an effort to keep the California gold rush a "white only" treasure hunt, public pronouncements made it clear to free blacks and Indians that if they wanted to pan gold, they could only do it as a slave to a white person. The hundreds of free blacks who traveled to California in search of gold, not re-enslavement, were blocked by local laws and white vigilante violence.

California was one of the few free states, so blacks, forced out of the gold fields, had few other places to go. Most starved to death, were lynched or died from exposure. The few who survived were forced to "inhabit the worst parts of the town . . . and lived commonly in . . . filth and degradation."[36] Like blacks, Indians fared badly. In 1845, four years before the gold rush started, approximately 150,000 Indians lived in California. After the gold rush ended, barely 35,000 Indians remained.[37]

> The intentional exclusion of blacks and Indians from acquiring wealth or a part of the "American Dream" had been established into national policy in 1836 by Secretary of War Lewis Cass, who rationalized: "We are all striving in the career of life to acquire riches of honor, power, or some other object, whose possession is to realize the daydreams of our imaginations; and the aggregate of these efforts constitute the advance of society. But, there is little of this in the constitution of our savages." [38]

But not all nonwhite groups experienced such systematic and exclusionary treatment. As word of the gold rush spread, large waves of Southern European, Chinese, and Mexican immigrants sought their fortunes in California. Whites considered Chinese more acceptable than Indians or blacks. Accordingly, state and federal government officials praised them as hard working and thrifty. The Chinese were accepted into the ranks of the gold seekers. Some staked claims and even found a little gold. Others worked in mining camps doing odd jobs. But most Chinese failed to find gold and had little choice but to open ethnic businesses or offer their labor at low wages.

Similarly, Mexicans had greater access to the gold fields than either blacks or Indians. The greater acceptance of Mexicans could have resulted from the Spanish culture that was prominent in California, or from the fact that

Mexicans had not been categorically and historically abused by white society, although Mexicans ranked lower than Chinese in preferred skin color. In the early 1850s, the total number of Mexicans was less than 3,000 in the entire nation. Therefore, they did not present either a challenge or threat to whites, as did the more than five million blacks.

Though Chinese and Mexicans were nonwhite, they supported European whites' practice of excluding blacks and Indians from prospecting for gold. A minister for this period reportedly observed that "The immigrants became the bitterest of Negro haters within 15 days of their naturalization as American citizens." Apparently, learning to despise blacks was an important aspect in the acculturation of immigrants. Blacks carried a heavy burden — they were the target of everyone's hostilities, but were totally unable to defend themselves or compete.

Neither Chinese nor Mexicans endured the kind of discrimination that blacks did. Only blacks were the systematic victims of cultural customs and laws that denied them legal freedom, the fruits of their labor, the right of property ownership, the right to protect their person, family and race, and a promising future.

Many social scientists and politicians justified the near total exclusion of free blacks from any land ownership and wealth-building activity on the basis that the U.S. Constitution declared them noncitizens and subhuman. But such reasoning does not hold, especially since there was a constant influx of non-English European, Hispanic, and Asian immigrants who were neither citizens nor white Anglo Saxon Protestants.

If free blacks were "ineligible" to own land, why did government encourage them to participate in every military conflict with a promise of land and other veterans benefits at war's end?

Black Vets Denied Access to Preferential Wealth

Many years later, the American government played another role in preferential wealth distributed to whites. The government passed wealth to its white veterans, both the living and the dead. Through the years, America has expressed its gratitude to its war veterans in a variety of ways, primarily through land grants, land bounties, and homesteading opportunities.

In 1642, the same year that Massachusetts introduced slavery into the colonies, Virginia enacted a law forcing blacks to join a militia and protect the larger white society. In 1763, Virginia became one of the first of the colonies to set aside a large section of territory west of the Alleghenies as bounties for veterans. Later, in the 19th century, a Veterans Land Program was established by the federal government to recognize and reward servicemen who had served in wars from the Revolutionary through the Spanish American War with Mexico. Blacks have participated to varying degrees in nearly every war in which this country has engaged since the year 1619. Yet blacks have received little monetary compensation of any form for their military services to this nation.

The Veterans Land Program offered veterans either a homestead site or six feet for a burial site. Since blacks were the only non-English racial or ethnic group that had fought in every major military involvement since the initial settlement in 1619, they were optimistic that perhaps they would be included in the Veterans Land Program. However, black veterans did not qualify for the homesteading sites. Until the 1960s, black veterans fortunate enough to be eligible for a free, six-foot burial site were discriminated against even in death. Preferential treatment at most cemeteries and grave sites enforced a "whites only" rule.

Affirmative Action for Special Interest Groups

After the Civil War, when nearly all of the land and wealth building resources had been claimed by members of the majority white society, conservative social forces began campaigns against any governmental program or policy that portended assistance or a redistribution of wealth to blacks. Convinced that the majority white society was well in possession or control of wealth, power and resources, conservatives promoted an ideology that the right people were already aboard the wealth boat, so keep the gangplank up.

In 1860, five percent of the population controlled approximately 25 percent of the country's wealth. One hundred and thirty years later, after a Civil War, two World Wars, a major economic depression, and a Civil Rights Movement, the major possessors of wealth remain unchanged. Five percent of the American population still controls 25 percent of the country's total wealth. Most of this wealth was passed on from generation to generation. The younger generations of whites resent being held morally or financially responsible for the racial sins of their ancestors, though, as whites, they still enjoy the inherited advantages and privileges of slavery.

Ironically, most wealthy conservatives today pretend that they earned their wealth, rather than admit that they got it the old fashioned way, through preferential government treatment, exploitation of black labor, expropriation of Indian land, or simply as an inheritance from those who acquired it through

Exhibit 8.

TIME LINE: 1857 - 1867

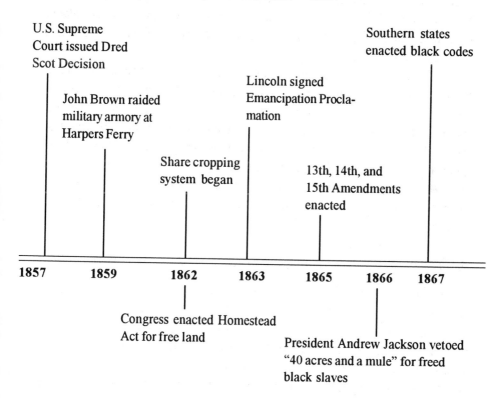

U.S. Supreme
Court issued Dred
Scot Decision

Southern states
enacted black codes

John Brown raided
military armory at
Harpers Ferry

Lincoln signed
Emancipation Procla-
mation

Share cropping
system began

13th, 14th, and
15th Amendments
enacted

1857   1859   1862   1863   1865   1866   1867

Congress enacted Homestead
Act for free land

President Andrew Jackson vetoed
"40 acres and a mule" for freed
black slaves

one or any combination of those three ways. Conservative elements oppose reparations or any government program that benefits blacks, but few acknowledge the existence of or oppose systemic government programs that distribute wealth to various special interest groups within the majority white society.

Despite current political rhetoric, blacks are not the primary recipients of federal grants, "giveaways," and subsidies. Historically, the largest recipients of federal government largess have been railroads, ranchers, farmers, and miners. Theoretically, public lands and resources within the United States are owned by or held in trust for all citizens. Accordingly, the federal government should manage these properties in a way that benefits all Americans.

However, the government has not managed public properties in an even-handed manner in the best interest of all the people. The federal government has systematically permitted a select wealthy population to use, exploit, and profit from these public resources. These programs frequently never required the recipients to pay anything, and when payment was required, the payment never approached the fair market value for the public resources. As such, these programs amount to massive taxpayer funded subsidies to the recipients. Due to the racial policies and feelings within the nation at the time these grants were made, the benefits were doled out along racial lines. These programs, some of which continue to this day can therefore be considered race-based government preferences for whites, even now.

But somehow, Americans have never allowed themselves to think this way. The term "preferential treatment" only applies when federal programs are targeted to provide assistance to disfavored groups. Meanwhile, preferential government programs that benefit the majority group are simply seen as either maintaining the status quo or as temporary assistance to a "vital" segment of the population in the interest of national security. Majority preference programs are so pervasive and so accepted that it is almost a radical notion to term it "white affirmative action." Yet if we apply the definition equally, this is clearly what these programs are. The following section discusses some affirmative programs for whites.

The Railroad Companies: Kings of Special Interests

The major purpose for building the railroad system across America was to move the slave-produced goods to domestic markets and to seaports for shipment to foreign markets. Centuries of sales of slave-produced cotton, tobacco, rice, and indigo had built the Southern economy and sustained the Northern businesses upon which the American domestic and foreign trade were based. In *The Use of Blacks in America*, historian Dan Lacy discussed how black labor subsidized the development and westward expansion of the railroads. According to Lacy, "The shiploads of cotton poured onto the docks of Liverpool [England] financed the factories and railroads of the United States and the vast settlement of the American West. In the economic life of 19th century America, with black labor, 'Cotton was King' and caused the nation to prosper and expand."[39]

To facilitate the shipment and sale of these goods and to support the cotton economy, government did everything possible to persuade the railroads and their stock holders to build lines across the country. Just between the years of 1850 and 1871, Congress gave railroads sections of land extending six miles on each side of railroad tracks across the nation and totalling more land area than the entire state of Texas. Politicians argued that if the railroads were persuaded with free land to build their lines across the country, then farmers and merchants would soon follow, and the general populace would be close behind. This great land giveaway to the wealthy white elite was done in the name of building America.

Railroad builders exploited their preferential status with the government by "upgrading" their free land for better lands. For example, before the 1900s, Congress enacted a law that permitted a railroad to exchange property it owned on an Indian reservation for federal land outside the reservation. Under this provision, for instance, railroads exchanged millions of acres of worthless or low-valued land for land located in the fertile valleys of Washington, Oregon, Idaho and Montana. These exchanges had nothing to do with building the railroad lines.

The railroads, such as the Illinois Central, were allowed to purchase additional millions of acres from the government at the price of 5 cents an acre to build additional tracks. These same railroads later made massive fortunes by reselling the land that they received free from the government to land speculators. Author Howard Zinn indicated the potential profits stating:

> "Within 10 years, the Illinois Railroad Line publicly announced that it had 1,100,000 acres, or less than one-half of its original grant, for sale in forty-acre lots and upwards, at prices ranging from $5 to $25 per acre, whereas the national domain was offered at $1.25 per acre."[40]

Of the approximately 2,600,000 acres that the Illinois Central Railroad received from the government through land grants, all but 450,000 acres were sold in less than 20 years. Whites holding corporate stocks and bonds in these railroads also received significant capital gains, though millions of acres of the best public land was first given to their company free of charge. They were then allowed to reap a second windfall capital gain by upgrading the land for better public land. Blacks, on the other hand, could not profit from the railroad land grants because they were slaves or poor freemen, who could not hold or purchase any of the land, railroad stocks, bonds, or hold corporate positions. The common perception of blacks as slaves made it nearly impossible for a black to get a paying job with the railroad lines.

Many railroad lines actually purchased slaves as property and business equipment. Railroads used slaves to do the heavy loading, maintain tracks and railroad cars. Other times slaves were purchased on speculation for capital gains. According to Stanley Lebergott, The North Carolina Railroad listed among it assets: real estate, tools, and two Negroes, worth $1,550. Even when railroads held public auctions or resold their land holdings, few, if any, blacks could afford to purchase any of the parcels. As a result, there were no freed black stockholders or heirs to railroad fortunes. Beyond not being able to own railroad stock, they could not get railroad service in their communities. The railroads would not establish train stations in black sections of any town or city, nor hire blacks for anything except the most undesirable, lowest paying jobs.

Ranchers and Grazers

Ranchers have also been a longtime beneficiary of federal funds. Much of the land in the western states was arid and profitable only for grazing livestock, but the small size of many of the holdings made ranching difficult. Beginning in the 1850s, corporations and individuals sought to acquire large tracts of land in the Louisiana Territory and westward to use the public natural resources for grazing. The large, open tracts of federal land represented extremely valuable property.

Many ranchers boldly grazed their livestock on these federal lands without permission or payment, and the federal government allowed it. As a result, the public range quickly became severely overgrazed. To prevent further overgrazing, Congress passed the Taylor Grazing Act in 1934, but the legislation only provided additional federal subsidies and benefits to the ranchers. For example, it provided preferential permits, low grazing fees, and federal funding for range improvements such as fencing and revegetation. As a result, taxpayers provided further subsidies to the ranchers. They now paid the bill for fencing off and replanting these federal lands so that ranchers could continue to use them.

The ranchers never paid fair market value for the use of these government lands, and allowed their greed to place personal gains over preserving the public's interest in these properties. The Bureau of Land Management, which supervises more than 500 million acres of federal lands, estimated in the 1970s that approximately 80 percent of the land in the far West that had been leased to ranchers had been overgrazed and damaged. The federally granted grazing rights gave the ranchers additional financial benefits beyond providing a financial windfall in free livestock feed.

Ranchers holding federally-issued grazing permits can use them to appreciate the value of their personal private farming or ranching properties. For example, if a rancher holds 20,000 acres under his name and leases another

Exhibit 9.

© 1993 by Herblock in *The Washington Post*

150,000 acres from the Bureau of Land Management, he can sell his 20,000 acres at a price that includes the value of the use of the other 150,000 acres of public land. This additional value can be passed from one generation to the next as a form of wealth. In addition, ranchers can use grazing permits as security for loans from local financial institutions.

Ironically, this lending practice enhanced the political power of the ranchers, since lending institutions had a financial incentive to oppose political proposals that would increase the cost or availability of federal grazing rights, and thereby reduce the profitability of these ranches. The political strength of the groups backing this federally sponsored handout was evident in recent short-lived attempts to reform grazing rights. Though blacks are cited as the primary recipients of taxpayer funded "freebies," blacks have been systematically denied participation in the establishment of this grazing subsidy system, and therefore, are still barred from participating in any of the subsequent benefits that still accrue to current ranchers.

Farmers

Farmers were also a major beneficiary of federal aid programs. Over the last century, various laws allowed agrarian homesteaders to claim millions of acres of public lands for farming. For example, the Homestead Act of 1862 gave 160 acres to any settler who would farm the land for five years. Nearly all of the earlier large farms were originally acquired through direct or indirect government homesteading assistance. These properties often remained in the family for generations, and their value was frequently augmented by additional government subsidies and tax advantages. This preferential treatment still exists.

When Ronald Reagan became President, the Federal Price Support Program had an annual budget of $4 billion per year. He increased the annual budget to a record $57 billion. From 1986 to 1989, Reagan spent, on average, $600,000 per farm.[41] This massive redistribution of public funds amounts to an expensive affirmative action program for rural white Americans.

Clearly, government-sponsored farm support programs have provided a steady source of income and a safety net for generations of farmers. Congress decided in 1967 that farmers could sell or rent their quota to other landowners. Once a quota is separated from the land, it becomes a commodity all its own, like silver or gold. Production quotas are sold at public auctions and advertised for rent in newspapers. It is ironic, but the country is adamantly opposed to the use of quotas to help blacks, but feels no such reluctance in establishing beneficial quotas on peanuts, for example.

Government has provided subsidies to non-black, special interest groups for more than two centuries. Some of the federal government's favorite annual subsidies and special interests are: a $188 million subsidy for fertilizer research with the Tennessee Valley Authority; a $32 million 40-year-old subsidy to honey producers; a $212 million 42-year-old subsidy to wool and mohair farmers; and the $470 million annual subsidy to farmers. Besides import commodity quotas, farmers profit from corn, wheat, tobacco, soybean, and peanut allotments and quotas. For example, in 1949, the U.S. Department of Agriculture established a minimum support price for peanuts that the government pays if the market does not. Under this income maintenance system, only farms with a peanut quota or allotment can produce peanuts for sale in the United States, and only a specific number of pounds.

Mining

Similarly, for nearly a century and a half, the federal government conducted a program that conferred federal subsidies and grants almost exclusively to white miners. Beginning in the mid-1800s, both individuals and major corporate conglomerates were allowed to exploit thousands of acres of public land for their own private benefit. Though the federal government held these lands in trust for all American citizens, the Mineral Act of 1866 and the General Mining Law of 1872, in effect, allowed a redistribution of land and mineral resources from the public trust to a select group of individuals and businesses.

The General Mining Law of 1972 opened all unreserved public lands to mineral exploration and extraction, allowing those who actually found minerals to stake a claim without notifying or obtaining permission from the federal land management agency; exclude other prospectors; and use whatever natural resources are available on the claim for necessary mining needs. Commentators observed that after several years of negligible work and payment of a modest fee, the locator could be granted a federal patent that entitled him or her to outright ownership of the former mining claim. Once a claim has been patented, the owner can do whatever he or she wants with the claim, including using it or selling it for non-mining purposes. At no time was the locator-patentee required to pay rent or a royalty to the United States. As a result, private mining companies gouged and scarred the public lands in search of coal, iron ore, aluminum, gold, and silver.

Such policies are not a thing of the past. In fact, some are still active. *The Washington Post* reported that Interior Secretary Bruce Babbitt finally stripped the Bureau of Land Management of its authority to confer low-cost mining rights on federal lands in 1993. He had found it offensive that politically connected miners could acquire federal land for as little as $2.50 per acre upon demonstrating that the land contained valuable minerals.[42]

Surprisingly, even foreign firms have been allowed to use U.S. laws to get preferential mining rights and mineral rights in American mines, while paying little, if anything, for them. For example, a Canadian firm, the American Barrick Resources Corp., controls the largest gold mine in America. Located in Nevada the mine has gold deposits and reserves valued at $8 billion.

The U.S. government wants to sell the mine land to Canada at $2.50 per acre, and charge no royalty on extracted gold, but federal court has ordered the Clinton Administration to sell to the Barrick Company.[43] For as little as $5 per acre, Barrick gets 1,949 acres of land worth billions of dollars. In the very same article, Rep. George Miller (D-California), chairman of the House Natural Resources Committee and a leading advocate for junking the 1872 law, reacted to the sale in a way that could easily be a summary of black Americans' feelings. He said, "The lesson is the law should have been changed a long time ago. It is absolutely unfair to the American people that you would continue a process that takes lands that are owned by them for their benefit and simply give them away for private profit without the American people sharing in any of it. It's a very sad and sorry state of affairs."

Though foreign firms like Barrick have been allowed to own and exploit the nation's land and natural resources, blacks have been systematically denied that opportunity. As far back as 1856, the United States Attorney General Caleb Cushing ruled that free blacks did not have the right to apply for or enjoy the benefits under the Land Preemption Act of 1841.[44] Until Emancipation, black slave labor was the primary tool in mining operations. Mining companies often owned and maintained their own slaves, but more frequently, they simply leased slaves from local owners for as little as $120 to $200 per year. Black slaves were the first and most preferred mine workers. Mining dangers and harsh labor requirements significantly shortened blacks' already short life expectancy. As the quality of mining conditions and salaries improved, blacks were replaced by European immigrants.

The Heritage Foundation, an ultraconservative, right-wing group, continues to rationalize and promote the redistribution of public lands and natural resources to wealthy elite as necessary for the public good and national interest. In its *Mandate for Leadership III: Policy Strategies for the 1990s*, which served as a political bible for the Reagan and Bush Administrations, the foundation suggested that the Republican administration should instruct the Department of Interior's Bureau of Land Management and Mineral Management Service to "provide private business with increased access to mineral deposits on public lands, and oil and gas leases in the Arctic National Wildlife Refuge; slacken due diligence requirements; and permit the marketplace to decide the value of land leases."[45]

Exhibit 10.

"WE DON'T TAKE KINDLY TO PEOPLE MOVING INTO THESE PARTS, MISTER"

© 1993 by Herblock in *The Washington Post*

The Heritage Foundation did not even attempt to hide its support for the centuries-old partnership between business and government, under which business provides campaign support for politicians, and in turn, politicians provide subsidies and tax loopholes for businesses. This partnership ensures that the white power elite would continue to receive wealth from the public's loss.

Conservatives argue that giving public money, natural resources, and other financial benefits to certain wealthy individuals and businesses in the private

TABLE 9		
Preferential Groups Receiving Federal Assistance in 1980s		
Industry	**Value (Millions)**	**Form of Assistance**
Maritime Industry	$600	Cash Payments
Business Aviation	$660	Cash Payments
Trucking Companies	$60	Tax Breaks
Multinational Corporations	$500	Tax Breaks
High Technology Firms	$650	Tax Breaks
Timber Companies	$470	Tax Breaks
Oil and Gas Companies	$1.9	Tax Breaks
Interstate Trucking	Limited Competition	Favorable Regulations
AM Broadcasters	Limited Competition	Favorable Regulations
Nuclear Power Industry	Limited Liability	Favorable Regulations
Exporting Companies	Low Interest Loans	Loan Subsidies
Source: Common Cause, Inc., 1981		

sector stimulates further investment within the economy. The benefits of this activity eventually "trickle down" to the less fortunate, thereby benefiting all Americans. Conservatives argue that federal grants to the less fortunate Americans are "bad economics" because the poor do not reinvest. The benefits of these federal grants do not, therefore, trickle up throughout the economy. Under this hypocritical reasoning, only the overwhelmingly white wealthy can and should be the beneficiaries of federal aid programs.

Corporate and Other Special Interests

In the 1980s, while poor blacks were denied educational and business opportunities, bank loans, home mortgages, food stamps, welfare payments, and other forms of assistance, the federal government, headed by conservative politicians, administered a system of financial incentives, cash payments, loans with favorable repayment terms, tax breaks, lucrative government contracts, and other giveaways for wealthy individuals and corporations. These policies, combined with business-friendly legislation, such as refusals to raise minimum wage, amounted to an affirmative action program for wealthy corporations. Common Cause compiled data on governmental preferential treatment policies for these wealth-producing industries (See **Table 9**).

Conclusion

Blacks were involved in every aspect of the development of the American nation. We cleared the land and produced the crops. We raised the food and the children of white families. We fought in every war and developed the land expropriated from the American Indians, though we were permitted to be buried only in certain nonwhite areas of this very land. Blacks produced the wealth that whites in both the Old and New Worlds possessed, and claimed to have achieved by the sweat of their brows.

The centuries of physical and psychological abuse that black people suffered were tragic, but even worse, the dominant white society has systematically hidden the fact that the foundations of the American, European, Latin American, and Caribbean economies are rooted in the labor and production of blacks. Black labor fueled the exponential growth in the economies of numerous nations around the world.

For centuries, slave-produced products were found in every home in every Christian and non-Christian nation. Slaves produced the raw goods that filled storage facilities, warehouses and merchant shelves in nearly two-thirds of the world. They provided fibers for textiles and clothes, food, alcohol, and raw materials for the factories. Black slaves and Jim Crow labor directly or indirectly generated not only thousands of jobs in vertically-integrated industries, but also provided what most people of this nation wore and ate.

The increased reliance on computers and immigrant labor has all but ended white society's dependence on black muscle power. Yet, the planned obsolescence of black labor will only exacerbate the 600-year black holocaust. Second class citizenship will only end when blacks can recognize political, economic, and social trends and policies that are detrimental to them as a group, and collectively demand either an end to such practices or inclusion as beneficiaries of such practices.

7

A National Public Policy on Black People

"Take up the white man's burden, A hundred times made plain,
To seek another's profit, And work another's gain."
— *Kipling, 1899* [1]

The totality of black peoples' existence and condition in America stems directly from a national public policy designed by white society to control and use black labor to build a new nation.[2] The public policy on the use of blacks developed incrementally until it became like an onion with many layers. It began taking shape in 1619 and evolved into a systematic, mandated social arrangement that dictated the behavior of both blacks and whites. The policy's core principle stipulated that blacks were to be used as a well-disciplined, uncompensated, subordinated, noncompetitive, permanent labor class that existed on the margins of society.

The national public policy determined black peoples' human worth and status as well as their educational and political opportunities and their cultural and family values. The dominant white society's national public policy explicitly and implicitly defined how blacks were to be treated and used.

Public policy is important for blacks to study because it gives clear insight into the process and methods that the dominant society used to establish absolute control over millions of blacks as a laboring class. But equally important, it shows blacks who are seeking to gain power through community organizing the way whites constructed a national black policy and plan. Understanding that plan is essential to the shaping of a new public policy for blacks.

The public policy was formulated from racial dogmas and doctrines that justified the policy. The doctrine of racial superiority legitimized the exclusion and segregation of blacks from mainstream white society. The doctrine of noninterference dissuaded governments and social institutions from using their resources and power to stop the abuse of black people. And the doctrine of expendability promoted the belief that black life was non-sacred and that there was nothing wrong with using blacks for the betterment and protection of white life. These policy doctrines and dogmas continue to determine the quality of life for whites and blacks in America today.

How the National Policy on Blacks Developed

European culture set the stage for the exploitative use of black Africans, and the social and physical conditions of life in the New World drove the English to construct an aggressive strategy to enslave them. No single factor compelled Europeans to seek out blacks to serve as the labor class of the New World. Many factors converged simultaneously.[3]

The English people, like most Europeans, harbored racist attitudes towards black people long before the first settlers arrived on the North American continent. The European traders and explorers to Africa had brought back stories about "The Dark Continent" and its dark-skinned "heathens." The 17th century Anglo-Saxon culture was filled with anti-black terms, and the first English settlers brought their prejudices with them to America.

The first 20 blacks entered Jamestown in 1619 on a Dutch warship. Whether or not these blacks were slaves is a matter of interpretation, because the records from that period are scant. But it is reasonable to assume that they were not considered slaves initially. They had been rescued from a Portuguese slave-trading vessel by the Dutch warship. They were brought to Jamestown and the Dutch captain exchanged them for food and ship supplies. If the Dutch captain indebted the blacks in the exchange, it was probably as indentured servants, because records revealed that within five years, these blacks were free to buy land, carry

Exhibit 11.

TIME LINE: 1877 - 1905

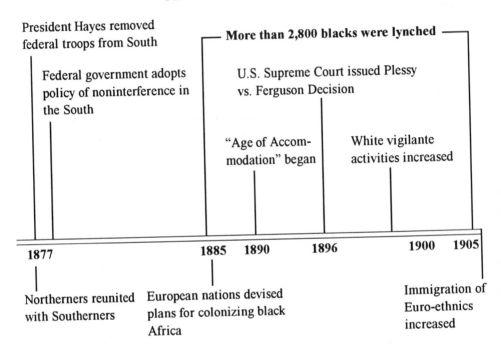

President Hayes removed
federal troops from South

Federal government adopts
policy of noninterference in
the South

More than 2,800 blacks were lynched

U.S. Supreme Court issued Plessy
vs. Ferguson Decision

"Age of Accom-
modation" began

White vigilante
activities increased

1877   1885   1890   1896   1900   1905

Northerners reunited   European nations devised   Immigration of
with Southerners   plans for colonizing black Euro-ethnics
                       Africa   increased

weapons, go to court, attend church and generally socialize with other
settlers until the late 1630s.

The cycle of black degeneration in the American colonies was well under way by the late 1630s. Labor was critical. No one was available to do
the backbreaking work, not even the free blacks. Word of the terrible
work conditions had gotten back to Europe and whites refused to come to
America as indentured servants. Colonial courts and legislative assemblies had begun to enact punitive legislation or rulings against blacks or
any whites who consorted with them.

As discussed earlier, the Maryland colony set the stage for black slavery in America by issuing a government policy that singled blacks out
for subordinate and exclusionary treatment. Based upon available records,
scattered incidences of Indian, white and black slavery were appearing in
the Maryland colony as early as 1634. But four years later, in 1638, the
first public edict or policy against blacks was issued by the Maryland

Colonial Assembly. That edict declared that neither the original 20 free blacks "nor their offspring shall be permitted to enjoy the fruits of white society." This Maryland edict became the founding public policy for the use and treatment of blacks from which white racism, Jim Crowism and segregation later grew.[4]

A Broad Community Need Shapes the Public Policy

An abundance of free land and a shortage of labor made involuntary labor the key to white survival. Those who owned the largest tracts of undeveloped land could not convert the huge tracts into productive, profitable agricultural businesses without the assistance of a disciplined, strong, expendable and preferably unpaid work force. Without such a labor force, it was questionable whether the colonies could survive, let alone prosper. Neither Indians nor white indentured servants would do the laborious work. A bound labor force was the logical solution.

The Maryland public edict on blacks took on greater importance as the colonial settlers realized that they possibly had the key to their common labor problem in the use of black people as their uncompensated workers. The labor problem was resolved in 1665, when all of the existing colonies enacted laws to enslave blacks.

The Maryland colonies' original edict was expanded into a public policy on blacks, stipulating that "black people shall constitute an available, uncompensated, noncompetitive, well-disciplined, permanently subordinated work force, which shall be separated from the white society." England supported the colonies' enactment of slavery laws by establishing a full-scale international slave trading industry to provide them with a dependable supply of black slaves.

The primary purpose of forced black labor was to bring whites' newly acquired land to productivity and value by clearing the forest, building the houses, raising the crops, tending the livestock, preparing the food and raising and comforting the white families. Second, the slaves were to supply England's industries with valuable cash crops and commodities.

After the 1660s, all of the colonies had written black enslavement into their statutes. England, as the mother country and the overseer of the colonies, was the first to codify the colonies' public policy on black slavery into an act passed in 1667 called the "Act to Regulate the Negroes on British Plantations."[5] Besides regulating the slave trading industry, this act introduced the concept of blacks as personal property and advocated strict and severe treatment of slaves. A doctrine of black expendability was explicitly advocated in this Act, which granted white society the right to brand, whip, or actually kill enslaved blacks.

Four years later, in 1671, another Maryland act strengthened the public policy by enacting the doctrine of noninterference. This doctrine notified religious organizations that religious conversions and baptisms of slaves, before or after importation to North America, did not entitle the slaves to freedom as some slaves had hoped. This noninterference doctrine was later expanded under the concept of "personal property rights," which soothed the fears of slave owners, who were concerned about losing their investment in any slaves who converted to Christianity. The colonies devoted the next 20 years to perfecting a public policy that defined, with mathematical precision, what individuals, races or ethnic groups would be slaves and how they were to be treated.[6]

By 1705, Virginia produced a codification of laws applying to slaves called "The Slave Codes," which standardized the public policy on blacks as well as white behavior towards blacks. The codes imbued the public policy on blacks with a new kind of social arrangement of accountability within the white community. It not only established rules of conduct with specified penalties for slaves, but it also implied a code of conduct for all white persons in their relations with blacks. It prohibited any white person from committing any act that elevated the status of blacks or demonstrated leniency in the treatment of slaves.[7] The Slave Codes were premised in the belief that humility and weakness in the treatment of slaves anywhere was a threat to slavery and white privileged life-style everywhere.

The Slave Codes reinforced the public policy, giving it substance and statutory authority. In the South, the policy gave rise to a unique racial code of etiquette that prescribed the status, role and expected behavior for both blacks and whites. The new racial etiquette gave respectability to the policy. Laws were enacted that required newspapers, businesses and social organizations to be ever mindful of the policy and to publicize the code of etiquette. Often clergymen were required to read both of them to their congregations.

The primary purpose of the code of etiquette was to support the public policy on the use of blacks by requiring that all whites act superior to blacks at all times and that blacks give deference to whites and act inferior to them at all times. The secondary purpose of the code and public policy was to make it possible for whites to exercise effective control

Exhibit 12.

TIME LINE: 1915 - 1954

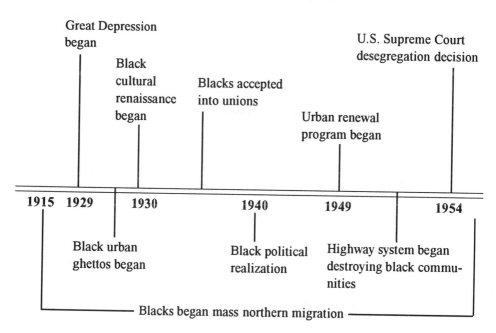

over blacks and to strengthen the sense of white unity.

In 1787, the drafters of the U.S. Constitution incorporated the colonial public policy on blacks into the founding documents of the new nation, making it the slave holder's friend by recognizing and legitimizing black enslavement. The concept of blacks as property and the doctrine of non-interference appeared as three interconnected clauses in the Constitution, which of course, served as the legal basis of the nation.

The Constitution declared blacks to be three-fifths of a person prohibited Congress from outlawing the slave trade for 20 years and bound the states to assist in returning fugitive slaves to their masters. The drafters made it clear that the government was the legal instrument of white society and that it should be powerless to interfere with black enslavement within the states or with foreign slave trading practices. Yet on the other hand, it was also mandated to exercise its full powers to protect the white slave holders' investments in slave properties.

Until the Revolutionary War, the public policy on the use of black labor evolved primarily from the tobacco-growing regions supported by commercial interests. The profitability of slavery declined until Eli Whitney invented the cotton gin in 1793. In the midst of Europe's Industrial Revolution, the cotton gin increased the popularity of cotton and black slavery. At the time, wool was the primary fabric because cotton was scarce and generally very expensive.

The cotton gin made American-produced cotton the king of agricultural products and the primary fabric of the world. This surge in cotton's popularity re-shackled blacks to America's plantations. Businesses and industries associated with and dependent upon black slavery sprang up throughout the North and South. The renewed economic dependence on black labor demanded support from the public and private sectors. White society became more dependent than ever on black labor for creating wealth and income. Moreover, it became more determined to keep blacks subordinated, unskilled, noncompetitive and excluded from white society.

The Civil War Modified the Public Policy

By the mid-1800s, the North insisted on change in the public policy on black labor because Northern workers could not compete with the uncompensated slave labor of the South. The South refused and the nation went to war. The national public policy was in limbo from immediately after the Civil War until the late 1890s. During this time period, the South had no official labor force or public policy on the use of blacks. Emancipation legally said blacks were no longer personal property.

Newly-freed slaves sought to break free of the old public policy. They demanded the 40 acres and a mule that they had been promised as compensation for their years of unpaid labor. Blacks wanted to leave slavery prepared to be self-sufficient and productive. However, to break free of the old national public policy would require the government to give millions of blacks unused public lands or portions of old Southern plantations for homesteading.

For the newly-freed slaves to be competitive, they needed quality school systems to help them shake off centuries of forced ignorance. And to protect them from the animosities of their old enslavers and enemies, the newly-freed slaves needed legal and police protection, since they were never permitted to bear arms. However, blacks received none of these things, because the national public policy on blacks as a labor force was unchanged by the Civil War. Both the North and the South had needs for a low-paid, intellectually noncompetitive labor force.

In reconciling postwar differences, the North adopted the public policy of its Southern brothers on the treatment of blacks. There was never any serious effort to give blacks any measures of economic independence or to compensate them for their generations of unpaid labor.[8] As a Washington, D.C. newspaper noted in 1868, "It is impossible to separate the question of color from the question of labor, for the reason that the majority of the laborers . . . throughout the Southern states are colored people and nearly all of the colored people are at present laborers."[9]

To change blacks' status as laborers would cause changes in society's political and social ordering of acceptability. Thus, the North and the South collectively agreed to continue, but modify, the basic tenets undergirding the public policy on blacks.

The black freedmen were penniless, uneducated, homeless and friendless in a hostile South. Without land reparations or tools, they had little choice except to offer the market their only resource — themselves. As an available, trained, cheap labor force, blacks stepped into a predictable future. The Southern states enacted the Black Codes, which revised the national public policy on blacks, forcing them into sharecropping on Southern farms under the control of former slave holders.

The Black Codes effectively modified the public policy by substituting sharecropping for slavery. It also fixed black people in a subordinate place in the social order and provided white society with a manageable and inexpensive labor force. The principle behind the national public policy remained intact and survives to this day.

The Public Policy During the Civil Rights Era

The latest great change in the national public policy came in the early 1960s and coincided with the Civil Rights Movement, which championed the awakening of black America during what became known as the "decade of progress" between 1955 and 1965. Blacks won the battle to attend white schools, sit at white lunchroom counters and sit in bus seats that had historically been reserved for whites only. Little notice was given amidst the celebrating, to the fact that the income gap between blacks and whites was widening, the two societies were growing more segregated than ever, blacks were losing their few businesses and disposable incomes to white suburban stores and black unemployment was beginning to skyrocket.

The integration accomplishments of blacks had coincided with the new phase of the public policy on blacks — obsolescence. For the first time in the history of the nation, blacks were "free" from white society's pre-scribed labor role. Major advances in technology became the magic bullet that freed the larger white society from dependence on black labor.

The two groups' newfound freedoms caused major adjustments in black-white relations. White society's shift away from its dependence on black labor was noted by Alvin Toffler in his book, *Powershift*. Toffler asserted, "The most important economic development of this lifetime was the use of a new system of creating wealth based no longer on muscles, but on minds."

Whites began moving towards a color blind society, where new labor-saving machines replaced the need for black muscles and sweat. Machines were less offensive and threatening. It was unlikely that new labor-saving machines would champion equality, integration or civil rights. Instead, new technology provided a bridge from the Old World to the New World and freed the dominant white society from its old ways of thinking about race relations, its old ideologies and its public policies.

New World technology pushed white society into a new public policy for blacks. Few unskilled jobs were left in white businesses and indus-tries. Simultaneously, conservative and liberal white politicians alike claimed that since the Civil Rights Movement had succeeded in giving blacks their social and legal rights, there was nothing else anyone could do for blacks. Blacks were therefore, finally free, but obsolete.

Implementing the Public Policy

Eight major factors appear to have driven the public policy on the use and treatment of blacks across the centuries.

- 1) The European colonies were predisposed by their native culture to have negative feelings about blackness and black people;

- 2) They established a public edict that was based around a common need, that, if resolved, would be beneficial to all members of white society;

- 3) White society refined and vigorously supported a coherent public policy on blacks that was transmitted from generation to genera tion, through laws and social customs;

• 4) The policy was codified by official governmental acts;

• 5) It was concertedly supported by all levels of government, schools, churches, businesses and the larger general society;

• 6) A sense of community accountability for supporting the public policy was established;

• 7) The public policy received total commitment from all segments of the community;

• 8) The public policy was continuously promoted and coordinated by institutions and other entities.

As a result of these factors, a consensus was reached on how blacks were to be treated. The public policy was expanded and modified incrementally. The adjustment continued over the centuries based upon the broad labor needs of white society. The nature of the modifications can be tracked to some extent by the historical developments of the nation. When new opportunities and challenges demanded human labor in the agricultural fields of the South, the range lands of the West, the factories of the North or the military battle fronts all around the globe, the appropriate government or white institution made sure that the black labor force was available and in the forefront.

Role of Societal Institutions

All of the societal institutions supported the established public policy for the use of blacks. The churches, schools, businesses and governments joined in the alliance against blacks. They were parts of a larger social network that systematically concentrated power, wealth, authority and resources in the hands of white society and consigned blacks to a subordinate and exploited status.

The churches offered biblical justification for black enslavement, denouncing blacks as heathens and bearing the mark of Ham. They preached the doctrines of white superiority and black inferiority and excluded blacks from or segregated them within the congregations. Within the churches

TABLE 10	
How Whites Conditioned the Blacks They Enslaved	
- Goals - **Blacks Were To:**	**- Techniques -** **Blacks Were Subjected To:**
Be taught discipline	Endless, hard, tedious, dirty labor
Be inferior to whites	Never seeing any blacks with power
Know their place	The Color Line and Jim Crow
Be backward/childlike	Planned ignorance and humiliation
Be fearful of master	Physical and psychological deprivation
Place master above self	Denial of humanity and hope
Surrender totally	Religious humility and hopelessness
See whites as superiors	Master's reward and punishment system
Be totally dependent	Improverishment; marginal existence
Be racially divided	Destruction of family and racial unity

founded by blacks, ministers internalized their conditions, taught blacks meekness and resignation and a nonviolent strategy for gaining access to their rights and white-owned and white-controlled resources.

Educational institutions carried out their essential purpose of servicing the economic ends of white society. They prepared white children to be leaders and masters of their own fate. White youths were taught academic skills, cultural values and the pragmatic responsibilities of leadership. The schools passed on the doctrines of white superiority and black inferiority to both races. Black children suffered centuries of planned ignorance. During slavery, it was illegal to teach blacks to read; today they attend inferior, ill-equipped schools.

American businesses played a role in tailoring the national policy on blacks to their wealth-building interests. They formulated new economic principles of capitalism that defined blacks as human commodities and their labor as cheap tools to produce great wealth.

American government functioned as a guardian of white wealth and power. White society used government power to enhance or maintain their own privileged positions and to reduce the social and economic status and potential of blacks. Government guaranteed white control over the fruits of black labor and control over the work process. Government later sustained the inequities by perpetuating the myth of equal opportunity.

Once the public policy for blacks was established, all members of the alliance were committed to vigorously supporting it, whatever the cost. A sense of commitment to the policy was a part of the broad sense of white community cohesiveness. Attacks on or violations of the policy anywhere were an offense against the policy everywhere. The South was so committed that its members preferred to secede from the Union and engage in a Civil War before altering the policy.

Psychological and Social Conditioning Process

The national public policy on blacks was structured to incorporate the psychological and social conditioning process for blacks and whites that evolved over the course of American history. Slave holders' absolute power over blacks allowed them to operate an efficient and effective slavery conditioning system. Slave holders constructed internal controls on slaves that minimized the external force necessary to control them. The government provided the environment for the legal framework that allowed the conditioning process to exist and to operate for 250 years.

The slave holders conditioned blacks to serve as good slaves. The effects carried over into the freed black society and affected the general behavior of blacks as a race of people. Table 10 indicates some of the major goals, techniques and strategies employed in the conditioning process that forged a helpless, submissive and manageable labor force.

The process was designed to instill in blacks strict discipline, a sense of inferiority, belief in the slave owners' superior power, acceptance of the owners' standards and a deep sense of a slave's helplessness and dependence. The slave owners strove to cut blacks off from their own history, culture, language and community, and to inculcate white society's value system.[10]

That blacks are still burdened by the legacies of such conditioning speaks to its effectiveness. Though some slaves resisted, the system worked because the majority of slaves gave passive approval and cooperation to the slave holder. That in turn made slavery more profitable and permanent. Had slaves been determined not to cooperate and to sabotage production regardless of the cost to themselves and their families, they undoubtedly would have changed the course of history, and perhaps, spared their descendants centuries of suffering.[11]

Meritorious Manumission

Meritorious manumission was the legal act of freeing a slave for good deeds as defined by the national public policy. Meritorious manumission could be granted to a slave who distinguished himself by saving the life of the white master, inventing a new medicine or snitching on fellow slaves. This was a destructive weapon in the slave holder's arsenal, and a powerful component of the public policy. The importance that whites placed on black informants is emphatically demonstrated by a rare monument that the town of Harper's Ferry erected to honor Hayward Sheppard, a black man, who was killed by the totally committed abolitionist John Brown and his raiding party shortly before the beginning of the Civil War.

Hayward Sheppard was shot dead by John Brown's party when he recognized John Brown and attempted to warn the town that they were there to free the slaves. In grateful recognition for placing the economic interest of the slave holders above the freedom of his own people, the town erected the only monument honoring a black man who could appropriately be described as a "Sambo." Since the black Civil Rights Movement of the late 1960s, the statue has been stored beside the city's major museum and covered with a wooden box.

Meritorious manumission was not only used as an instrument to reward blacks, but it was a device for destroying black unity and race loyalty. It created a very effective informant system. The meritorious manumission policy introduced a strong element of distrust among the slaves and made it more difficult for slaves to organize a revolt. The psychological techniques used were designed to drive wedges between slaves and to train them to trust no one other than the white slave masters. Meritorious manumission was first instituted in Virginia in 1710. According to Peter M. Bergman's, *The Chronological History of the Negro in America*, the technique of meritorious manumission was adopted by all of the colonies:

"The first use in Virginia of the legislative power to break the bonds of a slave was made in this year [1710]. A Negro named Will . . . [was cited for discouraging a slave conspiracy in the colony] and in recognition and reward of the public service, an act was passed conferring freedom upon him. This Act of Freedom read: "The said Negro, Will, is and shall be forever hereafter free from slavery . . . and shall enjoy and have all the liberties, privileges and immunities of or to a free Negro belonging."[12]

The Act of Freedom restored some of the liberties, privileges and immunities that Maryland's public edict took from blacks in 1638. This national discipline policy was so successful that in more than 250 years of slavery, there was not one successful slave revolt in North America. Of the mere 150 to 200 attempted slave insurrections, in nearly every instance, the slave revolts were prematurely exposed. Unfortunately, the informant in nearly every instance was a black person. [13]

Keeping Blacks in a Minority Status

White society has always placed a great deal of importance in maintaining power and control through numerical dominance. Since the public policy stressed keeping blacks in a controlled subordinate state, the national immigration laws, beginning with the first one in 1790, were used as control tools. Immigration policies and laws kept the black population below the white comfort level — usually less than eight percent.

During the 20 years preceding the Revolutionary War, the colonial settlers were extremely fearful of the uncontrolled number of black slaves being shipped into the country. By 1750, the percentage of the total national population that was black had reached nearly a third.

Black slave revolts were on the increase and British military officers encouraged slaves to rise up against the slave owners. Ironically, none did, though they had good opportunities during the Revolutionary War. In 1790, white society's fear of reprisals from blacks prompted the first Congress to enact a law that mandated taking a population census and publishing the results every 10 years. Census data monitored social, economic and political changes according to race and provided the government with a data base for designing public policies.

Table 11 outlines the legal means that were used by whites during the past 200 years to skillfully manipulate social circumstances to maintain

TABLE 11		
Federal and State Actions to Keep Blacks a Numerical Minority		
Total Black Population		**Actions Taken That Reduced Percentage of Black Population**
Year	Percent of U.S. Pop.	
1720	15.20	VA limited increases in blacks
1730	14.00	VA put 5% duty on imported slaves
1740	19.00	Georgians opposed slavery increase
1750	33.00	VA put 20% duty on imported slaves
1760	33.00	All Colonies petitioned to ban slaves
1770	33.00	Continental Congress banned slaves
1780	32.00	Revolutionary War halted slave trade
1790	19.30	First White-Only Naturalization law
1800	19.00	The North passed anti-slavery laws
1810	18.50	International slave trading outlawed
1840	16.00	Influx of white European Immigrants
1860	14.10	Influx Immigrants: Asian/European
1890	11.90	Influx of Immigrants: So. European
1910	11.00	Influx Immigrants: Jewish
1930	9.70	Quota for Black Immigrants: Zero

* Sources: The Immigration Acts of 1790, 1982, 1892, 1907, 1924 and 1936; "The Chronological History of the Negro in America" by Peter Bergman; and the "World Encyclopedia." [14]

the population status quo between them and blacks. The increase in the black population in the 1700s was counteracted by the enactment of the first immigration law in 1790, which sought European whites to reduce the total black population to a range that made whites comfortable — between 5 and 8 percent.

Though blacks had a birthrate that doubled that of whites, U.S. immigration laws annually brought in so many non-black immigrants that the nation's black population was reduced from 33 percent in the late 1700s to less than 10 percent at the beginning of the 1900s. Strict anti-black immigration laws assured the majority white society that blacks would remain a numerical as well as a psychological minority. Though immigration policies at the turn of the 20th century contained language that could have set a black immigration quota of one percent, for all practical purposes, until the late 1960s, immigration was closed to blacks.

As indicated in **Table 11**, whites consistently used a variety of measures to keep the black population below 8 percent. Immigration policies were the major device for keeping both the black percentages under control, especially after the successful Haitian revolt. Following 1790, immigration policies and the massive influx of illegal non-black immigrants drove the black population into the low teens.

There never has been and never will be a black refugee program, no matter how desperate or life-threatening the circumstances are that they are fleeing. The nation's total black population has climbed to 12.4 percent, which is above whites' eight percent comfort range and dangerously close to their take-action 15 percent tipping point. If history is any indicator, the majority society will initiate measures to reduce or increase their control over America's black population at their whim. Ironically, black Africa constitute's 12.4 percent of world population.

In order to develop a plan for self-empowerment, complete with goals and policies, blacks must understand the public policy model and doctrines that were used against them in order to empower white society. The model used by white America was very successful. Just as whites have done, blacks must now unashamedly protect their self-interest, pursue real power and wealth and shape themselves into a politically and economically competitive group in America.

The greatest challenge to black America is to do what blacks have never been permitted to do in the past. Through centuries of slave insurrections, civil rights demonstrations and urban riots, blacks have never had a public policy or clearly identifiable goal. They have not developed a public

Exhibit 13.

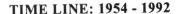

TIME LINE: 1954 - 1992

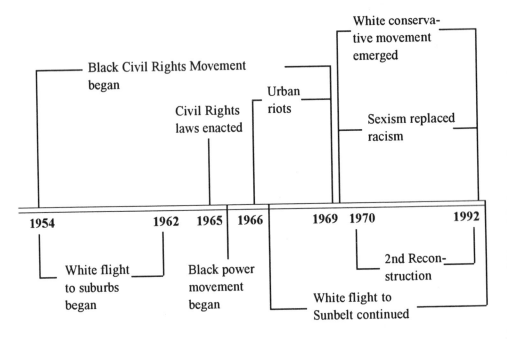

policy on how they are going to deal with racism, where they intend to go as a people and how best to get there. This public policy ought to be broadly disseminated to all blacks and interlinked with all levels of black communities across America. All segments — churches, schools, businesses and community organizations — should be involved in designing strategies and supporting the public policy. Rather than reinventing the wheel, blacks should use white society's model for establishing public policy, because it was very successful.

Conclusion

Black Americans have always been a compassionate and caring people. They should continue to do so. But it is now time for them to put their own interests first, if they are to have any chance of changing their negative living conditions. Black America must develop strategies and programs that serve their best interests and allow them to both develop and protect themselves within a society that historically committed harmful acts against them. Until black obsolescence was reached about 20 years ago, blacks had limited ability to organize, because they lacked capital, leadership and resources and they were restrained by an economic system that still had a use for them. Now that black labor is nonessential and expendable, blacks as a group are vulnerable and expendable.

A national plan for black empowerment should focus on blacks' becoming politically and economically competitive by acquiring increased wealth and resource power. The greatest challenge to black America is to do what it has never done before. Through the centuries of slavery, Jim Crowism, the Civil Rights Movement and the Black Power period, blacks have never had a public policy or racial goals to effectively deal with racism.

Instead of an empowerment plan, new generations of blacks have inherited the vestiges of a failed 1960s strategy. Three major failings deserve highlighting:

• First, black leadership mistakenly believed that by removing Jim Crow symbols that racism would effectively die;

• Second, they thought integration would make them equal and give them control of resources and power;

• Third, they failed to construct long-term institutions, with long-term goals that could transcend generational lines and produce a never-ending flow of competent, well-informed new talent. Young blacks must have a public policy and a plan for direction. All segments of the community— churches, schools, businesses and community organizations — must be involved in formulating and implementing the plan. But the plan must be coordinated nationally by an institute with an intellectual infrastructure.

Modelling the methods used by whites, blacks must develop an accountability system to make sure that all blacks support the goals of the plan. Blacks will have to be equally as determined and committed to public policy on black self-empowerment as white society has been to public policy on the use of blacks. Blacks must be willing to apply social sanctions and other penalties against those who violate the public policy for blacks.

The black empowerment plan must be based upon a vision of vigor-ously competing in a changing world. The plan must go beyond the dream of equality and integration, which hangs before them like a carrot on a stick.

8

Becoming Politically and Economically Competitive in America

"The gods see what is to come, wise men see what is coming, and ordinary men see what has come." — Apolonius [1]

A new era is dawning, bringing dramatic changes across the world. Within the next 20 years, these changes will place black people in the midst of one of the most important and turbulent periods in the history of mankind. There will be accelerated technological changes, unprecedented political upheaval, massive global population migration and merging national political economies. These global changes will produce new anxieties and uncertainties. There will be a marked increase in ethnic and racial hostility as racial groups compete for power, wealth, and the control of resources.

Throughout mankind's history, competitive struggles between ethnic and racial groups have regulated their populations and established a relative ranking of power among them. In power struggles, the strongest survive and prosper; the weak or noncompetitive groups disappear or live to serve the strong.

Black America is approaching the threshold of the 21st century as a noncompetitive, socioeconomic disaster. It is ill-prepared to compete with other racial and ethnic groups. Contrary to popular belief, blacks have made only relatively slight political and economic progress. Their quality of life has improved only because the general conditions of white society improved.

The crucial question now concerns not civil rights, voting rights, affirmative action or even equal opportunity. Instead, the question is whether or not black Americans are ready to face the socioeconomic realities that confront them. Do blacks understand what will happen to them if they do not pull themselves up by the year 2013? Do they understand that they are at risk of becoming a permanent underclass in America?

Developing political and economic forces do not bode well for blacks. Black America's frail state makes it vulnerable to international and domestic developments that could converge and do great injury to blacks around the year 2013. Conditions for blacks will be made more serious by:

• The hardening sentiments of the next white generation, which surveys predict will be more indifferent and harbor stronger anti-black attitudes;

• The merging of international superpower economies that will force blacks to compete with better prepared and united groups from around the globe;

• Higher unemployment and less public assistance resulting from downsizing and privatization in government services;

• Continued deterioration of black families, churches and other institutions;

• The loss of status of blacks from a majority-minority to a minority-minority (The tide of Hispanic and Asian immigrants should reach 81 million and 46 million respectively by the year 2013.);

• Deteriorating social and economic conditions that will spur a general increase of criminal activity with a major portion associated with blacks;

• The continuing impact of a 350-year-old national public policy on the use of blacks that basically made blacks obsolete three decades ago.

Developing Black Empowerment Strategies

Now is the time for black America to start developing strategies for becoming a more competitive group. The purpose of this book is twofold: firstly, to identify the historical genesis of white wealth and power and black poverty and powerlessness; secondly, based upon conclusions from historical analysis, to use white society as a model and recommend strategies that blacks can adopt in order to gain competitive wealth and power.

In this chapter, various strategies for improving the quality of life for black Americans are discussed, followed by analyses and recommendations. These strategies will demand from blacks a more focused and self-serving set of priorities and behavior patterns. They are absolutely necessary in order to give blacks real power.

Strategy I: Leadership

Humans, like all orders of life, seek leadership and find it naturally. But in America, white society has been the proactive institutional leader and black America has reactively followed with new leaders who arise in response to each new issue or event. The power and resource disparity between blacks and whites has caused blacks to have different standards for selecting, developing and recognizing leadership. Beyond the fact that there are numerous definitions of leadership, the most important factor in examining black leadership is the understanding that power and leadership are relationships based upon socioeconomic motives and needs.

Leaders are individuals who can induce others to cooperatively work towards certain goals that represent the values and motivations of both the leader and the followers. To fully understand the nature of leadership requires understanding the essence of power because leadership is a special form of power. The goal of forming new black leadership is to acquire for blacks, in this lifetime, economic justice, wealth, power and equal enjoyment of the rewards and benefits of the American dream.

Analysis:

• 1. In a competitive society, there are no mechanisms to give voice to unorganized and inarticulate groups. Mainstream society tends to oppose extra measures to include such groups. White society develops and conducts its substantive training on many fronts simultaneously within government, academia, the media and corporate and other institutional structures. They manipulate and manage these entities so that they will reflect white society's wishes and attitudes about all major socioeconomic issues, especially race. Blacks have limited access to and control of established institutions.

Black leadership too often does not spring forth from systems of leadership training, but rather results from a call into community service by a higher power to resolve a particular dilemma. It follows that the calling is answered usually from the ranks of the most independent sectors of black communities — churches, small business operators, and community agencies. Most individuals from these organizations have served their communities without the benefit of broad and competitive organizational resources behind them.

• 2. Lacking access to comprehensive data, talent banks, and well-trained organizational leadership, black America has no formal way to assess past accomplishments and potential leaders. It is difficult to distinguish between benevolent and self-serving leadership. Aspiring leaders, on the other hand, are sometimes forced to substitute rhetoric for research and emotionalism for planning. Those who are most charismatic and eloquent are elevated to leadership status. But to survive within their own communities, these leaders must remain constantly visible and involved with all levels of the black community, while being exposed to adversarial elements (negative press, conservative government policies, radical groups, etc.) outside of the black community.

• 3. Many blacks who are capable of leadership lack the tools of leadership — access to organizational power, media, and money. Blacks who accept the mantle of leadership often fail to significantly change the conditions of black America because they are reactive rather than proactive, single-issue or event-oriented and weak on long-term planning. After nearly 400 years, blacks have still not developed a comprehensive national public policy or master plan. Nor have they coordinated efforts between black communities and organizations to move black America toward self-sufficiency and empowerment.

• 4. The dream of black-white integration caused many blacks to abandon their interest in maintaining a strong sense of community or to know, trust, and be responsible for their neighbor's well-being. Many in the black middle class have joined in the tail-end of white flight to the suburbs and have failed to reconnect with their old communities, culture, and racial realities. Responding to the integration process, black civil rights leaders have sought to accommodate and access institutionalized white power and wealth, rather than seek to establish their own.

• 5. Black communities tend to seek out one leader or messiah at a time. Most often such an individual is the most visible person rather than the most able or committed. This lack of self-imposed standards for black leadership makes it easy for white society to use its powers to anoint leaders within black communities. Unwittingly or not, this method protects the interest of white society and allows it to manipulate which black leaders will be publicly acknowledged, respected or rewarded. Institutional powers are used to discredit or remove aggressive blacks, often labelling them as radical or offensive.

• 6. The world is rapidly changing, yet black leadership seems frozen in time. Forces focused on alleviating the symptoms rather than the causes of racism impede meaningful change. Too many black leaders continue to read from political and economic scripts that are hopelessly shortsighted in addressing the myriad of fast-approaching domestic and international changes. While keeping their eyes on the integration prize, black hopes, families and communities are being destroyed by rampant social pathology.

Blacks witness the steady decline in the quality of their lives and exhort that things have got to get better. They borrow from the conservative white agenda and blame the problems on the symptoms and the victims, rather then the systemic causes. Too many black leaders have the heart and commitment, but lack the vision and power.

• 7. Tomorrow's pluralistic and increasingly competitive society will demand black leadership that will neither grow old nor be bought off or assassinated. The national public policy on the use of blacks, by design, has kept blacks leaderless and weak in their pursuit of power and wealth. New black leadership must be just as devoted to achieving self-sustaining black communities within 10 years or less. Achieving this goal requires black leaders with vision, not dreams. The mind's eye of the new black leadership must be wide open.

Recommendations

• 1. Unlike a dream, the mechanisms of self-empowerment will not materialize on their own accord. New organizational leadership must arise and become the force behind a collective, national movement that will provide a unifying framework that all existing black organizations can use to harness their potential, formulate a common direction and prevent them from working at cross-purposes.

• 2. A new kind of black leadership institute is needed to buttress the current scarcity of black individual and organizational leadership. Blacks must establish a think tank with an intellectual infrastructure that focuses exclusively on formulating national policy blueprints for solutions to the multitude of conditions crippling black America. This institute should be an independent, nonpartisan, tax-exempt research foundation. It should provide proactive research and promote comprehensive prescriptive strategies for achieving black political and economic self-empowerment. It should be distinguished from other think tanks by the activism that should flow from its research, and focus on those issues that are common to all blacks, regardless of economic, social, or educational differences.

• 3. A national public policy and plan should go hand in hand with the training of new black leadership. All levels of black America need to understand how they would benefit as individuals and as a race in terms of wealth, power, peoplehood, and general improvement in the quality of life. Without black America's energetic participation, directed by new black leadership, the national obsolescence and marginal existence of blacks will continue.

• 4. New black leadership must use technological advances to create a national information network that could be designed to communicate with constituents and to broaden educational, scientific, economic, and technological cooperation among and within black communities. Data and research developed by institutional leadership could be accessible to decision-making blacks and others in the private and public sectors.

• 5. The new black leadership must develop a strategy for blacks to compete in domestic and international markets with the majority and other minority communities. Empowerment goals and timetables must be established and promoted throughout every black community. Issues and events ought to be prioritized and focused through a public policy template designed to produce what is best for blacks. A public policy template would not only simplify the decision making process, but would provide structure and ideological continuity.

• 6. The new black leadership must be able to discern and counter the new so-called color blind or race-neutral racism, which does nothing more than maintain the status quo. New racism hides the dominant society's indifference towards blacks by focusing the nation's attention on non-issues, such as sexism, minority parity, sexual preferences, privatization of public services, crime abatement, quotas, and affirmative action backlashes. These issues distract black leaders into wheel-spinning activities that diffuse and drain the black race's limited resources. They must understand and forcefully counter the political ploys of white conservative think tanks, which constantly develop and promote new code words for racism.

Strategy II: Wealth and Capital Formation

Centuries of compulsory black pauperism have created a power imbalance between whites and blacks. Dominant white society possesses nearly 100 percent of the wealth and the tools for accessing and amassing wealth. Dr. Martin Luther King, Jr., recognized the importance of the relationship between wealth and racial equality late in his career. He told the Southern Christian Leadership Council: "American society must have a radical redistribution of wealth and economic power to achieve even a rough form of social justice. We must recognize that we can't solve our problems now until there is a radical redistribution of economic and political power."[2] Until the wealth imbalance is significantly reduced black-white racial strife will continue unabated.

Analysis

• 1. The fall of the last great West African empire in the 15th century gave rise to the wholesale exploitation of the continent's natural and human capital by European and Arab traders. Black labor and Africa's mineral wealth became investment commodities as America's wealth increased primarily as a result of slave labor. As slaves and cheap labor, blacks were classified as valuable commodities that gave land its value. Land was the second major producer of white wealth but it did not surpass blacks until well after the Civil War. Until that time, wealth from black labor was the engine that drove world civilization for nearly 300 years.

Beginning in Europe and spreading into the New World, wealth produced by blacks fueled banking and industrial revolutions, generated new forms of government and economics, transferred massive amounts of wealth across racial, ethnic, and national boundaries, and fomented numerous civil wars. Black labor essentially fed, clothed, and enriched nations all around the world. Ironically, black-created wealth was used to sustain slavery, Jim Crowism, and provide an economic safety net for European, Hispanic and Asian refugees. Blacks have remained producers, but not possessors of wealth, even now, as the world progresses towards the threshold of the 21st century.

• 2. The U.S. government established and maintained preferential treatment laws, policies, and programs that gave and preserved wealth, power, and a privileged status for European whites. The government's preferential treatment programs and policies aggressively helped 16 generations of European whites to acquire free or cheap land, black labor, business and employment opportunities, and other forms of government assistance. At the same time, government-supported laws and customs denied blacks access to the same resources and prohibited them from competing with whites in education, labor, professional trades, and businesses.[3]

Without government assistance, black enslavement would not have been possible. Without black slave labor to make the New World productive, land would have had little value and the United States would not have developed into an economic and military superpower.[4]

• 3. Through inheritance, accumulated wealth is passed from one family's generation to the next. Wealth acquired by white families, based on expropriation of black labor and land ownership passed onto succeeding generations of whites until the original sources of wealth became hidden by time. With the conclusion of slavery, dominant white society increasingly turned away from blacks and towards alternative means of producing wealth. Much of this wealth was converted into corporate stocks, public bonds, and banking certificates, which were government-regulated and protected. The percentage of white wealth has remained unchanged from generation to generation. Those who inherited wealth will most likely remain wealthy and powerful.

• 4. Controlling less than two percent of the nation's wealth — primarily in the form of a primary residence, automobile, and saving accounts — blacks have little wealth to pass on. Due to the minuscule number of black businesses, few blacks ever inherit a business. Discriminatory policies within the banking industry, insurance industry and mortgage companies have impeded blacks' economic progress and the acquisition of wealth. Marginal incomes force most blacks into apartment renting or public housing tenancy, which provides neither tax shelters nor equity for future black generations to inherit. In essence, black heirs are likely to inherit permanent poverty and an unpaid debt.

• 5. For hundreds of years, whites have been attracted to black culture and music. Today, expropriated black culture and art forms are generically called American pop culture. Popular music is a worldwide industry with a $100 billion annual revenue, but blacks' monetary gains from their contributions to the industry are relatively minuscule. Even in the largest category of black music, Rhythm and Blues, blacks receive revenues of less than two percent of the annual $54 billion gross.

• 6. Traditional black history courses focus on the achievements of individual blacks instead of presenting information in a complete context. This teaching approach fails to discuss the circumstances or tell the story of the contributions that blacks have made as a group to this country's and the world's economic development. By and large, neither blacks nor whites know about blacks' full role in the development of the New World.

• 7. The American government owes its black citizens for the "Black Holocaust" that has lasted nearly 400 years as a result of governmental policy, decree and sanction. This includes the premature deaths of millions of blacks, the expropriation of black labor, the psychological and socioeconomic damage under slavery and Jim Crowism, and the assignment of blacks to a poverty underclass. White society in general, and government in particular, still owe blacks the 40 acres and a mule that were explicitly promised by the U.S. Congress, President Andrew Johnson and General William Sherman in 1865.

Providing reparations for blacks would not establish a precedent, for the U.S. government has a history of making restitution to American Indians and the Japanese. The German government is still making restitution to Jews who survived death and slavery in Nazi concentration camps.[5] The German government, through the Jewish Claim Conference, has allegedly paid nearly $55 billion to approximately 50,000 Holocaust survivors (more than $1 million per survivor), according to written reports.

Similarly, in 1991, the Japanese Recovery Act authorized the United States government to make restitution payments to Japanese Americans, who the United States relocated to internment camps during World War II. Reparations to Japan and Germany began immediately following the end of World War II. To rebuild the economies of the defeated Japanese and German peoples, America and the allied nations paid more than $14 billion in reparations.

The relocated Japanese were not enslaved, murdered, castrated or statutorily exploited. Yet, for their four years of inconvenience, indignity and material loss, the United States paid each Japanese claimant $20,000.

The Japanese government apologized to Asian women who were forced into prostitution during World War II. Neither blacks nor black African nations have gone to war with America or England, but they have yet to receive apologies or reparations from either nation.

• 8. A disproportionate number of Asian and Hispanic immigrants establish businesses and function as conduits for removing money from the black community. These merchants do not usually hire blacks, identify with, or live in black communities. They charge higher prices for their goods and do not patronize black-owned businesses.

Recommendations

• 1. It is time for blacks to make acquiring reparations from the American government a major national issue. Reparation payments should be directed into black communities in the form of infrastructure improvements, business and industry development loans, educational grants and stipends and expanded public services to repair the socioeconomic damages that the dominant society and government have inflicted on 16 generations of black Americans.

• 2. An immigrant fee should be charged to all new immigrants and channeled into an investment fund earmarked for the economic revitalization and industrial development of black ghettos. America remains the premiere destination for legal and illegal immigrants all around the world. It is clear that the government must stop the tide of immigrants seeking the benefits of first class citizenship who have neither paid any dues nor contributed towards building the quality of life they are seeking. Immigrants should no longer be given a "free lunch" upon the granting of citizenship. It is criminally unfair for generation after generation of European, Asian, and Hispanic immigrants to be brought into this country and allowed to enjoy benefits historically denied blacks.

Directing immigration fees into an investment fund would not be a novel initiative. The 1990 Immigration Act allows 10,000 visas each year for foreign investors who invest between $500,000 and $3 million in an enterprise that provides employment for at least 10 full-time U.S. workers. Blacks could use the Act as a model for establishing an immigrant investment fund to industrialize black communities and improve its economic conditions. With small modifications, the visas could be issued to investors who put money into black communities. Smaller immigration fees could also be established and directed towards black reparation programs.

The economic justice that would be inherent in such fees would not only be the repayment to black communities for its expropriated labor. The fees would also cushion the new immigrants' drain on social services, establish common ground between the immigrants and blacks and repair the economic drain that these ethnic businesses cause in black communities.

The investment fund strategy would also provide training and investment loans for blacks to start businesses. Furthermore, just as ethnic immigrants are using revenues generated from their black-oriented businesses in order to pay transportation costs of their relatives and friends from their homelands to America, blacks could use investment funds to cover the cost of bringing in and hiring immigrants of African descent. In fighting for such measures, blacks could make a national issue out of the racial injustice within American immigration policies.

• 3. There is no historical justification for providing affirmative action relief for groups such as Asians, Hispanics, the disabled, gays, abused wives or senior citizens. People in these categories haven't suffered throughout American history. Blacks must refocus the national agenda on race, then extricate themselves from the catchall category of "minority." As the dominant society's public policy on blacks continues to make blacks obsolete, government will increasingly function as the "drum major" for benign neglect towards black Americans.

Unless blacks step forward to challenge the government to amend its policies, affirmative action in name only, will be used to perpetuate the sham. There will be no affirmative action efforts that solely address the historical wrongs that still hound blacks. Instead, affirmative action programs will be nothing more than empty shells for addressing the needs of ambiguous amorphous groupings.

Affirmative action provisions should be meted out on a ranking or scale that determines the most needy and the most worthy. In addition, public policy remedies must be restructured for the narrow purpose of redress to blacks. The justification for such measures is this: Hispanics, white women and other minorities were not statutorily enslaved, Jim Crowed or racially segregated.

Redress should be directed towards specific, injured groups and not to non-injured classes, who now seek to benefit from the affirmative action programs that were originally designed to address the historical suffering of blacks. Qualifications for reparation-type programs should include a scale to measure the degree and extent of historical oppression as well as the magnitude of contribution the potential reparation recipients made towards the development of the nation. Applications for affirmative action or reparation benefits should also include a scale to both assess the extent to which applicants sustained statutory abuses by the government and measure the length of the potential recipients' residence in this country.

Strategy III: Wealth and Group Economics

Blacks are America's most impoverished population group but, when considered as a nation within a nation, they could generate disposable income to sustain black economies. Black America has approximately $280 billion annually in disposable income, but as a group they remain impoverished because they have failed to create their own internal economy, and therefore, they do not retain their capital within their communities. To survive in the rapidly approaching pluralistic society, blacks must create a black economy. To develop economically, black dollars must bounce or exchange hands eight-to-10 times before leaving the black community. Contained and recirculated dollars within black communities would stimulate business, create employment opportunities and expand tax bases.

Analysis

• 1. Besides correcting the classic problems surrounding the insufficient number and high failure of black businesses (lack of capital, management skills, experience), two other social factors impede the establishment and effective operation of black businesses in black communities: the withholding of support by whites and blacks; and the lack of a vertical network of supportive businesses (discussed in more detail in **Chapter 9**). It is difficult and in many instances impossible for black businesses to survive when both whites and blacks are boycotting them.

Regardless of any business know-how and capital a black business person might have, without a customer base the business cannot thrive. White society avoids doing business with blacks, however blacks now boycott black businesses also as they pursue the integration dream. Boycotting activities intensified after the 1954 desegregation decision.

Black businesses that survive boycotting have been hamstrung by the lack of supportive, vertical black businesses within their communities. It is very difficult for black retail businesses to be competitive when they are wholly dependent upon non-black distributors, manufacturers, warehousers, processors, and wholesalers for their products. Surveys have shown that these up-line businesses charge blacks 25-to-50 percent more for poorer quality merchandise that is delivered on an irregular and unpredictable schedule.

With overpriced, poor quality merchandise, black businesses cannot be competitive. Such conditions reconfirm black customers' inclination to look for the products from whites, believing that "the white man's ice is colder."

Many successful black businesses have survived by politically or economically "passing" in white communities. They got ahead of the customers' march to the suburbs by building their businesses in the suburbs and catering to non-black customers. By locating their businesses outside of the black community, they hoped to capture some portion of the white and black customers who routinely boycott black businesses and spend their disposable income in white communities. By appearing as non-black-owned companies, they became independent of black communities. These businesses are permitted to operate in white communities as long as they do so in a noncompetitive or nonthreatening fashion.

Should it become known that they are successful and black-owned, they would be in for serious problems with whites. Thus, black businesses that are totally dependent upon the larger white community are guests who exist on borrowed time.

• 2. The Doctrine of Unequal Exchange continues to be an effective strategy that whites use to gain access to black wealth. Blacks annually transfer their disposable income into white communities and receive little more than consumer satisfaction in return. Blacks currently retain about five percent of their total gross income. Of this five percent, approximately three percent is spent with non-black merchants, who take it out of black neighborhoods. Only two percent remains with black merchants. It is impossible for black communities to survive off of two percent of its annual income.

• 3. By spending their income with non-black businesses, blacks deprive their communities of a tax base for providing human services and jobs. In a capitalistic country, human worth is valued in terms of ownership and control of wealth, so blacks dis-empower themselves when they don't spend money with other blacks.

• 4. Employers, business owners and investors have five times the net worth of employees. Blacks in general had a greater number of businesses per 1,000 persons at the turn of the century than they have today. To turn this around, blacks as a group must employ discipline, and cooperation. They must utilize the principles of group economics and group politics. To improve the wealth base of black America, there must be an increase in the number and size of successful black-owned businesses and industries.

• 5. Currently, white businesses have a lock on natural resources throughout the world. It is important, therefore, that blacks pursue mutually supportive business ventures with blacks of other nations, especially resource-rich Africa, which represents the best source for black Americans to secure raw materials for vertical industrial development. A vertical black business structure (see **Chapter 9**) would include a network of linked businesses, from retail and manufacturing to the control of the resources. With the cooperation of government, blacks and black African nations could develop vertical industries. African nations have access to natural resources, but lack the professional middle-class and surplus disposable capital needed to capitalize on natural resources. Black Americans have the disposable income and the professional middle-class, but lack access to natural resources.

• 6. Compared to Asian, Hispanic and white communities, black communities appear to be the only ones that are unregulated and uncontrolled by its own residents. For example, white communities have councils or boards that establish and enforce community construction and business standards. In Japan, most communities vote on whether or not to accept foreign businesses into their communities. In the various ethnic communities in America, cultural barriers often establish standards and restrict business opportunities. In 1992, Cubans in Miami, Florida, publicly told Arab merchants that they could not establish businesses in the Cuban communities of Little Havana and Hialeah. The Arab merchants experienced no such difficulties in opening stores in a black community in Coconut Grove.

• 7. The Civil Rights Movement succeeded in giving blacks a boost in togetherness and increasing their access to white power. But, the movement produced horrific and unanticipated negative results as well. The integration process sapped the financial, intellectual, and political cohesiveness of black communities and organizations. The remaining black institutions — families, churches, and businesses — have grown progressively weaker. The integration process tore apart previously united communities. As the more successful and affluent blacks moved to the suburbs, the neighborhoods they left behind became more dysfunctional, disorganized, and leaderless.

Racial integration is the enemy of unity because it requires the integrating group to be subsumed, weakened and scattered as a minority in a society in which the majority rules. Mobility patterns strongly suggest that blacks are the only nonwhite ethnic group that aspires to integrate with the white society. The second generation of European ethnics, Hispanics, and Asians have the option of assimilating, not integrating.

Studies demonstrate that white flight from neighborhoods and schools begins when the percentage of blacks exceeds 5 to 8 percent of the population in those areas. If the maximum percentage of blacks that whites will voluntarily accept is 5 to 8 percent, what happens to the balance of the black population that cannot integrate? Or, on the other side of the question, what is the impact of the integration process on the social and psychological well-being of the 5 to 8 percent of blacks who successfully integrate into the dominant white society? When they abandon the larger black community to live as a fragmented, powerless minority in the dominant society, has a form of social-political suicide been committed?

Recommendations

• 1. To achieve self-sufficiency, blacks must master the principles of capitalism and group economics. The window of opportunity for achieving this goal will pass within the next decade. Civil rights, social rights and integration cannot produce group wealth and power.

• 2. Vertical integration of industries and businesses is a design that has the potential to create numerous individual, but linked businesses, and therefore should become the basis for an economic development strategy for blacks. Vertically integrated businesses should be constructed around consumer products that blacks buy in a disproportionate number or in areas where blacks are disproportionately represented in the production of the product.

For example, blacks are high consumers of seafood, compact discs, tapes and records, electronic equipment, expensive athletic wear, leather goods, distilled liquors, and movies. They are disproportionately represented in musical entertainment, education, and professional sports. All of these areas could represent opportunities for vertical businesses structures for blacks.

In a vertically integrated business structure blacks would control the businesses required on each level of the overall business structure, from manufacturing to retailing. Vertical integration provides business opportunities for warehousers, wholesalers, shippers, distributorships, truckers, dealers, insurance carriers, and other supportive businesses. The interrelatedness or vertical connection of the businesses establishes a network that protects the businesses from competitors, while guaranteeing an economically empowering flow of wealth via the services and products.

• 3. Although the size of the black consumer market is limited, that is not necessarily an insurmountable barrier to building businesses. Markets can be expanded to achieve economies of scale by exporting products from black communities to surrounding communities. With a strong sense of a national community, a product produced in one black community could be competitively produced for domestic or markets in black foreign nations.

• 4. Vertical business within black communities could reduce high underemployment and unemployment rates by hiring black people, enhancing their communities' tax base, and increasing their group's wealth and disposable income. As previously discussed, there is enough capital within the black community to support businesses. In addition, black businesses would not have to market themselves to blacks only. They simply need to have a solid base of black customers, just as all other ethnic and racial groups provide solid and dependable customer bases for their industries.

• 5. Black leadership must find opportunities for black businesses to gain access to raw materials, if the concept of vertical integration is to be viable. Since established white industries have controls on most natural resources and raw materials, blacks should focus their energies on black African or Third World nations. Africa represents both another market for expansion and a new source of natural resources that could fuel black business in America.

Blacks should seek business relationships with various independent African countries, primarily in terms of securing competitive control of resources for new vertically integrated industries. Blacks could then start businesses based upon new, valuable resources, such as hardwood from Cameroon for a vertical chain of wood milling and furniture manufacturing, rubber for an automobile tire company, or diamonds and gold for jewelry and industrial use.

• 6. Black municipal governments should establish a trade policy between black communities and white suburbs. It is not fair trade for white suburbs to simply ship products into black communities, but never purchase products produced within those black communities. Fair trade policies and practices with white suburbs should go hand-in-hand with establishing vertical businesses and industries. A trade policy will become more important as the number of industries within the inner cities increases.

Strategy IV: Black Underemployment and Unemployment

Black men, women, and children were kidnapped and transported all over the world for one purpose: to work and produce white wealth. Until the mid-20th century, they represented America's true and senior labor system. In nearly every instance, the white lower class functioned as a management class over blacks, though in modern times they referred to themselves as the working, blue collar class. The lower white class supervised blacks in jobs ranging from picking cotton and digging ditches to working on the assembly lines of large automotive plants. The value of black labor has always been controlled by the white community. Since blacks had few employment alternatives, they were relegated to the dirtiest and hardest work. Blacks' high rates of underemployment and unemployment were reflections of their expendability. They lived by the rule of being the last hired and the first fired.

Analysis

• 1. Capitalistic democracies have historically accepted a certain level of unemployment as a necessary public good and permitted businesses to use unemployment as a device for maintaining low wages. The acceptable range of overall unemployment is typically five percent. While recent white unemployment rates rarely exceed five percent, the National Urban League's Hidden Unemployment Index estimates that the jobless rate among black adults is four to five times higher than the jobless rate among white adults.

Meanwhile, more than 50 percent of eligible black youths can't find jobs. Though this systematic black unemployment criminalizes blacks and renders them noncompetitive, neither the government nor larger society has demonstrated a willingness to use their vast resources to eliminate the causative factors.

• 2. Over the years, blacks have consistently asked for, but seldom received, employment assistance from government. Following their 250 years of full employment as slaves, blacks asked that the government give each black slave family 40 acres and a mule. Government responded by reshackling them into nearly another century of semi-slavery, called sharecropping. In the dying years of the Civil Rights protest period, blacks held national demonstrations in support of the Humphrey-Hawkins Full-Employment Bill. A conservative backlash, led by major corporations and politicians, killed the bill by claiming that the government, not the private sector, would have to hire blacks. Approximately 70 percent of black college graduates are employed in government, because there is no black business infrastructure capable of absorbing them.

• 3. Entrenched high unemployment is a direct result of the fragmentation within the black community. They lack the resources and commitment to create employment opportunities and they don't spend their disposable incomes wisely. Even if they had full employment, it would not alleviate the myriad of problems facing them. Wealth is the primary problem. Employment is secondary. There is a big difference between having a job and having wealth. Jobs are not designed to create wealth. They are intended to keep employees one payday away from the poorhouse and to satisfy workers' basic consumer needs. Real wealth is accumulated via investment returns and ownership profits.

• 4. The 20 years between 1969 and 1989 saw the introduction of controversial affirmative action policies, supposedly to compensate black employees for past discrimination in the job market. Conservatives vehemently opposed those policies, charging that affirmative action unfairly advantaged and enriched blacks at the expense of whites. However, statistics suggest that affirmative action brought few real changes to the position of black employees. Between 1969 to 1989, black annual income increased by only $22 relative to white income. Moreover, from 1979 to 1989, overall black income increased by only one dollar.

• 5. Low-paying, minimum wage jobs are more attractive to immigrants than blacks. Immigrants see these low-wage jobs as temporary stops on their way to a better life. It is a way of paying their dues. Blacks have paid nearly four centuries of dues. But they never had reason to be optimistic that a minimum wage job would lead them up the economic ladder. For them, those jobs were not temporary; they were permanent. Minimum wage jobs for blacks are a form of labor exploitation, a waste of brain power and another cause of low self-respect.

• 6. Limited employment opportunity is a major difference between black and white communities. The lack of private sector employment opportunity within black communities forces blacks to seek income from government jobs, welfare assistance and sometimes criminal activities. All of these sources are condemned by conservatives. Yet, these same conservatives frequently resist policy changes that would create private sector alternatives in black American communities. Moreover, conservatives are the primary exploiters of government and the general public through their immoral and unfair business practices.

• 7. The lack of employment opportunities in black America is not a temporary aberration. It is permanent and endemic. It must be resolved by black America, because neither the government nor the larger society has incentive to create employment opportunities for blacks.

• 8. The black community suffers from brain drain. The best-trained blacks depend upon whites to hire them. Though historically they have had very little choice in employment options, it becomes racially self-defeating for blacks to devote their lives to professional careers in white businesses, in white communities, or in white-controlled government agencies. The three-century-old national public policy on the use of blacks stipulated that blacks would serve as a labor force for creating wealth and comfort for whites.

Little has changed, because blacks are still cooperating with the policy. The concern that should be foremost on the minds of blacks is, "Who's taking care of black businesses within the black community, while the best black brain power is taking care of the business of government and the larger community?"

Recommendations

• 1. Blacks must accept that nobody owes blacks jobs or full employment. Blacks must assume the burden of providing employment for their own people. The burden rests upon the shoulders of the black business community and those businesses located within black communities. Discrimination in hiring practices of businesses within the black community has long been a problem, especially with Hispanic and Asian merchants. These groups have cultures that stress hiring from their own group. They often hire people from their homeland, even for menial labor, before hiring blacks. That can remain their choice, but the black community must insist that these ethnic merchants reinvest in the community.

• 2. Blacks should initiate measures to halt the brain drain from their communities by creating employment, business opportunities, and incentives within black communities to attract and keep the best black minds within the community. With appropriate employment and business opportunities, the best black brain power could devote time, energies and intellect to taking care of black communities.

The handful of blacks working on Wall Street or in corporate boardrooms does not represent group progress. These advances may help individual blacks, but do little for blacks as a race. If a large number of blacks who received business training sought to develop their own businesses in black communities, rather than seeking to integrate into white businesses, the wealth of blacks in America would expand beyond its stagnant two percent range. And it is likely that these businesses would be larger and more powerful than the mom-and-pop operations that currently make up the majority of black businesses.

Strategy V: Black and White Psycho-social Behavior Patterns

Blacks have been acculturated, domesticated and integrated, but never assimilated into white society. Assimilation is the process by which a minority group learns the values and norms of the dominant culture and is then absorbed into the dominant society. After 400 years, blacks have not been absorbed. The legacy of separation remains very strong. It is unlikely that whites will ever freely absorb blacks, regardless of how blacks conform to the cultural standards of white America.

If conformity and acculturation were key criteria for black assimilation, then white society would have absorbed blacks years ago. Slavery and Jim Crowism were socializing and conditioning processes that stripped blacks of their sense of humanity and self-sufficiency. Blacks responded to these conditioning processes by developing behavior patterns that reflected a unique black personality. They were systematically rewarded for displaying behaviors that conformed to white standards, especially those that helped whites maintain their power and privileged positions. For example, black slaves were rewarded for helping white slave holders to maintain control over slaves by informing on any activities among their fellow slaves that might have endangered whites.

Though it may be uncomfortable for some to acknowledge, there are some blacks who are still "selling black America" for personal gain. They clothe themselves in the uniform of the day — sexism, conservatism, and various other "isms." But in each instance, among such blacks the welfare of the larger black community comes last, if it is considered at all.

Analysis

• 1. Humans have enslaved other humans for a variety of reasons as a result of indebtedness, religious differences and military defeats. Skin color was never a major factor until around the 14th century. Color entered the enslavement equation from two opposing directions.

Firstly, the Mamelukes, who were the last known group of whites to be enslaved, revolted forcefully and vengefully against the Arabs and generally signalled an end to white enslavement. When the white indentured servant system started several hundred years later, it was managed via contract and mutual agreement, with limited terms, no punishment systems, and bonus compensation at the close of the contracts.

Secondly, Arabs imposed slavery, the Islamic faith, and the Swahili language on black Africans to get access and control of their wealth and natural resources. Arabs began enslaving and trading blacks around 800 A.D. According to various sources, Arabs are still using color as the basis for enslavement and are still slave trading in the countries of Saudi Arabia, Mauritania, Sierra Leone, Libya and Sudan.

• 2. Black slavery was totally unlike any other form of slavery. Various Asian and Hispanic nations were colonized, but the inhabitants were never animalized, commercialized and traded as slaves in international markets. Although blacks failed the lesson that the Mamelukes taught the world, the American Indian did not. When European whites attempted to enslave the American Indians, the Indians simply refused to perform the role of slaves. Only blacks were branded as slaves for the world, and the explanation for that must be more than whites' loathing of black skin color.

There were East Indians, Moors and Arabs who were just as dark, if not darker, than West African blacks, yet they were not enslaved. In the opinion of this writer, blacks alone were branded as slaves primarily because:

• Africa remained disunited as a result of tribal structures in Sub-Saharan Africa, while their natural wealth made all tribes targets of hostile foreigners

• Sub-Saharan Africans alone would submit to brutal slavery and a perpetual subordinate status. After centuries of oppression, blacks have yet to come together as a strong community and conduct self-empowerment activities that would free them from oppression. Instead, blacks have such little self respect that they continue to pursue integration, a process that fragments and weakens them.

• 3. The rewards of meritorious manumission, the law that rewarded black slaves who sold out their brothers and sisters, has created a legacy that is still with us. Blacks have no balancing social devices that punish those blacks who sacrifice members of the race for their own personal advantage. Nor do blacks have a device for rewarding whites who extend themselves to assist blacks. Black America is void of social accountability policies and enforcement devices.

• 4. It is highly unlikely that white conservatives will permit government to assist blacks, because true social changes would give blacks access to all of the resources and privileges enjoyed by whites as well as cultivate the potential for black empowerment. Such a transfer or sharing of resources would create new labor, business and political competition that would threaten the middle-class status of whites. Consequently, recorded history indicates that blacks should not count on the goodwill or moral obligation of white society.

Since blacks made marginal gains in income and educational achievements in the 1960s, whites have grown increasingly callous and indifferent to blacks and their problems. They urge blacks to heal themselves, yet simultaneously block access to the resources necessary for such healing. They resist any form of civil rights legislation for blacks, even when the impact of the legislation would be minimal. A survey by the American Jewish Committee indicated that even in 1990, most white Americans believe that any changes in blacks' present conditions would be too much and too fast. They oppose any kind of government-sponsored social engineering that is designed to redistribute wealth to blacks or relieve the oppressive conditions of black America.

• 5. Most whites have yet to understand that their current privileged status resulted from government assistance and black exploitation. It is easier to believe that they acquired their status as a result of hard work and natural social ordering. Dominant culture has taught them that blacks, by nature and desire, are where they are supposed to be in the human social order. Though all whites do not have wealth and political powers, those who do not take comfort in their belief that those who have power will exercise it in their favor at the expense of blacks.

• 6. Many whites harbor subconscious fears that blacks will acquire power and become economically competitive. Many whites appear to harbor a strong dislike for blacks, though most cannot offer a rational justification for their feelings. These feelings are so deep that for centuries, whites have allowed into their society immigrants from countries that were formerly or are currently hostile towards Americans. Surveys indicate that as much as 50 percent of adult whites prefer not to have blacks in their neighborhoods, schools, or churches. Practically none would be willing to accept a black person marrying into his or her family.

• 7. Recent efforts to equate sexism with racism have stymied the black Civil Rights Movement. Lumping sex discrimination together with racial discrimination gives power holders more palatable choices for gaining civil rights credits among voters. Instead of bringing blacks into the power and wealth circles, white men satisfied their civil rights obligations by expanding the rights of white women, who were their wives, daughters, sisters, and mothers. As a result, all of the political, social, and economic gains of the women's movement served to increase the power and wealth available to white families. Contrarily, black women have not been able to use the feminist movement to create any appreciable change in the lives of black families.

• 8. Whites have long been attracted to black music, dance, language and sexuality. Black cultural products are sought, sanitized by white entertainers and writers, and adopted as America's "pop culture." On the other hand, blacks have received neither cultural recognition, nor increased wealth for their cultural products.

Recommendations

• 1. Blacks must first establish cultural standards of acceptable social behavior and jettison behavior patterns that render them economically noncompetitive. Blacks must openly acknowledge that certain behavior is detrimental to the race and must be changed. They can no longer excuse destructive behavior by hiding within the frail walls of civil rights issues or charging it to poverty politics or the legacies of slavery.

• 2. Blacks should strive to participate more equitably and fully in all aspects of American society. To do so, they must exercise greater responsibility in the development and control of their communities. They must sever their dependence upon white communities for solutions to their problems. America is a competitive society and the chances of it being changed simply to accommodate noncompetitive blacks are remote. Blacks must acquire enough wealth and political power to change their conditions. The realization of these goals will require leadership that is trained, experienced, devoted, visionary and representative of the best black minds.

• 3. Black institutions — churches, schools, families, and other social organizations — must assert themselves regarding the problems facing black America. They must establish and promote codes of conduct to protect their communities from black antisocial and dysfunctional behaviors. These foundation institutions should cooperatively use a variety of social tools to persuade members of the black race to comply with certain behavioral standards. Social tools, including sanctions, rewards and punishments must not only encourage respect and unity for the group, but should also instill trepidation in potential violators.

Black institutions must define and teach those roles, values, and beliefs, but must also house enforcement powers. Neither law enforcement, politicians, nor the military can bring about community togetherness. The lessons of the civil strife in Somalia, Haiti and Bosnia should soon make this point clear. Only those who live in the community can make it a safe, positive and enjoyable place to live.

Strategy VI: Building a Strong Sense of Community

Since for many years blacks lacked sufficient power to protect themselves, their families and their communities, they were unable to develop a strong sense of community. However, their sense of community and peoplehood was stronger prior to the 1954 Supreme Court desegregation decision than it is today. Prior to the decision, segregation forced blacks to be interdependent and more unified. They were concerned about the welfare of others in their group. They valued and respected black role models and aspired to emulate them. They imposed sanctions and consequences upon members who caused disruptions. For instance, elders were more willing to admonish and help teach neighborhood children right from wrong.

Analysis

• 1. The minority and immigrant labels, when applied to blacks, are not only misleading, but injurious, because they mask the unique history and status of black Americans. Blacks were never immigrants by definition nor in terms of the treatment that has been accorded them. And they have systematically been kept in a minority status to prevent them from acquiring power and wealth. Even when they were the majority in Louisiana, Mississippi, Georgia, Alabama and South Carolina, they were still powerless. And today, as majority populations in large cities, they are still powerless as a group.

• 2. Integration, in its present form, deters blacks from establishing and maintaining a strong sense of community togetherness and peoplehood. It engenders abandonment of the strong cultural traditions and values of black heritage. The process contains some of the same conditioning techniques employed in slavery. For instance, integration places blacks in a position of numerical weakness, subject to being monitored and controlled, rewarded or punished by whites. It forces blacks to be loyal to and identify with the dominant white society. Some blacks, perhaps out of a lack of racial pride or naivete, do not see the negative results of integration in its present form and continue to pursue it regardless of how often they are rejected or exploited.

• 3. Integration gives the illusion that a racial or ethnic group's numerical size is unimportant. Nothing could be further from the truth. Democratic societies operate on the basic principle that the majority wins and unity is power. In competitive group politics and economics, the integrating group is disabled, especially when it doesn't stick together. By fragmenting its members, they become permanent losers.

• 4. Integration works only when blacks stay in their assigned subordinate, powerless, scattered positions. Whites generally support integration as long as it doesn't increase the presence of blacks beyond 5 to 8 percent. When that happens, they generally feel that their positions, personal security, prestige and wealth are threatened.

• 5. A strong sense of community springs from group power. Institutions must be constructed within black communities to attract and retain wealth, information, and power. Institutional power is more potent and lasting than individual power. For instance, white wealth and political power is manifested through a wide variety of organizations and institutions. These entities are financed and directed by governments and corporate leaders who protect and enhance the privileged social position of their race.

Recommendations

• 1. Blacks must cease using the term "minority" and resist any other categorical, ambiguous terms that equates them with other racial, ethnic, gender or class groups. Centuries of statutory enslavement, exploitation, and subordination have imposed unique problems and conditions upon blacks. By using blacks as a model for redressing grievances, any group that perceives itself as aggrieved gets the thrill without the bill. In other words, they get the advantages of being perceived as victims, without having endured the historical suffering of blacks, and they gain greater acceptance within main stream society by being self-sufficient and conservative.

• 2. All black self-empowerment activities must contribute to building a strong sense of peoplehood and commitment to the acculturation principle of taking care of oneself, one's family and one's race. A true sense of peoplehood is not the same as the rhetoric of "brotherhood and sisterhood." Like whites, blacks will have differences of opinion and intraracial differences and disagreements. But black lives are interconnected by virtue of their color. So blacks must be committed to moving towards mutually beneficial goals.

This principle extends to international business, and dealings with African and Caribbean nations. Black Americans and black Africans should first learn to deal with black nations to which they have natural links before dealing with white colonialists. Power will increase in direct proportion to the degree of unity among black people.

• 3. Blacks should develop a sense of community togetherness patterned after white society. For centuries, white society has been solidly committed to European ethnic culture and attitudes about race and power. Their strong sense of peoplehood has permitted them to go to war with other members of their community, yet regroup and fight common enemies. Whites' sense of community helps them to prioritize issues and people and to decide how best to employ their wealth and power for the good of their group.

• 4. Blacks must recapture the sense of a national black community that they had before the 1960s civil rights protest period. Black cooperation and unity are essential tools for building empowerment, especially within the critically short time frame that remains. There will be little time for petty power struggles during the next decade. A Washington-based black think tank, The Harvest Institute, is currently being formed to provide some guidance in this area.

• 5. Blacks must recapture this nation's conscience by building and operating a Black Holocaust and Black History Museum in the Nation's Capital. It should be designed to convey the psychological, socioeconomic and political impact of slavery and Jim Crow. Considering the contributions that blacks made to America and modern civilization, such a museum should stand as an equal to this nation's most revered museums and monuments. Moreover, it would elevate the black historical role from a footnote to the major text. It should submerge visitors in the dreadfulness of the black American experience and the amazing productivity of a people under siege.

• 6. Black Americans must alter the way they see themselves economically, socially, and politically, if they are to change the way others see them. Black history must be taught in totality and in a new context. It must emphasize the outstanding productivity and the contributions blacks have made to capitalism, the industrial revolution and American society in general.

Black history ought not to be limited to the contributions of a few blacks. Instead, it should demonstrate blacks' massive labor and wealth productivity. It should focus on how they produced wealth, food, clothing and shelter for generations of non-blacks around the world. The history ought to show the uniqueness and enduring strength of the black culture that gave America its only true art forms — black music, dance, art and language. A black Holocaust and History Museum would provide a proper context for long overdue recognition of America's original labor class.

• 7. New black leadership must establish a national vision and articulate an acceptable code of conduct. Behavior that is injurious to other black persons and property must be strictly prohibited. Though America is a nation of laws, centuries of imposed criminality have rendered some black communities nearly uninhabitable. Blacks must retrieve their communities from the various outlaw elements within and around it, by legal, extralegal and any other means necessary.

• 8. As a part of a strong sense of community, an accountability mechanisms for rewarding and punishing offenders of the community will be needed to bring rampant black-on-black crime under control. Accountability standards to be imposed by the community will have to be designed. They should include social sanctions and other punishments.

• 9. Blacks, in accordance with the national public policy became an obsolete and endangered race in the 1960s. Since blacks are less acceptable, more vulnerable and more powerless than Jews, it is important that blacks develop the capability of an organization like the B'Nai B'Rith Anti-Defamation League that would monitor and report all anti-black activities anywhere in the world. Such a capability would not only keep black America well-informed, but would dissuade groups from engaging in destructive activities against blacks.

Strategy VII: Role of Institutions

Black institutions, such as churches, community agencies and fraternal organizations are needed to reestablish a broad sense of community and peoplehood. Their historical roles and resources must be broadened and linked via a national plan.

Analysis

There is no inter-linking of black churches and social and political organizations, thus they continue to operate independently, taking money out of black America rather than bringing it in. These organizations spend millions of dollars annually on travel, meetings, hotels, entertainment and food. Little, if any, of this wealth goes back into the black community. They have no master plans designed to alter the marginal existence of blacks.

Recommendations

• 1. Though the social-political role of black churches has diminished over the past two generations, they are still a unifying force. They can play an even more important role by not only providing religious training, but assisting in the economic development and rebuilding of black America. With a new commitment to a broad black community, black churches could initiate a mandate to call back the black Americans who drifted from the churches or joined white churches. Church services should be spiritually uplifting, but they must also be sources of information and motivation about the requirements for unity.

With its audience of millions, the black church would not only be able to pool large amounts of money, but could also communicate the need for blacks to become better educated and more thrifty. It could also sponsor scholarships; stimulate economic development through developing credit unions, food cooperatives, urban land programs and other enterprises. Some churches have started to move in this direction and provide models that others can follow. Other social and political organizations could pursue the same goals via similar activities.

• 2. Black church members should insist that their churches become more accountable for the billions that they annually extract from black communities through tithes and contributions. Some of these funds should be directed towards strengthening the community. They could be made available to black entrepreneurs through capital formation pools or regional economic development banks controlled by various denominations. Black ministers could assist further by preaching about the need for blacks to practice capitalism and group economics. The nursery schools and kindergartens should teach unity and economic self-sufficiency.

Strategy VIII: Government Resources

White society has always maintained full control of government and used it as a tool for acquiring and maintaining wealth. Though assisted by government in their maldistribution of power and wealth, conservative forces oppose any use of government to correct the imbalances by helping blacks to gain wealth. Taxes are the only established device for redistributing wealth in America. Antigovernment forces understand that without tax revenues, government would not be able to assist blacks, who have been abused by the powerful.

Analysis

• 1. The conservative movement to privatize government services could have serious negative consequences for blacks, because limited private sector employment opportunities force a large percentage of working blacks to earn their income from government jobs. Meanwhile, unemployed blacks depend upon government for assistance and benefits.

• 2. Black Africa is beginning to privatize. Free of European colonial powers and socialistic ideologies, African nations have begun to privatize or sell state-owned assets as business opportunities for entrepreneurs. Black Americans should explore the opportunity to purchase some of these properties. They should also seriously explore opportunities to establish vertical businesses with Africa. Cuban and other Hispanic groups are already developing plans to gain control of privatized resources in Africa. John Naisbitt and Patricia Aburdene, in *Megatrends 2000*, identified industries within various African states that are in the process of privatization:[6]

- Nigeria plans to sell its stake in 160 state-owned banks, breweries and insurance companies.

- Kenya plans to divest the state's interest in more than 400 enterprises.

- Mozambique has reportedly privatized more than 20 industrial plants since 1985.

- Tanzania plans to seek managers to take over state-run hotels and game lodges.

- Angola, Benin and Congo plan to sell mining, fishing and construction companies.

- Togo began privatizing services and companies in 1988.

- Many African countries are privatizing aspects of telecommunications and seeking new communications technologies and program sources.

These business opportunities could provide blacks with a vital link to industrial development. But let the buyer beware. This will not be a giveaway and due diligence is required. Some of these businesses may be overpriced or have poor products and obsolete equipment. Yet even in view of potential shortcomings, these African sell-offs are worth investigating.

   • 3. In America, local governments could establish quasi-public lending institutions funded by assets converted from confiscated properties and funds programs. In 1988, the Federal Drug Enforcement Agency reported that it had confiscated properties worth nearly $700 million. These programs could produce revenue by converting inactive funds and property into funds directed towards the good of the community from which the funds came. The funds could be made available to black entrepreneurs through low interest, long-term loans. The black businesses would pay interest and taxes to city governments and create jobs.

• 4. Local governments could offer land grants and headrights on abandoned ghetto properties to black individuals or corporations that need land for industrial or business development. Additionally, tax incentives, as discussed earlier, could encourage development.

• 5. Government could formulate partnerships with black businesses and industries by purchasing a specific amount of services and goods from black businesses situated within various municipal boundaries.

• 6. Government could offer subsidies to black industries that hired hard-core underemployed and unemployed blacks. Funds could be redirected from funds currently used to pay government assistance to the needy in black communities, and from the confiscation of funds described earlier.

Strategy IX: Political Empowerment

What is the political system about? And why is the possession of political power important to a group? Group power is important because the distribution of economic, social rewards and benefits within the broad society is the major role of a political system. The group with the greatest political power will receive the greatest benefits. For nearly 400 years, the United States' immigration policies have been used to contain black populations at nonthreatening and controllable levels. Black percentages exceeding 5 to 8 percent generated white backlashes.

In a democratic society founded on the principle that the majority wins, the racial or ethnic group with the largest population always gets its way. National immigration policies and the integration process have restricted black immigrants from entering the country and scattered them as minorities among whites. Such practices have consigned blacks to a constant numerical minority and therefore to a perpetual loser status.

After Emancipation, blacks struggled harder than any other group in the country to overcome barriers erected to prevent their participation in the political process. Voter registration and education drives were major components of the Civil Rights Movement. The black vote became a decisive factor in all levels of elections. Blacks could proudly take credit for electing white candidates as members of state legislatures, mayors, governors and presidents. They were equally successful in delivering black candidates to public offices. However, increased political gains do not mean improved conditions for blacks.

Analysis

• 1. The Voting Rights Act of 1965 increased black voting strength and opened the doors to unprecedented growth in the number of black elected officials. Unfortunately, the material benefits to blacks did not increase in proportion to the increase in black representation. Even in large urban areas with a strong tradition of black participation in local, state and national government, it appears that material dividends to blacks have been either minimal or nonexistent. Judging by the meager rewards and benefits that blacks have received from the political system, the real question now is: Should blacks continue to participate in politics as they have in the past?

• 2. Throughout history, black officeholders have been neither numerous nor especially influential. Most entered and left office without altering black America's conditions. More often, they lacked power and direction and had few resources from which to draw support.

• 3. There has been little quid pro quo for the blacks who put candidates into public office. This results primarily from the fact that white society controls nearly all aspects of government and it will not easily let government be used to help blacks. Another drawback is black political appointees. The reality of the political process makes it easier for them to bury themselves in the business of taking care of the general public's business rather than proposing issues and programs to specifically improve the quality of life for blacks. They feel safer being good public servants rather than black employees with an agenda of their own. There is often little noticeable difference between them and their non-black predecessors or counterparts. They lose sight of the reasons that blacks fought for the right to vote.

Blacks do not vote solely for good government. They vote for candidates who they think will bring them proportional returns. When elected officials or their appointees fail to support black people's interest, blacks must do whatever is necessary to bring the candidate and his appointees to task.

• 4. Politicians are becoming more open in expressing opposition to black issues. They sense that these issues have been successfully closeted or placed on the back burner. After a major election is over, mainstream society expresses fatigue from hearing about race issues. Blacks comfort them by discussing mainstream issues in public and political forums. The Republican Party, for instance, espouses that it is interested in increasing black membership under their Big Tent platform. In truth, their interest in black voters stops at the point where they feel that they have diluted the black block of votes that traditionally supports the Democratic Party. They don't want to attract hordes of blacks because they do not want to tarnish themselves with too many black Republicans.

If a massive number of blacks registered as Republicans, most whites would become Democrats. If a large number of blacks registered as Democrats, most whites would become Republicans. If blacks split their registration evenly between both the Democratic and Republican parties, whites would be very happy. If blacks developed a national plan and began acquiring self-sufficiency, wealth and power, whites would be unable to predict the black vote and would be forced to develop other strategies.

Recommendations

• 1. Without wealth-power, blacks as a numerical minority cannot hold public officeholders accountable. An officeholder needs the majority of the votes and campaign financing. If blacks cannot offer both, they have no control over the candidate except when a narrow amount of support is needed to tip the scales. Even then, a white candidate has to be careful not to be overly identified with a group perceived as poor and powerless. Blacks must unify and form a critical mass that politicians cannot dismiss and must reward.

• 2. The damage inflicted by non-accountable office holders will eventually compound and render blacks even more nonthreatening. They must financially support their candidates and demand accountability for their investments. Like wealthy Jewish or corporate groups, they must hold politicians accountable by withholding their support during subsequent elections.

• 3. In their political activities, blacks should stress that the most important issue for them is not political partisanship. The issue is race. There are blacks who swear by one political party or another, while whites switch political parties to make the bottom line come out right. During their enslavement, blacks did not belong to any political party. From the end of Civil War until after the Great Depression, blacks primarily belonged to the Republican Party, but they were subordinated, lynched, and segregated.

From the late 1940s until today, about 85 percent of all registered black voters have been Democrats, and black America is still excluded and subordinated. This suggests that regardless of the degree of black political involvement, black conditions remain unchanged. Therefore, blacks ought to consider starting their own party and run their own candidates for public office.

Blacks would have very little to lose since very few black public office holders win elections on the white vote. If nothing else, an independent political party would get blacks public forums, financial support, candidates committed to the black community and white respect for having some backbone.

• 4. Black businesses must shoulder their share of the responsibility to support black political candidates. Black businesses are the first to ask for political favors and usually give the least in return. Consequently, black political candidates are weakened because they have to depend upon white contributors. It is difficult, if not impossible, for black public office holders to be outspoken and supportive of black causes if they are dependent upon white dollars. Whites only support black candidates who are non-threatening to the power, wealth and privilege of a white life style.

9

Cultural Foundations for Economic Power: Black Artists and Athletes

"If I didn't have hard luck and trouble, I wouldn't have any luck at all."
— Old Blues Song

O bviously, a major premise of this book is that black America's future is inseparably connected to its past. The majority of this book illuminates the facts and characteristics of the systematic and racist exploitation of blacks. This chapter takes the reader back into history one more time, but for a different purpose — to suggest ways by which blacks can use their history and culture to create wealth and power through vertical business development.

Vertical businesses can be built within any industry where one group has major control, if not a monopoly, on certain resources. Music entertainment and sports represent probably the best, if not the only two, excellent areas where black Americans have great potential advantage to develop vertically-linked and controlled businesses.

Black Americans have a long and intimate involvement with American music and sports. Yet, they have not reaped a full share of the financial rewards created via their talents. Music and sports are multi-billion dollar industries and hold the potential to produce tremendous wealth, not just for black enter-tainers and athletes, but for a significant number of other blacks as well. Blacks can apply vertical business integration in these industries by harness-ing their physical gifts — some of which were manipulated and exploited by whites through slave breeding — and their musical genius — which was also manipulated by whites — and now use them to build economic self-suffi-ciency and power.

In the concept of vertical integration, a single entity or group controls all aspects of the creation and sale of a service or product, including obtaining the raw materials, processing and manufacturing, then distributing, market-ing and selling the finished products. Through vertical integration, the group that controls raw resources and markets can reap the profits without sharing its proceeds with middlemen and others outside of the group. The group has the chance to take its profits or reinvest them in the business. Either way, it becomes stronger.

The black community could adapt these concepts to the music and sports industries and thereby spread millions of dollars into black businesses through-out the nation. In such a vertically integrated economic chain, money for goods and services would flow up and down the black chain. Each link would ben-efit from, but also contribute to rebuilding the black economic infrastructure by providing employment, new business, an improved tax base, and a more economically independent community. This process would build a stronger community, because all fortunes would be connected and grow together.

The concept would provide both entrepreneurial and investment opportuni-ties for blacks, and could be applied to many other industries. In sports, for example, black athletes could band together and demand that black businesses receive manufacturing contracts for sports equipment, concession businesses at stadiums and arenas and a large share of the legal work, travel and trans-portation contracts, janitorial contracts and whatever else is needed to sup-port the industries that center around their talents.

Similarly, black musical artists could create or use black-owned recording studios, printing and pressing facilities, and other businesses necessary for the recording process. Music and sports are expressions of black culture, and black athletes and artists have inherent power to control access to the most valuable raw resources in these industries — their unique skills. If a system of integrated businesses could be built around their services, then black athletes and artists could use monopoly control of their skills as leverage to create further business opportunities for others. The historic exploitation of black music and other art forms provides a strong philosophical reason to target these industries as visible examples of a new black economic agenda.

Immigrant groups have always built vertically integrated businesses within their communities and around their cultures. They have commercialized and controlled their culture, retained the resulting capital within their communities and created employment opportunities for their people. Nothing prevents black people from doing the same.

Building Wealth Through Black Music

Much of American popular music — from Rock and Roll to Jazz, Swing and Gospel — is rooted in black music. Most other African art forms were destroyed by slavery or diluted to such an extent that the original distinctive characteristics were lost. But the musical aspect of black culture survived slavery and has prospered. Though many black individuals have become successful as artists, they have failed to fully access or control the money generated by the music industry. They have not had a strong presence in the production, distribution, marketing or sale of music or the related legal or business work.

Black music is the basis for one of the world's wealthiest industries. It has a unique role in popular world culture. The wealth and power of the music industry offer the most compelling reasons for blacks to recapture control of this cultural resource.

The Roots of Black Music and Dance

White society's interest in black culture and musical art forms is deeply rooted in history. Whites were fascinated by African customs, especially native dance and song. The black Africans' physical movements were rhythmic, uninhibited, and sensuous. Whites found their dancing, singing, chanting, cries and other sound effects compelling, erotic and emotionally stimulating. Whites liked to observe blacks performing, not only because black art forms conveyed a sense of contentedness, but because whites were *entranced* by the black style.[1] They liked what they saw, they liked what they felt and they found ways to manipulate it, control it, imitate it and make money from it.

The conversion of African music to New World or black American music began aboard the slave ships, as the music was transformed in response to the horrible conditions of enslavement. The slaves expressed their physical and psychological pain through song, music and dance. Captains of the slave ships gave slaves opportunities to sing, dance and express their sorrows. These releases of emotion were like a drug that raised the slaves' spirits and burned off surplus energy, quelling pent up hostilities, that represented a constant danger to their white captors. During the long voyages from Africa to the New World, both the slaves and the crews looked forward to these release rituals, which became known as "dancing the slaves."[2]

For added enjoyment, some slave ships provided musical instruments, such as tambourines, harps, fiddles, and banjos for the slaves. Ships without musical instruments often permitted slaves to make music by using pots and pans. The most commonly used accompanying sounds were vocal harmony, hand-clapping, or foot-stomping. The long voyages and brutal conditions generated deep new emotions in the slaves, who modified their traditional African songs, music and dances to convey how they felt about their forced voyage from Africa. The white slave traders were fascinated by the emerging new sounds and dances.

In the New World slave markets, the slaves retained and continued to modify their music and dance heritage. European settlers began to openly express their interest in slave music. Some plantation owners gave slaves musical instruments. The gifts were investments that provided entertainment as well as profits. Advertisements for slaves sometimes touted musical and dancing talents, because such skills increased a slaves value. By the Revolutionary War, the Virginia Act of 1776 called blacks into military service to be "employed as drummers and fifers."[3]

In rural plantation areas, slave musical performances were the primary entertainment, and dancing was the favorite form of recreation. Throughout the South, slaves played fiddles, banjos and drums at their masters' special plantation balls. Whites developed an appetite for the distinctive way that blacks played "the jig" and other Negro tunes. During holiday seasons and weekends, whites customarily gathered their slaves into the yards to sing, dance and make music to entertain the master's family members and guests.

The singing and dancing of slaves added to the security and comfort of the slave holders. They disliked and did not trust silent blacks. They wanted slaves to sing while they worked and to at least give the impression that they were happy. Black work songs developed into some of America's first folk music and became blacks' statements to the world. These work songs described the hard, unhappy lives of slaves. With primitive tools, little food, and no monetary compensation, they sweated their lives away in the cotton fields, mines, or on the railroad lines, producing wealth for the white class. The burdens and pains of slavery and Jim Crowism were eased by the music and the occasional chance to dance. It gave blacks the strength to endure.

The Emancipation Proclamation brought short-lived joy and celebration into the lives of the slaves, who sang and danced for days, ecstatic about their new legal freedom. But, the failure of Reconstruction made life harder for the newly-freed slaves. Confused and abandoned by the North, the ex-slaves continued to make emotional statements in the only ways open to them — new musical forms. They sought emotional comfort and release in the churches. The ex-slaves' inability to read the hymn books or musical notes gave them the freedom to play and sing what they felt in their souls. Outside of the churches, blacks blended the spirituals with old slave work songs and called it the Blues. Whether it was the church or the street corner, blacks accentuated their music with emotion. The black Blues singer was a storyteller who powerfully conveyed the deep sorrows and pains of a black nation imprisoned within a white nation.[4]

Often, white society responded to the new black music in a manner that reflected their emotional dilemma. They were attracted to it and simultaneously repulsed. The more religiously conservative whites affixed derogatory labels to black music. They called Blues "race music." By the 19th century, New Orleans had become the center of a new form of black music called Jazz, which was a shortened label for what whites called "jack ass music." In their happier moods, blacks created Dixieland and Ragtime music. Ragtime was labelled "coon music" by whites. Gospel music is a product of the 20th century and similar to black secular music, especially Blues and Jazz. The gutsy cries and grunts in Rhythm and Blues music took on the label of "soul music." Blacks passed their music down from generation to generation. It expressed their hopes, determinations, and assurance that there would be a better life.

Popular country and western music has heavy black roots, coming from the musical background established by black slave entertainers and vagabonds. Segregation in rural areas of the country maintained an archaic form of European speech patterns and a culture that resulted in Blue Grass and Western music, which were more closely identified with rural whites. However, popular and progressive Country music has been incrementally updated with black sounds through the years.

The Exploitation and Minstrelization of Black Music

From the beginning, black music and dance continued to thrive in an atmosphere of detraction, oppression, distortion, and theft. White minstrels in the 1800s gave rise to some of the first imitative exploitation of black music and dance. With black-face makeup, whites mimicked blacks and provided whites with black entertainment without blacks. These white performers provided whites with a safe window to the cultural and emotional world of black people and made money. They capitalized on white fascination and attraction to black art forms.

The exploitation of black art forms has changed very little from the earliest instance of Jim Crowism. On a Cincinnati street in 1830, Dan Rice, a famous white "black-faced" minstrel performer, saw a ragged little black boy singing, "Jump, Jim Crow, Jump" and copied the dance in his performances to the great pleasure of whites.[5] Rice and other vaudeville black-faced minstrels grew popular and wealthy imitating black songs, dances, and comedy acts that contributed to creating negative stereotypes of blacks.

By the Civil War, minstrel shows had become the most popular form of entertainment in the North, in part, because they ridiculed blacks and justified Northerners' indifference to black enslavement. A few blacks who had learned to mock themselves broke the minstrel tradition by the 1890s. Some black entertainers even whitened their faces — turning the paradox of skin color full circle.[6]

By the turn of the century, white vaudeville started to tone down its harsh mocking of blacks. This slight change was occurring primarily because talented black pioneers, like Bob Cole, wrote music and sketches for white vaudeville shows.[7] This allowed white entertainers to use black songs, dances, jokes, and slang expressions without being too offensive. But black-facing would not die. White minstrels remained popular in certain sections of the country well into the third decade of this century.

Paradoxically, in the early 20th century, blacks could not perform their own music and dance before white audiences due to segregation laws. Many black entertainers traveled to Europe and entertained the more liberal and enthusiastic audiences there. White performers capitalized on the fact that blacks did not have vertical commercial control of their music.

When black entertainers left the country, they left a void that was filled by a new form of white minstrelization. White performers began to try to sound black. By the Roaring Twenties, blacks had lost Ragtime, Dixieland and Jazz to big band white musicians such as Jack Teagarden, Benny Goodman, and the Dorsey brothers, who expropriated the art form under the label of Swing.[8] Music and dance went together. Black dances, such as the Charleston, Tap, Jitterbug and Cake Walk were copied in white dance halls.

By the 1930s and 1940s, a black-faced singer named Al Jolson achieved national recognition by mimicking blacks. Kneeling on one knee and singing "Mammy" and "Swannee River," Jolson's performances depicted the bewildered black yearning for the plantations of the past.

The integration movement that began in the mid-1950s opened the door for whites to totally appropriate black music. Until that time, black music was primarily available only in black clubs and underground. Blacks did not own radio stations and only one or two white stations would play real black music. It was not sold in white record stores. Only black mom-and-pop shops sold it. White singers scoured black sources for new music and again minstrelized it for white audiences, this time without using black-face makeup. They made fortunes in white markets by imitating popular songs of Rhythm and Blues artists. Elvis Presley became known as the King of Rock and Roll.

Much of the music sung by Elvis and Bill Haley and the Comets was music that was written and previously sung by black Rhythm and Blues artists. The title Rock and Roll came from an old Blues song of Big Joe Turner called "Shake, Rattle and Roll," which Haley and the Comets popularized among white audiences.

Hardly any black musical artists received respect, credit, or copyright compensation for their music, from Jazz, Blues, Dixieland, Gospel, Ragtime, Swing, BeBop, Boogie Woogie or Rhythm and Blues. Stripped of their music and revenue in the United States, black musicians increased their efforts to establish new markets in Europe in the late 1950s, just as their black predecessors had done in the 1920s. By the early 1960s, Europeans had been exposed to black music and dance and could imitate blacks. The mid-1960s witnessed an influx of black-influenced European musicians and singers, such as the Beatles, the Rolling Stones, the Bee Gees, and Elton John.

The Rock and Roll Hall of Fame in Cleveland, Ohio actually honors many of the whites as musicians and performers as artists who "discovered" black music, rather than as imitators who renamed it. Michael Bolton is the current popular white singer of black music. In responding to a letter from a reader, *Parade Magazine* (January 2, 1994) expressed its belief in the mainstream popularity of Bolton saying, he is "a white wailer who merely re-does old black soul ballads."[9] When a nationally known black television station informed Bolton that blacks felt he was mimicking black singers and exploiting black music, he assured the newscaster that he loved black music and was paying it the highest respect by singing it.

Naturally, some black artists, such as Fats Domino, Ruth Brown and Little Richard, regular targets of white musical imitators, did not see such actions as respect and sued white artists who became rich and famous by copying their music. A few have been successful in their lawsuits.

Blacks' lack of capital, production technology, marketing networks, and access to copyright and artistic protection not only left them exposed to the exploitation of imitators, but also left them absolutely no control over their cultural product. When major white record companies refused to contract with black performers, a few smaller white companies filled the void and developed R & B record labels and promoted black music to black markets. The return on their investment was high, not only because they created monopolies on black talent, but because they paid black performers a pittance for their valuable product.

Economic Control

Blacks have used music to earn a living in America for many years. Performing was the single most profitable occupation for blacks prior to the Civil War. As far back as 1850, census data indicated that nearly 24 percent of all free blacks classified themselves as professional musicians.[10] However, until Berry Gordy demonstrated how to control and commercialize black culture by forming Motown Records in the late 1950s, few blacks had found a way to form a lifeline between music and the wealth-building opportunities it provided.

Gordy practically cornered the market on contracting black singing talent. His artists dominated the record industry for decades, re-popularized black music, and controlled this black art form. Motown provided vertical opportunities for black singers, promoters, writers and musicians. It was an important symbol of blacks' controlling and profiting from black culture and producing wealth and power. Unfortunately, in 1993, it was reported that this unique repository of black history and culture would be purchased by Polygram Music, a Dutch corporation.[11] Though Motown passed from black hands to white hands, it still stands as the prime model for using black culture to build a sense of racial togetherness and pride, and economic success.

Building Black Wealth on Black Art Forms

The record industry sells $7.5 billion annually in compact discs, tapes, record albums and other products and services centered around music, according to *Black Enterprise Magazine*. That figure nearly matches the total gross annual revenue for all black businesses combined for the same time period. Black performers could leverage their status within the industry to create new business opportunities for black investors and aspiring black entrepreneurs. They could use their wealth and popularity as leverage to foster vertical business opportunities from talent agencies and music distributorships to nightclubs and record stores. The more economic involvement in the industry, the more personal power and wealth black entertainers could hold for themselves and their people.

Developing Sports into an Area of Economic Strength

Sports historically have been used to provide forms of recreation and relatively harmless ways to let off steam, gain attention, and foster specific attitudes and behavior patterns among blacks.[12] From slavery to the present day, these purposes have remained unchanged. Sports were not perceived as avenues for the black community to acquire wealth and income. In terms of an example of vertical business opportunities for the black race, sports are second only to black music, but only if blacks perceive the industry with new eyes and seize the opportunity to gain more control of it.

Unlike black music, dance, and language art forms, American sports are culturally unique and were not produced by blacks. Blacks were introduced to sports in America to benefit whites. Blacks did not invent boxing, basketball, baseball or football, but they have dominated these particular sports. Blacks are attracted to sports for a great variety of reasons. First, sports, unlike music, represent opportunities for black athletes to regain the humanity that slavery and Jim Crow stripped away. For many black Americans, sports fill an emotional need and presents an opportunity to measure oneself against opponents, especially non-black ones. For a long time, sports were the only area in which a black person was allowed to be a winner.

During slavery, some competitive activities were regularly planned and others were spontaneous. Boxing, wrestling, horse racing, foot racing, wood cutting, and a variety of dance contests were very popular. Black slaves often created their own contests in betting on who could pick the most cotton or do the most work in a certain period of time.

Sports Produced Benefits to Slave Masters

Saturday night sports contests between black slaves from different plantations were held routinely for fun and profit. They provided the slave the opportunity to demonstrate his physical prowess, and permitted the white slave
holders to enjoy themselves and make more money. At the more popular events,
whites placed large wagers on the slaves of their choice and earned money
from the contests. The activities were designed to promote blacks as uniquely
endowed with physical attributes best managed by white overseers.

Permitting blacks to engage in sports activities was also a major part of the
conditioning process. For not only did the black sports contests entertain and
make money for whites, but free play activities effectively drained off the
slaves' excess physical energies, thereby reducing the level of potential threat
to the slave owners and overseers.

Similarly, the sports events kept blacks preoccupied until they resumed
work in the fields and factories. Slave holders sometimes purposely overin-
volved slaves in sports activities, so that they were happy to give up their
temporary freedom and were anxious to return to routine chores.

Cruel and abusive whites created sports that used blacks like footballs or
ducks. To entertain themselves and make money, whites developed a game
called "coon hunting." The game was also used to reinforce fear and discipline within blacks. Blacks could avoid being used in the games by making
sure that they always obeyed whites. In the coon game, blacks' extraordinary
running abilities and endurance were pitted against white hunters' skills. Whites
joined the game with rifles and hunting dogs. A slave with whom a white
owner was dissatisfied was covered with a scent and set free to run in the
woods at night. The slave holders released their hound dogs to track and tree
the slave. Bets would be placed as to whose dogs would catch the slave first.
Once caught and treed, the slave was usually shot from the tree like a raccoon.

During the first few decades of the 20th century, in Rosewood, Florida a
wild game of coon hunting lasted for as long as eight days, with more than
100 blacks being killed. Nearly a century later, the Caucus of Black Legisla-
tors in Florida successfully pushed through for the first time ever, a monetary
reparations bill for the survivors of the hunt.

For blacks, there was a direct path from the cotton fields to the athletic
fields. While a black person was despised for his color, most were respected

for their endurance, strength and athletic abilities. Blacks began to gain recognition in certain sports. One of the first was horse racing. As early as 1783, Count Francesco dal Verme, in a letter to his father, remarked that in North Carolina, young teenage blacks were jockeys and rode horses bareback. Blacks groomed and cared for most of the plantation stables and developed a great deal of expertise in raising, training and racing horses.

By the latter part of the 19th century, black jockeys dominated the horse racing industry. Jockeys such as Isaac Murphy had achieved preeminence in national races. He won the Kentucky Derby in 1884, 1890, and 1891. Murphy also won the American Derby in 1884, 1885, 1886, and 1888. A lesser-known black jockey, Jimmy Lee, won all six of the races at Louisville in 1907. Within a couple of years, black jockeys' salaries had reached as high as $10,000 to $20,000 annually.[13] Noting that it was not appropriate for blacks to earn such levels of wealth, the racing industry, held accountable by the larger white community, eventually removed all blacks and replaced them with white and Hispanic jockeys. The only public reminder that blacks developed and once dominated the horse racing industry are the statues of black lawn jockeys that years ago decorated lawns and guarded driveways across America.

As blacks entered other sports, they quickly came to dominate them as well. The first black boxer, Tom Molyneux, was a slave who was freed because of his outstanding boxing skills. One of the most famous black boxers was Jack Johnson, whose boldness so inflamed white society that they sought a "Great White Hope" to remove him from the boxing ring. Joe Louis dominated boxing for nearly two decades, and he too was challenged in the 1930s by a great white hope, Max Schmeling, a German boxer. But Joe Louis, like nearly all black boxers and black athletes, finished his career impoverished. Few black athletes were successful in gaining access to the management and promotional aspects of organized sports.

The black man's role in athletics was symbolized by the Harlem Globe Trotters. Integration led to the demise of the all-black basketball league in the 1940s. Major league white basketball teams eventually hired a few of the black players on a quota basis. To salvage the black talent that was being wasted, Abe Saperstein signed the best players to be Harlem Globe Trotters and showcased their antics and skills around the world. Just as with black music, people in different nations were excited by the physical dexterity of the black-skinned players. During the past 50 years, individual black players moved beyond simply being paid as clowning athletes. However, the larger share of the profits still go to whites involved in ownership and team management.

Expanding Black Business and
Wealth Opportunities

Sports offer an opportunity for blacks to practice successful group economics and a chance to convert professional dominance and black consumer
spending into wealth power. Blacks are prolific consumers of sports equipment and sports clothing, and they spend a sizable amount of money watching
sports. Blacks make up approximately 80 percent of the professional boxers,
75 percent of the professional basketball players, 50 percent of the professional football players, and 40 percent of the baseball players. Very few blacks
own any entities connected to the sports industry.

More of the vertical wealth, employment, and entrepreneurial opportunities
from sports-related businesses could accrue to blacks if they challenge the
many foreign businesses that manufacture and produce sports equipment and
clothing. Blacks are heavy users of these consumer items. It is ironic that
there are few Koreans, Taiwanese, Chinese or Japanese in professional American sports, and even fewer Asian spectators. Yet, these groups are the major
manufacturers of the athletic equipment and clothing that is sold in the United
States. In effect, black athletes and black spectators are subsidizing business
development in other nations.

With the support of black spectators, black athletes could negotiate more
than higher salaries. They could leverage their popularity and fan support to
create structural business opportunities for blacks at all levels of the industry.
As a group, black athletes could negotiate for a percentage of the opportunities created by their team's purchases of sports equipment, marketing and
promotions, stadium concessions, insurance coverage, players' pension programs, banking deposits, accounting, legal services and stock sales, all of
which would provide wealth to blacks seeking business opportunities in sports.
The practice of group economics would give individual athletes leverage and
open economic opportunities that would strengthen blacks as a group.

Without the collective pressure of black athletes and spectators, the sports
industry will have no incentive to alter its present practice of excluding black
business persons.

Conclusion

Vertical business opportunities, like trees, grow best when they have strong,
deep roots from which to draw nourishment and support. Music and sports

represent such business opportunities for blacks, for in these industries, black peoples' roots are indeed strong and deep. In addition, the raw resources are readily available. Missing are the capital, entrepreneurs, and the black community's commitment to pursue economic empowerment by using its valuable resources for its own advantage and self-sufficiency.

Epilogue

*"No oppressed group in history has achieved deliverance,
without having taken the lead role" — Source Unknown*

I t is my hope that the reader has heard within the text of *Black Labor,
White Wealth* a simple call to action for black America. I hope that it
has helped to clarify the past for the purpose of illuminating a path towards a
more desirable future. Although the socioeconomic problems within black
America are devastating and all indicators show that conditions will worsen,
they are not insurmountable.

Black America has the cultural and economic wherewithal to become a
competitive racial group. But successful competition on a global scale will
require a new kind of leadership, changes in social behavior patterns, the
practice of group economics and politics and a strong sense of community.

Blacks should capitalize on their potential strengths, beginning with those
areas where they are dominant or can control basic resources, such as in the
areas of music, entertainment, government municipalities, urban lands and
buildings, the approximately $300 billion of annual disposable black income,
and the 35-million-strong black consumer market. The hope of black empowerment begins at home, in black communities, not in jobs within the 500 major
corporations or in white suburbs.

To the credit of black America, some positive signs have appeared that
strongly suggest that blacks are aware of the importance of the task before
them. While not yet a concerted effort, some black efforts are beginning to
signal proactive choices and an unwillingness to depend upon the support of
others to resolve problems. In a rapidly approaching pluralistic society, if
there can be coalition building, fine. But coalition building with other racial

groups cannot be used to seek self-sufficiency and self-empowerment within black America.

In the final analysis, blacks, and blacks alone, will have to solve black peoples' wealth and power problems. The socioeconomic and political strategies offered in this book clearly should be tried, because they are based upon lessons from the past and are designed to reverse the impact of both racism and the "crabs in a barrel" syndrome, which has crippled blacks from within for centuries.

Black efforts to develop vertical business enterprises are few, but encouraging. Black entrepreneurs have successfully started or acquired businesses with significant potential for generating other black businesses in the entertainment and beverage industries. Whether their ultimate impact results in personal gain only or has a community impact by creating more black business and job opportunities remains to be seen. In entertainment, black producers create black-oriented movies and cable shows that feature black comedians and employ black talent.

In professional sports, a retired football player is pursuing an expansion ownership opportunity that would place a national football team in a major black city. If he is successful, he would be the first African American to acquire ownership in professional football. Professional boxing has at least one major boxing promoter who syndicates fights on television Home Box Office.

In politics, there is also promising movement. During the September 1993 Congressional Black Caucus Annual Forum, a black leadership alliance was established between the Caucus, the NAACP and the Nation of Islam. The alliance was an attempt to put aside personal and religious differences and to work together to establish a black united front. However, there is serious doubt that a functional alliance will materialize.

Another significant conference for black America occurred during the month of June 1993 when 5,000 participants and observers met in Gabon, Africa for the Second African-African American Summit. The summit's goal was to forge a common strategy between black Americans and Africans that would promote economic development and progress in education and health care for sub-Saharan Africa.

According to *The Washington Post,* the first summit, held in the Ivory Coast in 1991, helped secure agreements that eliminated more than $1 billion of Africa's debt and resulted in multi-million-dollar black U.S. business investments in African development projects.

These are but a few small steps in a long journey. But they are very important steps towards black socioeconomic maturity and a new sense of community. Whether blacks can beat the clock is another question. Individual efforts, while important, must be maximized and become part of a plan for cohesive group development. An outgrowth of the research and networking stimulated via the writing of this book was the establishment of The Harvest Institute, a Washington-based, national black think tank.

The chief goal of The Harvest Institute is to construct a black intellectual infrastructure to formulate a black national policy and empowerment plan, with comprehensive strategies for getting black America from where it is today to where it needs to be. The Harvest Institute's short-term goals are to achieve competitive group economics and political empowerment for black America as quickly as possible.

APPENDIX

Boundary Safeguards and Restrictions in Southern States

Year	States' Legal and Social Restrictions	Purpose of Restriction
1619	Maryland Segregation Policy	Recommended that blacks be socially excluded
1642	Virginia Fugitive Law	Authorized branding of an "R" in the face of runaway slaves
1686	Carolina Trade Law	Barred blacks from all trades
1691	Virginia Marriage Law	Prescribed banishment for any white woman marrying a black.
1705	Virginia Public Office Law	Prohibited blacks from holding or assuming any public office
1710	Virginia enacted Meritorious Manumission	Rewarded slaves with freedom for informing on other slaves
1712	South Carolina Fugitive Slave Act	Criminalized runaway slaves to protect owners' investments
1715	North Carolina Anti-interracial Marriage Law	Forbade and criminalized black and white marriages
1717	South Carolina Anti-interracial Marriage Law	Forbade and criminalized black-white marriages
1723	Virginia Anti-Assembly Law	Impeded blacks from meeting or having a sense of community
1723	Virginia Weapons Law	Forbade blacks from keeping weapons
1740	South Carolina Consolidated Slave Act	Forbade slaves from raising or owning farm animals
1775	Virginia Runaway Law	Allowed sale or execution of slaves attempting to flee

- Continued - No. 2 Boundary Safeguards and Restrictions in Southern States		
Year	**States' Legal and Social Restrictions**	**Purpose of Restriction**
1775	North Carolina Manumission Law	Forbade freeing slaves except for meritorious service
1790	First Naturalization Law	Congress declares United States a white nation
1792	Federal Militia Law	Restricted enrollment in peace time militia to whites only
1793	Fugitive Slave Law	Discouraged slaves from running away; protected planters' invested capital
1793	Virginia Migration Law	Forbade free blacks from entering the State
1806	Louisiana Migration Law	Forbade immigration for free black males over 15 years old
1809	Congressional Mail Law	Excluded blacks from carrying U.S. mail
1811	Kentucky Conspiracy Law	Made conspiracy among slaves a capital offense
1813	Virginia Poll Tax	Exacted a $1.50 tax on blacks who were forbidden to vote
1814	Louisiana Migration Law	Prohibited free blacks from entering the State
1815	Virginia Poll Tax	Required free blacks to pay a $2.50 tax so whites could vote
1816	Louisiana Jury Law	Provided that no black slave could testify against a white person
1819	Missouri Literacy Law	Forbade assembling or teaching black slaves to read or write

- Continued - No. 3 Boundary Safeguards and Restrictions in Southern States		
Year	**States' Legal and Social Restrictions**	**Purpose of Restriction**
1820	South Carolina Migration Law	Prohibited free blacks from entering the State
1826	North Carolina Migration Law	Forbade entry of free blacks; violators penalized $500
1827	Florida Voting Law	Restricted voting to whites
1829	Georgia Literacy Law	Provided fine and imprisonment for teaching a black person to read
1830	Louisiana Expulsion Law	Required all free blacks to leave State within 60 days
1830	Mississippi Employment Law	Forbade blacks employment in printing and entertainment
1830	Kentucky Property Tax Law	Taxed blacks; forbade their voting or attending school
1831	North Carolina License Law	Required all black traders and peddlers to be licensed
1831	South Carolina enacted Licensing Prohibition	Free blacks were denied any kind of a business license
1831	Mississippi Preaching Law	Forbade free blacks to preach except with permission
1832	Alabama and Virginia Literacy Laws	Fined and flogged whites for teaching blacks to read or write
1833	Georgia Employment Law	Prohibited blacks from working in reading or writing jobs
1833	Georgia Literacy Law	Provided fines and whippings for teaching blacks

- Continued - No. 4 Boundary Safeguards and Restrictions in Southern States		
Year	States' Legal and Social Restrictions	Purpose of Restriction
1833	Kentucky Licensing Prohibition	No free person of color could obtain a business license
1835	Missouri Registration Law	Required the registration and bonding of all free blacks
1835	Georgia Employment Law	Prohibited employing blacks in drug stores
1837	South Carolina Curfew Law	Required blacks to be off streets by a certain hour
1838	Virginia School of Law	Forbade blacks who had gone North to school to return
1838	North Carolina Marriage Law	Declared void all interracial marriages to 3rd generation
1841	South Carolina Observing Law	Forbade blacks and whites from looking out the same windows
1842	Maryland Information Law	Felonied blacks demanding or receiving abolition newspapers
1844	Maryland Color Tax	Placed a tax on all employed black artisans
1844	South Carolina Amusement Law	Prohibited blacks from playing games with whites
1845	Georgia Contracting Law	Prohibited contracts with black mechanics
1846	Kentucky Incitement Law	Provided imprisonment for inciting slaves to rebel
1847	Missouri Literacy Law	Prohibited teaching blacks to read or write

- Continued - No. 5 Boundary Safeguards and Restrictions in Southern States		
Year	**States' Legal and Social Restrictions**	**Purpose of Restriction**
1848	Virginia Incitement Law	Provided death penalty for advising slaves to rebel
1850	Fugitive Slave Law Enacted	Stronger enforcement provisions
1852	Georgia Tax Law	Imposed annual $5 per capita tax on free blacks
1853	Virginia Poll Tax Law	Levied tax on all free black males 21-to-55 years old
1856	Virginia Drug Law	Forbade selling poisonous drugs to blacks
1857	Dred Scott Decision	Supreme Court dehumanized and disenfranchised blacks
1858	Maryland Recreation Law	Forbade free blacks and slaves from boating on the Potomac
1868	Southern Black Codes	Deprived blacks of right to vote and hold public office
1883	Civil Rights Law of 1875 Weakened	Supreme Court challenged the constitutionality of the law
1898	The Grandfather Clause	Deprived blacks of the right to vote in Louisiana

- Continued - No. 6 Boundary Safeguards and Restrictions in Northern States		
Year	States' Legal and Social Restrictions	Purpose of Restriction
1660	Connecticut Military Law	Barred blacks from military service
1664	Maryland Marriage Law	Enactment of the first anti-interracial marriage statutes
1667	British Plantation Act	Established codes of conduct for slaves and slave holders
1705	Massachusetts Anti-Miscegenation Law	Criminalized interracial marriages
1705	New York Runaway Law	Prescribed execution for recaptured runaway slaves
1721	Delaware Marriage Law	Forbade marriage between white women and black men
1722	Pennsylvania Morality Statement	Condemned blacks for sexual acts with whites
1722	Pennsylvania Anti-Miscegenation Law	Criminalized interracial marriages
1784	Connecticut Military Law	Forbade blacks from serving in the militia
1800	Maryland Agricultural Laws	Prohibited blacks from raising and selling agricultural products

- Continued - No. 7
Boundary Safeguards and Restrictions in Northern States

Year	States' Legal and Social Restrictions	Purpose of Restriction
1804	Ohio Anti-Mobility Law	Enacted "Black Laws" that restricted blacks' movement
1804	Ohio Registration Law	Required blacks to register and anually post a bond
1805	Maryland Licensure Law	Forbade blacks from selling tobacco or corn without license
1807	Maryland Residence Law	Limited residence of entering free blacks to two weeks
1810	Maryland Voting Law	Restricted voting rights to whites only
1811	Delaware Migration Law	Forbade migration of blacks; levied $10 per week fine
1818	Connecticut Voting Law	Disenfranchised black voters
1821	District of Columbia Registration Law	Required blacks to register annually and post bond
1827	Maryland Occupation Acts (Petition to Legislature)	Prohibited blacks from driving or owning hacks, carts or drays
1829	Illinois Marriage Law	Forbade black and white marriages
1831	Indiana Mobility Law	Required blacks to register in order to work and post bond
1836	District of Columbia Business License Law	Prohibited licensing blacks for profit-making activities
1844	Maryland Occupation Acts	Excluded blacks from the carpentry trade

Notes and References

CHAPTER 1

1. J.M. and M.J. Cohen, *A Dictionary of Modern Quotations* (New York: Penguin Books, 1971). The anecdote following this quotation is a fictional interview.
2. Quotes from Narrative of Solomon Northrup. *Twelve Years a Slave*, 1853.
3. Leonard P. Curry, *The Free Black in Urban America, 1800-1850* (Chicago: The University of Chicago Press, 1981), 136-137.
4. Ibid., pp. 129-130.
5. Note from author: Socioeconomic data on black employment, income, wealth, crime, businesses, and educational achievements were aggregated from the U.S. Census Bureau's 1990 census data; The National Urban League 1988 and 1992 reports on the state of black America; and a 1990 published report from the Joint Center for Economic Studies.
6. Harold Cruse, *Plural But Equal* (New York: Quill-William Morrow, 1987).
7. Lewis Lipsitz, *American Democracy* (New York: St. Martin's Press, 1986), 37, 38, 155.
8. Andrew Hacker, *Two Nations: Black and White, Separate, Hostile, Unequal* (New York: Charles Scribner's Sons, 1992), 23-24.
9. Hacker, Ibid., p. 60.
10. Joseph Boskin, *Sambo: The Rise and Demise of An American* (New York: Oxford University Press, 1986).
11. Harriet Beecher Stowe, *Uncle Tom's Cabin* (The New American Library. Bibliographic copyright, 1981).
12. Hacker, op. cit., p. 23.
13. Harold Cruse, *The Crisis of the Negro Intellectual* (New York: Quill-William Morrow, 1984), 478.
14. Harold Cruse, *Plural But Equal* (New York: Quill-William Morrow, 1987), 148.
15. Cruse, Ibid., p. 136.
16. August Meier and Elliott Rudwick, *From Plantation to Ghetto* (New York: Hill and Wang, 1970), 194.
17. Cruse, op. cit., p. 297.
18. Tom W. Smith, "Jewish Attitudes Towards Blacks and Race

Relations," *Jewish Sociology Papers*, (New York: The American Jewish Committee, 1990), 5.

19. Smith, Ibid., p. 5.
20. Cruse, op. cit., p. 63.
21. Smith, op. cit., p. 6.
22. Alphonso Pinkney, *The Myth of Black Progress* (New York: Cambridge University Press, 1984), 8-9.
23. Pinkney, Ibid., pp. 8-9.
24. Lipsitz, op. cit., p. 37.

CHAPTER 2

1. Chancellor Williams, *The Destruction of Black Civilization* (Chicago: Third World Press, 1987), 298.
2. Lewis Lipsitz, *American Democracy* (New York: St. Martin's Press, 1986), 12.
3. Stanley Lebergott, *The Americans: An Economic Record* (New York: W.W. Norton Company, 1984), 71.
4. Daniel J. Curran and Claire M. Renzetti, *Social Problems 2nd ed.* (Mass: Simon and Schuster, Inc., 1990), 149-150.
5. Curran and Renzetti, Ibid., pp. 149-150.
6. John E. Farley, *Sociology* (New Jersey: Prentice Hall, 1990), 241.
7. Farley, op. cit., p. 246.
8. Peter Bergman, *The Chronological History of the Negro in America* (New York: A Mentor Book, 1969), 39.
9. Data on black prisoners, unemployment, income levels and elected officials were aggregated from National Urban League, *The State of Black America*, (1988, 1993); "The Social and Economic Status of the Black Population in the United States: An Historical View," 1790-1978. U.S. Department of Commerce, Bureau of Census, Special Studies Series, (June, 1979); Bill McAllister (February 27, 1990) "Study: 1 in 4 Young Black Men Is in Jail or Court-Supervised," *Washington Post*, A3; U.S. Department of Commerce, Bureau of Census publications (1982, 1992) and Andrew Hacker, *Two Nations: Black and White, Separate, Hostile, Unequal* (New York: Charles Scribner's Sons, 1992).
10. James Jennings, *The Politics of Black Empowerment* (Detroit: Wayne State University Press, 1992), 34.
11. Harold Cruse, *Plural But Equal* (New York: Quill-William Morrow, 1987), 134
12. Harriet Beecher Stowe, *Uncle Tom's Cabin* (The New American

Library. Bibliographic copyright, 1981).

13. Jennings, loc. cit.

14. Arthur S. Evans and Michael W. Giles, "Effects of Black on Blacks' Perceptions of Relative Power and Social Distance," *Journal of Black Studies* 17.1 (September, 1986): 3-14.

15. August Meier and Elliott Rudwick, *From Plantation to Ghetto* (New York: Hill and Wang, 1970), 245-247.

16. Meier and Rudwick, Ibid.

17. Meier and Rudwick, Ibid.

18. Cruse, loc. cit. p. 35.

CHAPTER 3

1. Harold Cruse, *The Crisis of the Negro Intellectual: A Historical Analysis of the Failure of Black Leadership* (New York: Quill Books, 1984), 7-8.

2. John A. Garraty, *The American Nation: A History of the United States to 1817 7th ed.* (New York: Harper/Collins Publishers, 1991), 145.

3. Eric Black, *Our Constitution: The Myth That Binds Us* (Boulder: Westview Press, 1988), 21.

4. Madison and Jay Hamilton, *The Federalist Papers,* ed. Clinton Rossiter (New York: Mentor Books, 1961), 301.

5. Howard Zinn, *A People's History of the United States* (New York: Harper Perennial, 1990) 254.

6. Black, op. cit., p. 8.

7. Norman E.W. Hodges, *Black History* (New York: Monarch Press, 1971), p. 99.

8. August Meier and Elliott Rudwick, *From Plantation to Ghetto* (New York: Hill and Wang, 1970), 191.

9. Vann Woodward, *American Counterpoint: Slavery and Racism in the North/South Dialogue* (New York: Oxford University Press, 1971), 40-41.

10. Zinn, op. cit., p. 255.

11. Note from the author: W.E.B. Dubois made the remarks in a speech on black business development, in 1915, in Atlanta, Georgia.

12. Note from the author: These remarks were taken from a taped interview with Tony Brown, the host of *Black Journal,* in a Black History presentation entitled, *Contributions: African-Americans and The American Mosaic.* The taped series was made possible by Philip Morris Companies, Inc. and produced by Radio America.

Tony Brown's *Black Journal* is a long-running nationally syndi-
cated television program that addresses black issues.

13. James R. Kluegel and Eliot R. Smith, *Beliefs About Inequality*
(New York: Aldine De Gruyter, 1986).

14. Orlando Patterson, "Black Like All of Us," *The Washington Post,*
February 7, 1993.

15. Leslie Burl McLemore, "Toward A Theory of Black Politics - The
Black and Ethnic Models Revisited," *Journal of Black Studies*
(March, 1972), 323-329.

16. Harold Cruse, *Plural But Equal* (New York: William Morrow,
1987), 363.

17. Black, op. cit., p. 127.

18. Eric Foner, *Reconstruction 1863-1877: America's Unfinished
Revolution* (New York: Harper & Row, Publishers, 1988), 256.

19. Foner, Ibid., p. 256.

20. Howard Zinn, *A People's History of the United States* (New
York: Harper Perennial, 1990), 121.

21. Jamie Malanowski, "Racism for Feminism. The Odd History of the
Civil Rights Bill," *(The Washington Post,* Feb. 6, 1994).

22. Haki R. Madhubuti, *Black Men: Obsolete, Single, Dangerous?*
(Chicago: Third World Press, 1990), 85.

23. Peter M. Bergman, *The Chronological History of the Negro in
America* (New York: A Mentor Book, 1969), 197.

24. Leonard P. Curry, *The Free Black in Urban America, 1800-1850*
(Chicago: The University of Chicago Press, 1981), 136-137.

25. John E. Farley, *Sociology* (New Jersey: Prentice Hall, 1990), 272.

26. Farley, Ibid., p. 212.

27. Farley, Ibid., p. 212.

CHAPTER 4

1. Note from the author: From C. Eric Lincoln, *My Face Is Black*
(Boston: Beacon Press, 1964), 72-90, which was reprinted by
permission in *Old Memories, New Moods,* ed. Peter I. Rose, 359.

2. Note from the author: The actual figures for the number of blacks
captured, enslaved and shipped out of Africa is unknown, but estimates vary from a minimum of 20 million to a high of 60 million. The
differences in estimates result from the scarcity of records. The
lower figure is an estimate of the number of blacks enslaved in
North America, the Caribbean, or the Latin American countries.
Higher figures include the black Africans who were killed resisting

capture, died enroute, or were shipped into European or middle-eastern countries. Most histories commonly agree that two-thirds to seventy-five percent of all captured Africans died before reaching the slave markets throughout the world. Sources of the differences with explanations of the varied estimates of the number of Africans shipped out of Africa, can be found in the following books: Howard Zinn, *A People's History of the United States*; C. Vann Woodard, *American Counterpoint: Slavery and Racism in the North/South Dialogue.*

3. David Brian Davis, *Slavery And Human Progress*, (New York: Oxford University Press, 1984).

4. David Mills, "A Look at Slavery Then and Now," *The Washington Post*, October 7, 1993.

5. Harold Cruse, *The Crisis of the Negro Intellectual: A Historical Analysis of the Failure of Black Leadership* (New York: Quill Books), 1984.

6. Norman E.W. Hodges, *Black History* (New York: Monarch Press, 1971), 29.

7. Howard Zinn, *A People's History of the United States* (New York: Harper Perennial, 1990), 29.

8. Zinn, Ibid.

9. Winthorp D. Jordan, *White Over Black: American Attitudes Toward the Negro, 1550-1812* (New York: W.W. Norton & Company, 1968), 18.

10. Thomas Sowell, *The Economics and Politics of Race* (New York: Quill Publishers, 1983).

11. Chancellor Williams, *The Destruction of Black Civilization* (Chicago: Third World Press, 1987), 153.

12. R.A. Schermerhorn, "Power As A Primary Concept in the Study of Minorities." *The Sociology of Race Relations*, (New York: The Free Press, 1980).

13. Robert William Fogel, *Without Consent of Contract: The Rise and Fall of American Slavery* (New York: W.W. Norton and Company, 1989), 202.

CHAPTER 5

1. Carl N. Degler, *Neither Black Nor White* (New York: MacMillian Publishing Co., 1971), 260.

2. Dan Lacy, *The White Use Of Blacks In America* (New York: McGraw-Hill Company, 1972), 3.

3. Andrew Hacker, *Two Nations: Black and White, Separate, Hostile, Unequal* (New York: Charles Scribner's Sons, 1992), 10.
4. Douglas G. Glasgow, *The Black Underclass: Poverty, Unemployment, and Entrapment of Ghetto Youth* (California: Jossey-Bass Inc., Publishers, 1980), 35.
5. Norman E.W. Hodges, *Black History* (New York: Monarch Press, 1971), 44.
6. James F. Davis, *Who is Black: One Nations' Definition* (Pennsylvania: The Pennsylvania State University Press, 1991), 12.
7. Harold Cruse, *Plural But Equal* (New York: Quill-William, Morrow, 1987).
8. Winthorp D. Jordan, *White Over Black: American Attitudes Toward the Negro, 1550-1812* (New York: W.W. Norton & Company, 1968), 255.
9. Degler, op. cit., p. 245.
10. Jordan, op. cit., p. 263.
11. C. Vann Woodward, *American Counterpoint: Slavery and Racism in the North/South Dialogue* (New York: Oxford University Press, 1964), 13-46.
12. Note from the author: Data aggregated from 68th Cong., sess. I., chs. 185, 190; the 1924 Immigration Law quotas as contained in the U.S. Department of Justice Immigration Records; *Displace Persons Act of 1948,* 80th Cong., 2nd sess., chs. 646, 647, (June 25, 1948). Amendment of the *Displaced Persons Act of 1948;* 81st Congress, 2nd Session, Chapters 262, June 16, 1950; Numerical Limitations; Annual Quota Based upon National Origin; Minimum Quotas. Title II, Immigration, Chapter 1, Quota System. Public Law 414-June 27, 1952; and Howard Zinn's book, *Peoples History of the United States,* p. 371.
13. John A. Garraty, *The American Nation: A History of the United States to 1817,* 7th ed. (New York: Harper/Collins Publishers, 1991), 372.
14. Dan Lacy, Ibid.
15. Andrew Hacker, *Two Nations: Black and White, Separate, Hostile, Unequal* (New York: Charles Scribner's and Sons, 1992), 9. Data for table was extracted from the United States Department of Commerce, Economics and Statistics Administration, Bureau of the Census, Money, Income of Households, Families, and Persons in the United States, (1991), p. XIII.

CHAPTER 6

1. J.M. and M.J. Cohen, *A Dictionary of Modern Quotations* (New York: Penguin Books, 1971).
2. Sources of included: August Meier and Elliott Rudwick, *From Plantation to Ghetto* (New York: Hill and Wang, 1970), 30; Norman Coombs, *The Black Experience in America* (New York: Hippocrene Books, 1972), 19; and Chancellor Williams, *The Destruction of Black Civilization* (Chicago: Third World Press, 1987), 204.
3. August Meier and Elliott Rudwick, Ibid.
4. Chancellor Williams, *The Destruction of Black Civilization* (Chicago: Third World Press, 1987), 56.
5. Norman E.W. Hodges, *Black History* (New York: Monarch Press, 1971), 20.
6. Williams, op. cit., p. 184.
7. David Brian Davis, *Slavery and Human Progress,* (New York: Oxford University Press, 1984), 45.
8. August Meier and Elliott Rudwick, op. cit., p. 37.
9. David Mills, "A Look at Slavery Then and Now," *The Washington Post,* October 17, 1993.
10. Meier, Rudwick and Combs, op. cit., p. 24.
11. Howard Zinn, *A People's History of the United States* (New York: Harper Perennial, 1990), 1-2.
12. Zinn, Ibid., p. 2.
13. Zinn, Ibid., p. 4.
14. Peter M. Bergman, *The Chronological History of the Negro in America* (New York: A Mentor Book, 1969), 3.
15. Mortimer Chambers, et al., *The Early Modern Period: The Western Experience 3rd ed.* (New York: Alfred A. Knopf, 1983), 420.
16. Chambers, Ibid., p. 671.
17. John A. Garraty, *The American Nation: A History of the United States to 1817* 7th ed. (New York: Harper/Collins Publishers, 1991), 14.
18. E.N. Elliott, *Cotton is King and Pro-Slavery Arguments* (New York: Negro Universities Press, 1969).
19. Zinn, op. cit., p. 13.
20. Note from the author: For nearly three centuries, land was free for white European immigrants. Millions of acres of public land were sold at relative cheap prices. Peak land prices occurred in 1836 and 1854, which coincided with the prices of slaves. Land never exceed

$2.00 per acre until after slavery ended. Land did not surpass the greatest wealth producer, until well after the Civil War. For the various prices of land see: Sakolski, A.M. *The Great American Land Bubble.* New York and London: Harper & Row, 1932; Clawson, Marion. *The Land System of the United States.* Lincoln: University of Nebraska Press, 1968, pp. 56,57, 68; Garraty, John A *The American Nation: A History of the United States to 1817.* (7th Edition) New York: Harper/Collins Publishers, 1991, p. 57.

21. Elliott, op. cit., p. 104.
22. William Loren Katz, *Black Indians.* (New York: MacMillian Publishing Company, 1986), 53-54.
23. *World Book*, Field Enterprises Educational Corporation, 1976, 7:228e.
24. Katz, op. cit., pp. 64-65.
25. John A. Garraty, *The American Nation: A History of the United States to 1817* 7th ed. (New York: Harper/Collins Publishers, 1991), 146.
26. Mortimer Chambers, op. cit., p. 668.
27. Data for Table 8 was taken from Elliot, E.N. *Cotton Is King;* Garraty, *The American Nation;* Fogel, Robert W. *Without Consent or Contract.*
28. Robert William Fogel, *Without Consent of Contract: The Rise and Fall of American Slavery* (New York: W.W. Norton and Company, 1989), 82.
29. Hodges, op. cit., p. 116.
30. Bergman, op. cit., p. 64.
31. Eugene D. Genovese, *The Political Economy of Slavery* (New Hampshire: Wesleyan University Press, 1991), 166.
32. Elliot, loc.cit.
33. Fogel, op. cit., p. 100.
34. C. Vann. Woodward, *American Counterpoint: Slavery and Racism in the North/South Dialogue* (New York: Oxford University Press, 1964), 99; Fogel, Ibid, pp. 119-120.
35. Bergman, op. cit., p. 209.
36. George M. Fredrickson, *The Arrogance of Race* (Connecticut: Wesleyan University Press, 1988), 36.
37. Garraty, op. cit., p. 352.
38. Zinn, op. cit., p. 130.
39. Dan Lacy, *The White Use of Blacks in America* (New York: McGraw-Hill Paperbacks, 1972), 62.
40. Zinn, loc. cit.

41. Sharon LaFraniere, "Windfall Subsidies For Just Peanuts," *The Washington Post,* July 14, 1993.
42. Tom Kenworthy, "BLM Stripped of Authority Over Mining Land Sales," *The Washington Post,* March 11, 1993.
43. Kenworthy, Ibid.
44. Bergman, op. cit., p. 210.
45. Heatherly and Pines, op. cit., p. 141.

CHAPTER 7

1. E.W. Norman, *Kipling, 1899* (Reprinted from Hodges, E.W. Norman story. New York: Simon & Schuster, 1971), p. 11.
2. Dan Lacy, *The White Use of Blacks in America* (New York: McGraw-Hill Paperbacks, 1972).
3. Winthrop D. Jordan, *White Over Black* (New York: W.W. Norton and Co., 1968), 72.
4. Jordan, Ibid. p. 74.
5. Peter M. Bergman, *The Chronological History of the Negro in America* (New York: A Mentor Book, 1969), 16.
6. Bergman, Ibid., p. 17.
7. Jordan, op. cit., p. 82.
8. Lacy, op. cit., p. 85.
9. Eric Foner, *Reconstruction 1863-1877: America's Unfinished Revolution* (New York: Harper & Row, Publishers, 1988), xxvi.
10. Norman Coombs, *The Black Experience in America* (New York: Hippocrene Books, 1972), 40.
11. Jordan, op. cit., p. 189.
12. Bergman, op. cit., p. 25.
13. Jordan, op. cit., pp. 117-118.
14. Note from the author: Chart constructed based upon data aggregated from the Immigration Acts of 1790, 1882, 1892, 1907, 1924, and 1936 which effectively restricted or totally excluded people of African descent from acquiring citizenship. The National Origins Laws imposed a 1% quota based on racial percentage of citizenship in America in 1750. Since neither enslaved nor free blacks were citizens, the black quota was zero. Supportive information was also found in Peter M. Bergman's book, *Chronological History of the Negro In America,* (New York: A Mentor Book, 1969); and *The World Book Encyclopedia* (Chicago: Field Enterprises Educational Corporation, 1976), vol. 7.

CHAPTER 8

1. J.M. and M.J. Cohen, *A Dictionary of Modern Quotations* (New York: Penguin Books), 1971.
2. Harold Cruse, *Plural But Equal* (New York: Quill-William Morrow, 1987), 261.
3. Peter M. Bergman, *The Chronological History of the Negro in America* (New York: A Mentor Book, 1969).
4. William N. Parker, *The Structure of the Cotton Economy of the Antebellum South* (Washington, D.C.: The Agricultural History Society, 1970).
5. "The Last Holocaust Victims," *The Washington Post,* May 18,1993.
6. John Naisbitt and Patricia Aburdene, *Megatrends 2000: Ten New Directions for the 1990s* (New York: William Morrow and Co., 1990).

CHAPTER 9

1. Joseph Boskin, *Sambo: The Rise and Demise of An American* (Jester New York: Oxford University Press, 1986), 49.
2. Boskin, Ibid., p. 44
3. Peter M. Bergman, *The Chronological History of the Negro in America* (New York: A Mentor Book, 1969), 54.
4. Note from the author: The early development of various forms of black music presented in journal articles by James Dugan and John Hammond, *An Early Black Music Concert From Spirituals to Swing, The Black Perspective In Music,* Lazarus E.N. Ekwueme, *African-Music Retentions, The Black Perspective In Music* and William Ferris, *Blue Roots and Development, The Black Perspective In Music.*
5. Langston Hughes and Milton Meltzer, *Pictorial History of the Negro In America* (New York: Crown Publishing Company, 1963), 39.
6. Richard A. Long, *African Americans* (New York: Crescent Books, 1985), 56.
7. Harold Cruse, *Plural But Equal* (New York: Quill-William Morrow, 1987), 28.
8. James Dugan and John Hammond, *An Early Black Music Concert From Spirituals to Swing, The Black Perspectives In Music,* 191.
9. Walter Scott, "Personality Parade," *Washington Post,* Sunday Section, (January 2, 1994), p. 2

10. Leonard P. Curry, *The Free Black in Urban America, 1800-1850* (Chicago: The University of Chicago Press, 1981), 23.

11. "The Heart of Soul to Be Sold," *The Washington Post,* August 4, 1993.

12. Boskins, op. cit. p. 52.

13. John J. Macionis, *Sociology* (New York: Prentice-Hall, 1989), 23.

14. Note from the author: For some of the historical information on black athletes in professional sports see: Rayford Logan, *The Betrayal of the Negro* (New York Collier Books, 1965), 357; and Peter M. Bergman, *The Chronological History of the Negro In America* (New York: Mentor Books, 1969).

Index